HARDSHIP, GREED, AND SORROW

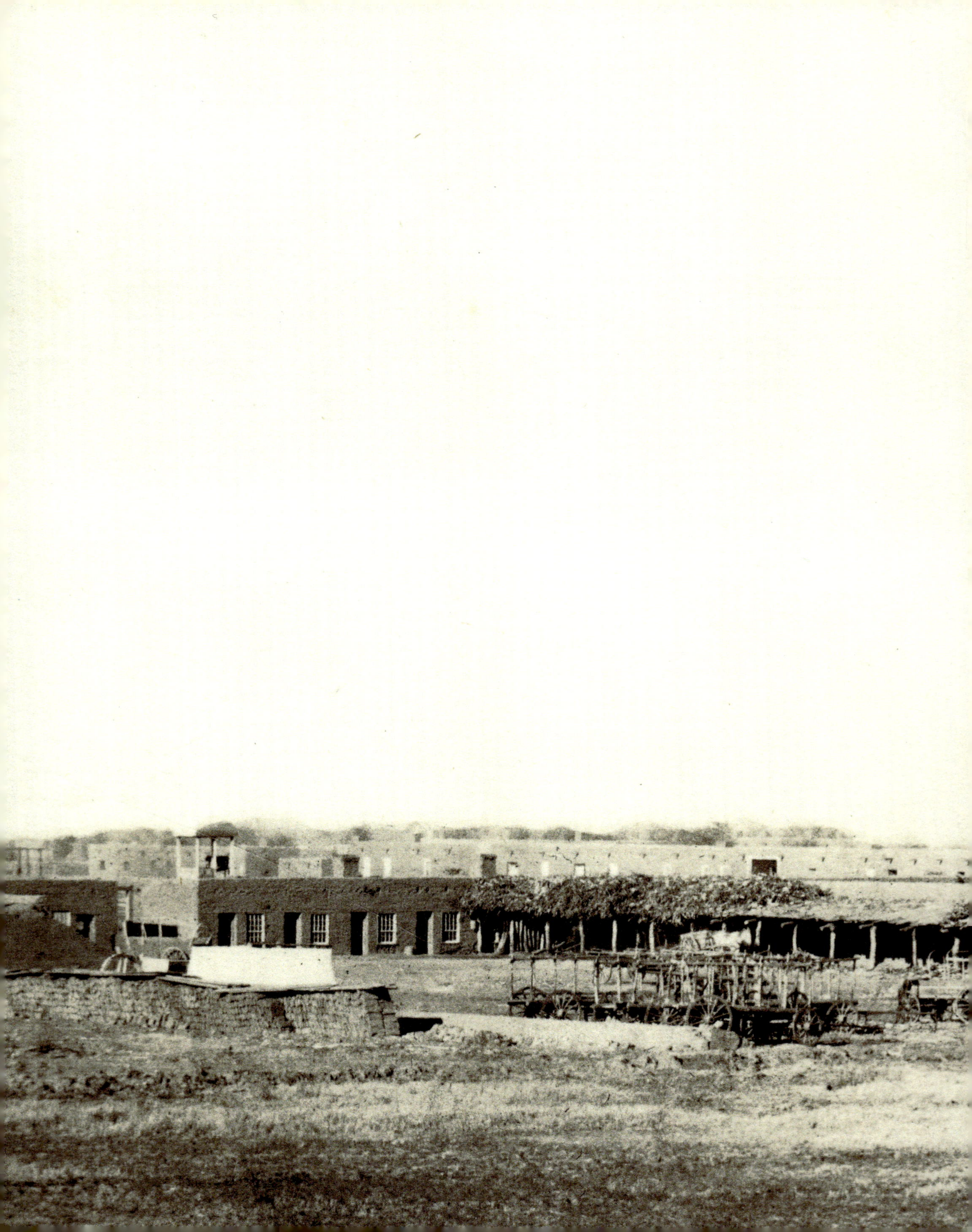

HARDSHIP, GREED, AND SORROW

An Officer's Photo Album of 1866 New Mexico Territory

DEVORAH ROMANEK

Foreword by Jennifer Nez Denetdale

Preface by Daniel Kosharek

UNIVERSITY OF OKLAHOMA PRESS : NORMAN

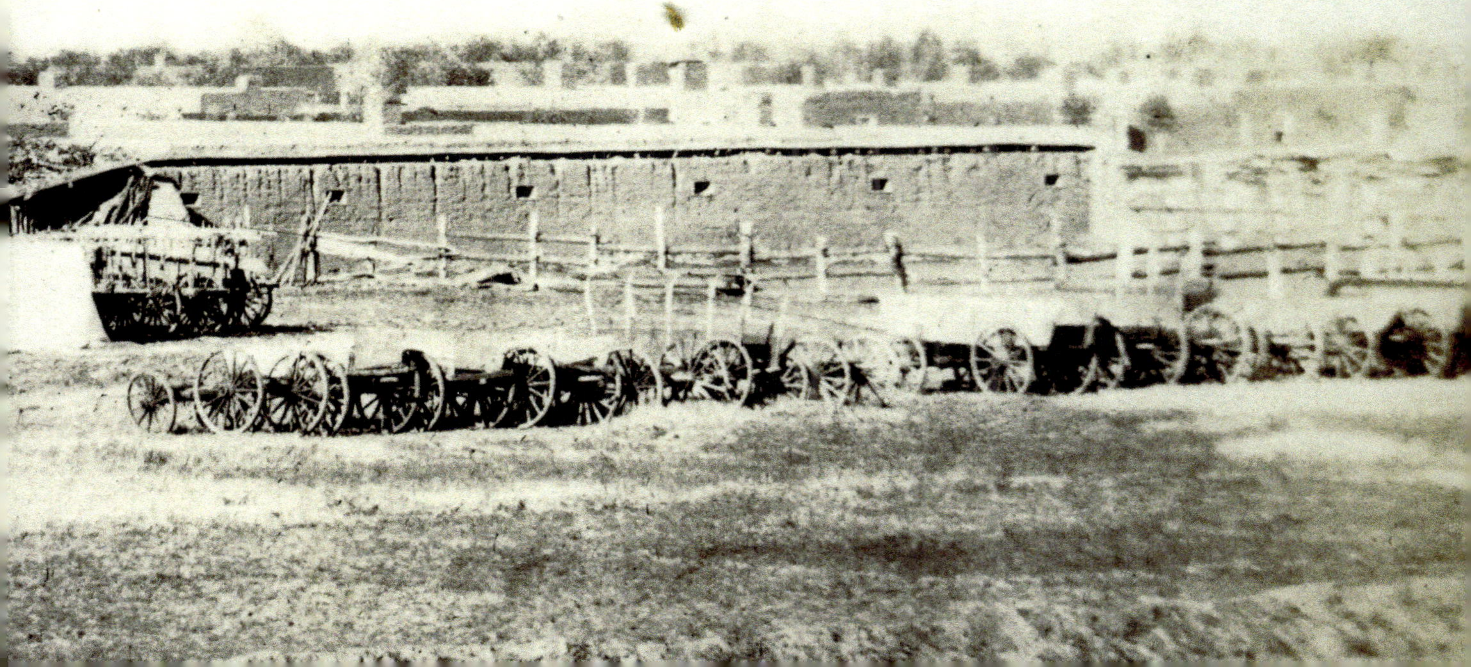

This book is published with the generous assistance
of the New Mexico History Museum, Santa Fe, and
the New Mexico Council on Photography.

UNCAPTIONED IMAGES APPEAR ON THE FOLLOWING PAGES AS NOTED:

Pages ii–iii: (detail, plate 46) Fort Sumner, New Mexico Territory, ca. 1865
Page vi: (detail, plate 15) Government repair workshops, Fort Union, New Mexico Territory, ca. 1865
Page viii: (detail, plate 53) Navajo men en route to or at Fort Sumner, New Mexico Territory, ca. September 1866
Page 67: (detail, plate 58) Navajo Indians at Fort Sumner, New Mexico Territory, ca. 1865

LIBRARY OF CONGRESS CATALOGING-IN-PUBLICATION DATA

Names: Romanek, Devorah, 1964– author. | Denetdale, Jennifer, writer of foreword. | Kosharek, Daniel, writer of preface.
Title: Hardship, greed, and sorrow : an officer's photo album of 1866 New Mexico Territory / by Devorah Romanek ; foreword by Jennifer Nez Denetdale; preface by Daniel Kosharek.
Description: Norman : University of Oklahoma Press, [2019] | Includes bibliographical references and index.
Identifiers: LCCN 2018060156 | ISBN 978-0-8061-6393-2 (pbk. : alk. paper)
Subjects: LCSH: Souvenir of New Mexico. | New Mexico—History—19th century. | Frontier and pioneer life—New Mexico. | Photography—New Mexico—History—19th century. | Portrait photography—New Mexico—History—19th century. | New Mexico—Social conditions—19th century. | New Mexico—Description and travel—19th century. | United States. Army—Military life.
Classification: LCC F801 .R66 2019 | DDC 978.9/04—dc23
LC record available at https://lccn.loc.gov/2018060156

The paper in this book meets the guidelines for permanence and durability of the Committee on Production Guidelines for Book Longevity of the Council on Library Resources, Inc. ∞

To my parents,
Enid and Walter Romanek,
who taught me to love the world
and its people and places

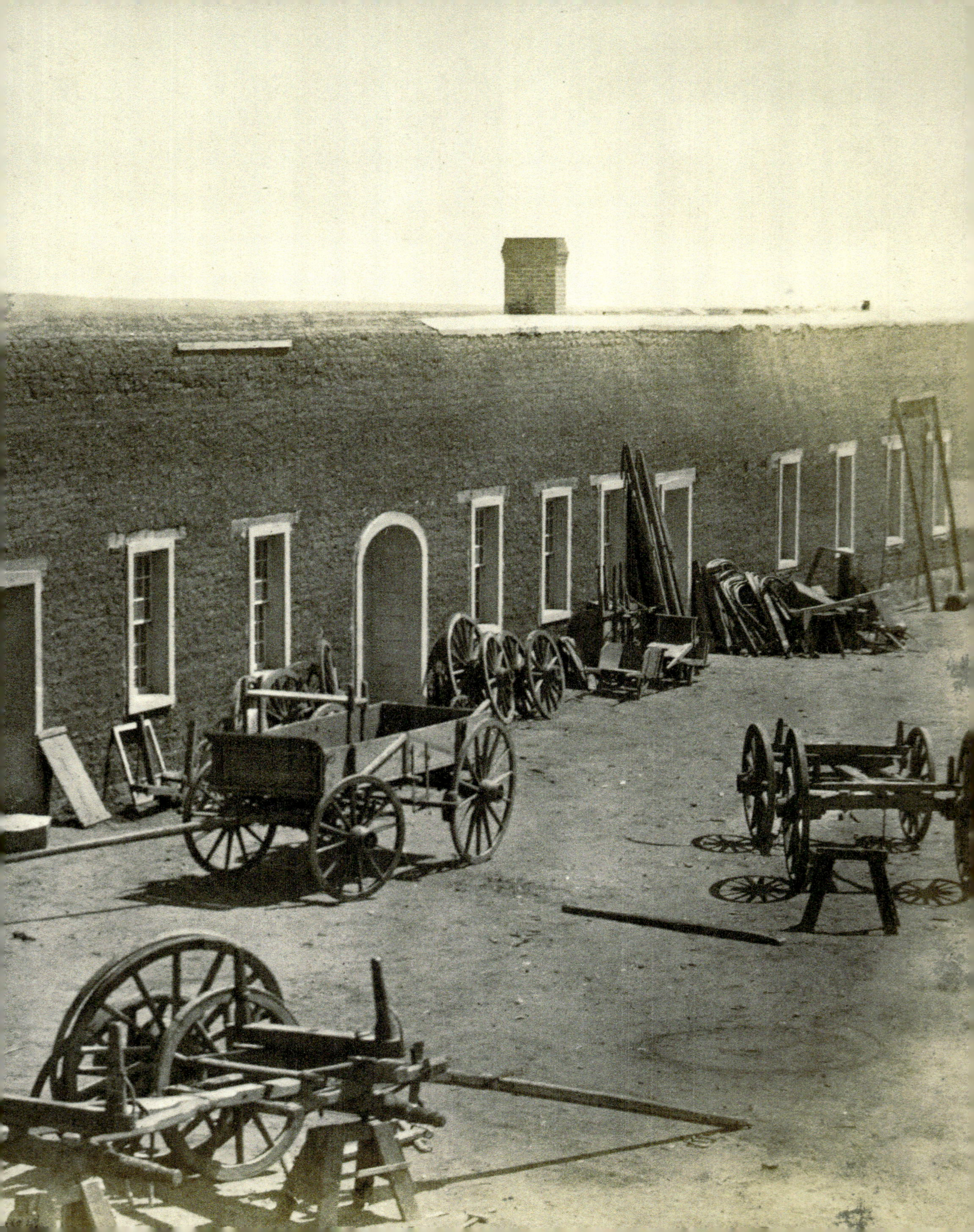

CONTENTS

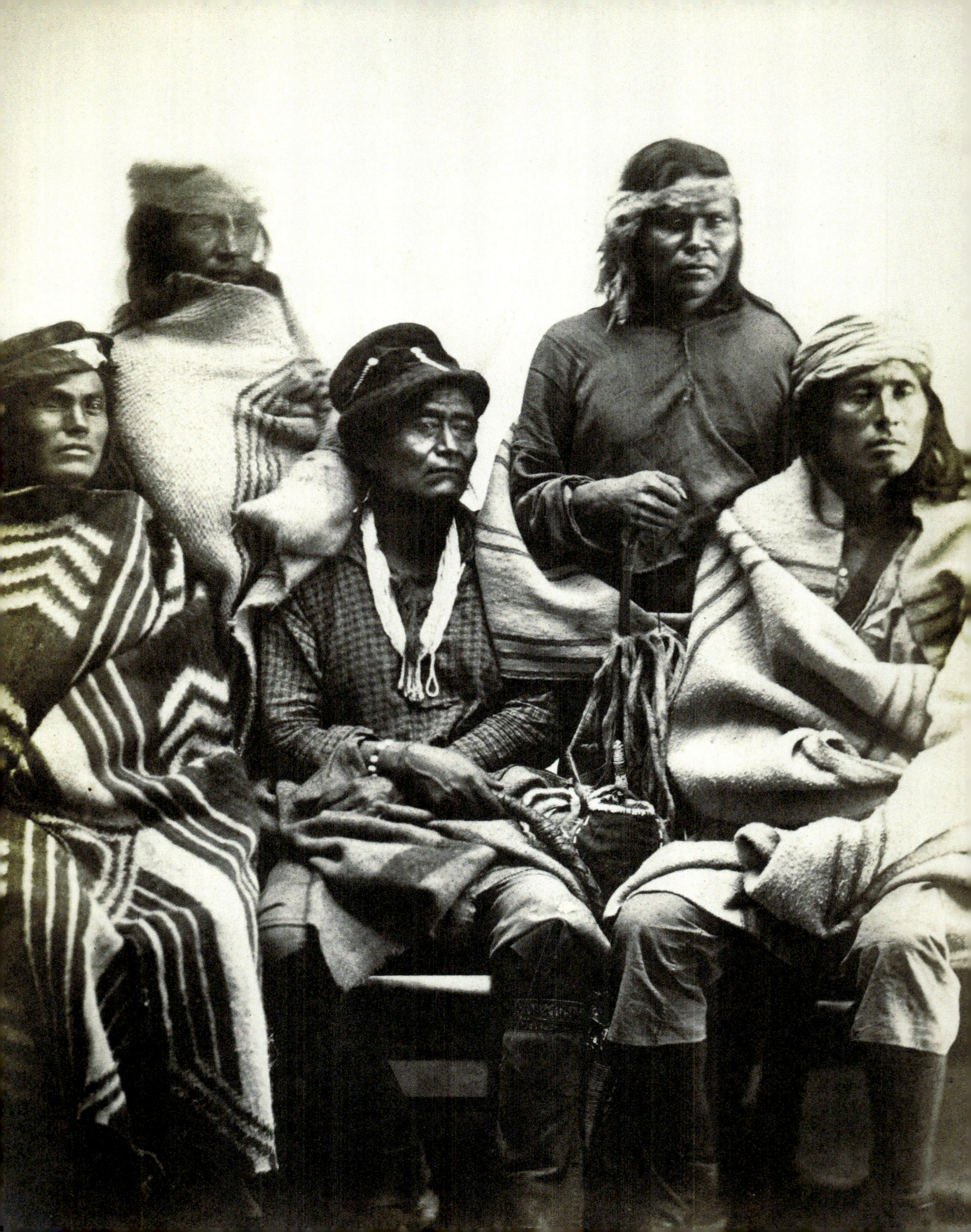

FOREWORD

Jennifer Nez Denetdale

My introduction to photographs of Diné began when an archivist at Northern Arizona University shared George Wharton James's *Indian Blankets and Their Makers* with me. James, as part of a tradition of introducing Native peoples to an American public, illustrated his book on Navajo textiles with photographs of weavers. One of those weavers was my great-great-great-grandmother, about whom my mother had shared stories, which in turn led me on a journey to learn as much as I could about the Diné past. The early twentieth-century photograph in James's book of my great-great-great-grandmother, who is best known in history as Juanita, wife of the Navajo leader Manuelito, was one of several photographs taken of her across several decades. The earliest photographs of her were taken in the mid-nineteenth century, the era in which the photographs in these pages were shot. The original album, very likely compiled by a U.S. Army officer, was called a "souvenir," an interesting remark on the owner of this album's time in the Southwest. It features photographs, placed chronologically, that reflect on American claims and tenure in the Southwest. It further represents a traveler's foray into strange and exotic places to show how others lived, and, foremost, it makes statements about American presence in claimed territories wrested from Mexico in 1848; in turn, American efforts to claim the Southwest also chronicle indigenous resistance. This album, then, can be "read" in different ways: One reading relates to the United States' claims to Mexican territory and how American presence was established—through relations with Mexico, the forts that enforce claims to land, and how indigenous peoples like the Diné/Navajos and Apaches would be treated if they resisted American occupation. Native peoples, in their own "reading," have also responded to these historic photographs, using them in their artistic visions—like those of the Diné photographer Will Wilson—and to draw insights about their ancestors and a time past.

Nineteenth-century photography introduced indigenous peoples to the view of non-Indians, and these images would be how non-Indians would come to know indigenous peoples. Frontier photographers like Nicholas Brown, who may have taken a number of the photographs at Fort Sumner, set up in towns like Santa Fe and established makeshift studios at various forts. These photographs come to us across many decades and include portraits of military officers and Mexican officials, offering a way to consider relations between Mexico and the United States in the nineteenth century when the United States announced a "peaceful conquest" of the territory and its inhabitants.

This book begins with portraits of Mexican officials and U.S. Army officers, recalling the history of the American takeover of Mexican-claimed territories in 1848 and relations between Mexico and the United States at the time. In the early nineteenth century, American traders were allowed into the Southwest because of the goods they provided, and they sometimes married the daughters of elite Nuevomexicanos, thereby cementing an alliance that fostered economic and political ties with Mexico. Portraits of Mexican officials like Benito Juárez (1806–72) and images of frontier forts tell the story of American expansion west. Forts that melted back into the earth with time once announced the U.S. claims to lands and the government's commitment to protect white settlements from indigenous threats; they also allow us to consider what the forts looked like and how they operated on a daily basis.

Fort Marcy in Santa Fe is depicted in some of the photographs in this album, which provides the occasion to think about a fort's daily operations. Fort Union has been of interest to me because during the Long Walk—the name given to the forced marches of Navajos and Mescalero Apaches from 1863 to 1866. It was a destination for Navajo captives who had surrendered to the United States, and it was on the route the captives took to their final destination, the Bosque Redondo Indian Reservation at Fort Sumner, New Mexico Territory, beginning in the spring of 1863 for the Mescalero Apaches and in the winter of that same year for the Navajos. On several occasions, I have stopped to view the remains of Fort Union, which lies south of the Colorado state border in northeastern New Mexico. Not much is left of the old fort: a few walls, some timeworn paths, and a compact visitors center. The center does not provide much information about the fort's operations and nothing about Navajo prisoners who were marched there and then south to Bosque Redondo. Once the prisoners left forts established in their homeland, they trekked toward the Sandia Mountains, forded the Rio Grande, and then were forcibly marched on different routes past what is now Albuquerque, north past the mountains toward Santa Fe, and then south to Fort Sumner and Bosque Redondo. Another trail went past Santa Fe, north to Fort Union, then south to Fort Sumner. It was by far the longest route for the captives. Historians have not found reasons for why the prisoners were marched so far before they arrived at Bosque Redondo.

The portraits include American military officers like James Carleton, the architect of the Bosque Redondo reservation "experiment." Many of these were taken in the style of commissioned painted individual portraits. Carleton was just one of many American military officers who had such portraits taken. Like others, his portrait perhaps supports American narratives about the responsibilities these officers bore to ensure protection of white settlements and safe travels to what is now California, from which stories of fabulous wealth reached the East.

Scholars of photography, however, ask the question of what lies outside the frame of a visual image; what lies inside can be recognizable as evidence of the truthfulness of American life, but we should be inquisitive of what lies outside the frame and question what we think we know about the West and indigenous peoples. The earliest photographs of the Diné date to their imprisonment at the Bosque Redondo reservation from late 1863 to 1868. It was only when Navajos had been thoroughly militarily subjugated by the U.S. Army that they came under surveillance and were metaphorically captured again by the camera lens. Photographs would come to be a significant means through which Diné would be known.[1] Nineteenth-century photographs capture Navajos as prisoners of war just as in other incidents of war against a group of people. For example, during the Japanese internments of the 1940s, the military and federal officials allowed only certain kinds of images to be photographed and then disseminated. Likewise, Navajo prisoners were shown as being well on the road to assimilation. Apache prisoners are seen laying sod bricks for various buildings, including the soldiers' barracks. Navajos are assembled for the distribution of ration discs. In these portrayals, the captives appear industrious; they are learning about the benefits of American values and also about American beneficence, since, as prisoners, they have been sent to a foreign place where they do not have access to even the most basic tools for survival and must depend on the federal government to shelter, clothe, and feed them. In truth, Navajo oral history recounts how the captives lived in proximity to the fort along the southern side of the Pecos River, where their encampments stretched at least ten miles along its embankment. Instead of building hogans to live in, they were left to dig pits into the earth and cover them with bits of wood and coverings provided by the army for shelter. Ration days are also photographed as the prisoners huddle in groups and stare into the camera from a distance. In these portrayals, the captives all seem to be dressed properly, most often with blankets covering them. Historians consistently remark on the ways that Navajos devised to receive more rations, including making counterfeit ration stamps. Rather than indicating how devious Navajos could be in their efforts to garner more food using whatever means possible, this practice speaks to the desperation of the captives, whose rations meant for a week were often consumed in a day. Another set of narratives told by Navajos relate how the women were reduced to selling sex for a handful of cornmeal. Although the photographs don't indicate how Navajo women were forced to offer sex in exchange for food, a strategy of survival, it does need to be acknowledged that the nineteenth-century U.S. wars against indigenous peoples did indeed include sexual violence as an integral component to conquest. As indigenous feminists point out, war against indigenous peoples has also meant war against women, for rape is integral to the conquest of a people, and today tribal nations and peoples continue to face violence against indigenous women as a legacy of settler colonialism.

The studio-style portraits of Navajos and Apaches taken at Fort Sumner are the first visual images that come to us from that era. Just as photographers created individual portraits of army officers, so, too, did they turn their lenses toward individual Navajos and Apaches, who are posed similarly. These portraits often do not name the individuals and include only those who were seen as leaders who interacted with American officials. Thus, we have portraits of important Navajo male leaders like Barboncito and Manuelito, both of whom were at Hweéldi, the Navajo name for the prison camp at Bosque Redondo. As Devorah Romanek notes, Manuelito is the only named Indian in this album, and he looms large in American histories about western expansion.[2] Military officials declared that only when American soldiers captured or killed this Navajo war chief would they consider the Diné to be defeated.[3] This portrait of Manuelito, who is better known to his own people as Hastiin Ch'il Hajiin (Man from Black Weeds), is one that has been reproduced, with the same posture, by Ben Wittick and then through popular Navajo culture. This image may bring up images of Edward Curtis's "noble savage" and also point to the irony that James Faris references when he observes that this sort of pose, in which indigenous men are positioned with implements of war when their people have been militarily subjugated by the U.S. Army, is about imperial nostalgia.[4]

The first time that Navajos actually saw themselves in photographs such as the ones in this album probably occurred with the federal government's use of visual media in the aftermath of the livestock reduction, when Milton Snow was hired by the Navajo Service in the late 1930s to photograph lands denuded as a result of Navajo sheep herds overgrazing the land. Snow's job was first to provide photographic evidence of what federal officials had given for the draconian livestock reduction policy—it was indeed Navajos who, with their too many sheep, had caused such environmental deterioration. The photographs were used to educate Navajos about land rehabilitation and good farming and ranching practices and, ultimately, to demonstrate that Navajos were receptive to the requirements for American citizenship. The photographs taken at Bosque Redondo were the predecessors of this message.

So many Diné died at Hweéldi—over two thousand—that for decades they refused to speak of their experience. Ironically, even as the most traditional Diné reprimanded their relatives who spoke publicly, the collective memory is filled with stark details of this period. Stories tell of soldiers' brutality; of women and children captured by slave raiders, who accompanied Kit Carson into the field and took payment in the form of the captives taken; of starvation, illness, and poverty. One has to reflect on the urgings of Diné elders not to speak of Hweéldi, while at same time marvel that the memories remain so vivid, as if it happened last week. The power of memory and the strength of stories to persist in oral form is indeed remarkable. The stories preserved in clan kinships and relayed through matrilineal clans continue to circulate and have become part of Navajo national memory. When told, these narratives have the capacity to reduce listeners to tears as they hear about the pain and anguish our ancestors endured. In a Navajo national context, the stories are points of reference to think about the past, the present, and the future. For example, in a 1968 Navajo centennial collection, photographs from this era were placed in juxtaposition with photographs from the modern period, ostensibly to induce the American and Navajo public to think about the progress Navajos have made in the hundred years from 1868 to 1968.[5] Some of the photographs are of individual Diné and Apaches; others, with their scant labelings, hint at how indigenous peoples were thought of at the time. For example, one of the photographs of a Navajo women indicates that she was a "belle," not a word used to describe "proper" women. Another photograph of two Navajo men clasping each other in a way that Navajos still do not approve of, because it is "not Diné" to show intimacy in public, is labeled "Navajo thieves."

These photographs inspire different responses when shown to a Diné audience. When I was interviewing my grandparents during the course of my research on Navajo history, I used photographs as an avenue to inspire conversation and prompt memory. When I showed a photograph of our grandmother to my grandfather, he looked at the image and said he has been thinking about our ancestors and Hweéldi. As he gazed at the picture, we were reminded of the courage of our ancestors, for they had survived extermination. Thus, at the same time, photographs of our ancestors can be used to remind us of tragedies and hardships and inspire us with memories of our ancestors. The stories of Diné experiences under U.S. colonialism are embedded within the photographs because viewing them bring about reflections on what our ancestors endured at the hands of the U.S. government and its citizens. Diné life depicted in the photographs—clothing, hairstyles, jewelry, moccasins, wearing blankets, poses—becomes a space to think about the past and the present. Who were we as a people? How have we changed? What circumstances are the causes for change? What stays the same? What do we mourn and celebrate? These questions become part of the act of gazing at these photographs.

Photographs are often seen as windows to the past, but as scholars of visual culture have demonstrated, photographs frame certain stories. In the case of these nineteenth-century photographs, they glorify stories of U.S. westward expansion, narratives that still do not acknowledge the treatment of indigenous peoples and the massive theft and dispossession of their lands. And yet, the photographs are also a medium through which indigenous people like the Diné are reminded of the past and what they still hold dear and cherish. The photographs renew storytelling and affirm the courage of our ancestors who survived.

NOTES

1. James C. Faris, *Navajo and Photography: A Critical History of the Representation of an American People* (Albuquerque: University of New Mexico Press, 1996), 28, 39.
2. Devorah Romanek, "A Certain Regard: 'Souvenir of New Mexico,'" *The New Mexican* (Santa Fe), August 21, 2014. *Pasatiempo* Sec. Print.
3. Jennifer Nez Denetdale, *Reclaiming Diné History: The Legacies of Navajo Chief Manuelito and Juanita* (Tucson: University of Arizona Press, 2007), 74, 75.
4. Faris, *Navajo and Photography*, 14, 15.
5. See, for example, Martin A. Link, *Navajo: A Century of Progress, 1868–1968* (Window Rock, Ariz.: K. C. Publications with the Navajo Tribe, 1968).

PREFACE

Daniel Kosharek

Since my arrival at the Palace of the Governors Photo Archives over a decade ago, I have frequently encountered historically significant photographs attributed to the "Meem Album" or "Souvenir of New Mexico." The source of these rather haunting photographs documenting the history of New Mexico and the West, showing military installations, Native Americans, and other scenes, always eluded me, as the originals were not in the archive, only copy negatives. What I did know was that somewhere out there was a 150-year-old album of photographs titled *Souvenir of New Mexico, ca. 1861–1868,* holding images that had been passed around for decades. These were usually poor-quality and badly attributed copies never properly identified as to true subject or source.

The story would have been lost to time if the album had not been donated to the Photo Archives in 2007, a windfall for the archive and the beginning of a mystery ready to reveal itself. Originally purchased by the architect John Gaw Meem in the 1930s from a rare book dealer in New York, the album chronicles the history of the West, a souvenir, if you will, of a very tumultuous time that included the Civil War, the Long Walk, and the French Intervention in Mexico.

But the story really begins to unfold when in 2014 the arts and culture magazine *Pasatiempo* at the *Santa Fe New Mexican* published an essay with photographs from the album to coincide with the annual Southwestern Association for Indian Arts annual market. Reading the album like a detective novel, Devorah Romanek and Khristaan Villela began shedding light on the mysterious origins of this important photographic document by identifying people and possible photographers. That photo essay drew the attention of the New Mexico Council on Photography, which generously donated the funds to expand the research started in this article and publish a book on the subject by the University of Oklahoma Press.

In *Hardship, Greed, and Sorrow*, Romanek has undertaken exhaustive research to tell the story of this photo album. The foreword by Jennifer Nez Denetdale, great-great-great-granddaughter of Navajo headman Manuelito, and his wife Juanita, who were held at Bosque Redondo, provides personal perspective on the story. Publication of this book is a testament to the value photo archives contribute to our shared visual history, and as they say, a picture is indeed worth a thousand words.

ACKNOWLEDGMENTS

Many librarians, archivists, curators, and scholars have contributed in a variety of ways to the research for this book. There are too many to name, but I thank some here.

I am thankful for the generous assistance of the New Mexico History Museum, Santa Fe, and for the New Mexico Council on Photography's Beaumont Newhall Grant in support of this book's publication.

Those who deserve special thanks are the great supporters and progenitors of this project: Jonathan Frederick Walz, Director of Curatorial Affairs and Curator of American Art, The Columbus Museum, Georgia, and enabler of community and scholarly connections, without which this book would have not come to be; Khristaan Villela, Director, National Museum of International Folk Art, who initially invited me to write about this topic with him; Daniel Kosharek, Photo Curator, Palace of the Governors Photo Archive, New Mexico History Museum, who supported and shepherded this project from start to finish with great enthusiasm and patience; Hannah Abelbeck, Archivist, Palace of the Governors Photo Archive, New Mexico History Museum, who dove in and worked with me on research, making some of the greatest recoveries of photographs that had been lost to history but for her sleuthing; Jennifer Denetdale, Associate Professor of American Studies, University of New Mexico, who participated in many conversations about Navajos and photography, as I know we will continue to do; Will Wilson, photographer, Head of Photography, Santa Fe Community College, who looked at the *Souvenir* album with me and offered great insight, and who continues to be willing to engage in an ongoing conversation about photographs; Dave Phillips, retired Curator of Archaeology and former Interim Director of the Maxwell Museum of Anthropology, and a great friend and supporter.

Others for whose help and support I am ever grateful include Jane Blyth, Jennifer Schmandt and William C. Jennings, descendants of Charles T. Jennings;

Elaine Rosen, daughter-in-law of Evelyn Rosen; John Wolfenstein, great-grandson of Valentin Wolfenstein; Audra Bellmore, the John Gaw Meem Archives of Southwestern Architecture, University of New Mexico; Diane Bird, Museum of Indian Arts and Culture; Dennis Daily, New Mexico State University Library; Deb Slaney, Albuquerque Museum; Anneke Groeneveld, Nederlands Fotomuseum; James Faris, anthropologist; Jennifer Brathovde, Library of Congress; Gina Rappaport and Daisy Njoku, Smithsonian Institution National Anthropological Archives; Paula Fleming, retired *Smithsonian* photo archivist; Emily Moazami and Nathan Sowry, Smithsonian Institution National Museum of the American Indian; Jonathan Eaker, Library of Congress; Danny Gonzalez, El Paso Public Library Border Heritage Center; Jason Stratman, Missouri Historical Society; Wendi Goen, Arizona State Library, Archives and Public Records; Bill Becker, director, photographymuseum.com; Clare Vasquez, Marianne Cavanaugh, Pat Boulware and Alex Marr, Saint Louis Art Museum; Anna Lee Pauls and Gabriel Swift, Rare Books and Special Collections, Princeton University Library; Cynthia Mackey and Katherine Meyers Satriano, Peabody Museum of Archaeology and Ethnology at Harvard University; Teresa Coble, Kansas Historical Society; J. Dale West, Civil War historian; Lori Wheeler, AHEC/USAMHI; Alan Chilton, Wilson's Creek National Battlefield; Eric Duncan, Cowan's Auctions; Nicholas Natanson, National Archives and Records Administration; Carol Johnson, independent researcher; Lee Burke, independent researcher; Donovan Quintero, Navajo Times; Fernando Herrera, independent researcher; Jaime Bourassa, Missouri History Museum; Sarah Walpole, Royal Anthropological Institute; Matthew Daniel Mason, Beinecke Rare Book and Manuscript Library, Yale University; James Eason, Newberry Library; Dylan Joy, University of Texas at Austin; Barbara Angus, El Paso Museum of History; Aaron Roth, New Mexico Historic Sites; Mitch Barker, volunteer research librarian, Fort Union National Monument; Kate Fitzpatrick and Rebekah Tabah Percival, Arizona Historical Society; Rachel Adler, New Mexico State Archives; John Waggener, University of Wyoming; Grace Roybal, Bosque Redondo Memorial; Wesley Thomas, School of Diné Studies; Lydia Nibley, independent filmmaker; Will Roscoe, independent researcher and activist; Coi Drummond-Gehrig and Abby Hoverstock, Denver Public Library; Nancy Blomberg, Denver Art Museum; Harris Francis, Diné elder; Clarenda Begay, Navajo Nation Museum; Klara Kelley, anthropologist; Jeremy Rowe, independent researcher; and Steve Lansdale, Heritage Auctions.

Great thanks are also due to the two editors who worked on this project, Nancy Warrington and Sandy Nelson, as well as to the anonymous readers.

HARDSHIP, GREED, AND SORROW

INTRODUCTION

THIS IS A STORY TOLD IN PICTURES taken by an anonymous photographer and annotated by an anonymous scribe. The still images assembled by the officer of the title capture moments from a turbulent and painful time in post–Civil War New Mexico, when the Territory was torn by the crosscurrents of war, conquest, appropriation, and exploitation.

This book reveals the connections suggested in the images, taken singly and collectively. It's a story bookended by greed and sorrow, with hardship shot throughout, most poignantly reflected in the images of those most uprooted and devastated—the Navajo people.

Souvenir of New Mexico, which is the center of this story, is an album of sixty-three mounted photographs taken circa 1866 by one or more photographers and assembled under that title by a U.S. Army officer stationed in New Mexico Territory after the American Civil War.[1] Since 2007, it has been a treasured but relatively unknown part of the Palace of the Governors Photo Archives collection in Santa Fe, New Mexico.

A number of the photographs from the album have been widely reproduced, often without much attention paid to their original context or how and why they were created, as well as often being improperly or inaccurately attributed. The photographs perhaps most reproduced are those of forts, as original-era copies of those photographs can be found in numerous archives. However, almost all of the portraits in this album are found only in this album as original-era prints, and therefore exist only in the Palace of the Governors Photo Archives. In only a couple of instances (i.e., the portrait of Benito Juárez and five of the portraits of Navajos) are any of these portraits found as original-era prints in other photo archives. A handful of archives hold original-era prints related to these portraits, but when these images are found in archives elsewhere, or when they are distributed in publications or online, they can almost always be traced back to this album.

The story of the provenance of the album reads like a mystery in which some loose ends remain untied and some elements unsolved. This book will reveal what is known about the collection, its compiler, and the photographer or photographers who captured images of a freighted and complex moment in the history of the American Southwest. By drilling down into the historical context of the images, and by connecting the seemingly disparate histories the distinct groups of portraits seem to display, a microhistory of time and place is presented as a way to grapple with the larger historical questions and themes the photographs touch on. While the themes dealt with in this book, as depicted in the album, have been discussed individually in other scholarly works, never have the numerous themes of the day and particular historical events illuminated in the album been dealt with in one place, linked together as they inextricably were in their own time.[2]

Souvenir of New Mexico was donated to the Photo Archives by the daughter of the legendary New Mexico architect John Gaw Meem, who purchased the album in the 1930s from the New York rare-book dealers Samuel Dauber and Nathan Pine of Dauber and Pine.[3] It's unclear how the album came into the booksellers' possession or where it was in between its compilation and its rediscovery, but notes that accompany the album by Frederic H. Douglas, curator of Indian Art at the Denver Museum of Art in the 1930s, explain how Meem acquired the collection. Meem's deep sense of history and place, his role as a preservationist, and his awareness of important cultural currents are evident in his decision to buy the album.

Each photograph measures seven by nine inches and is mounted on its own page, with captions written in pencil or ink. The images were made using the wet-plate collodion technique and reproduced as either salt or albumen prints. The album that contains the images was likely sold premade with blank pages that the owner filled according to his own plan; a custom-made album of the time would not have blank pages at the end or lack special endpapers, as this album does.

Given the subjects and themes—Mexican politicians, capitalists, soldiers, military installations, and Native Americans—it's safe to surmise that the images were collected by a U.S. Army officer serving at one or more of the depicted forts and posts to remind him of the places and faces he encountered during his time in New Mexico. His serendipitous decision to document such memories and experiences offers a rare and evocative, if not cataclysmic for some, glimpse into an eventful year in New Mexico history and in the lives of the people pictured.

The album is arranged by theme, suggesting both historical context and chronology of events. It begins with studio portraits of Mexican president Benito Juárez and members of his cabinet taken in El Paso del Norte (today's Ciudad Juárez) while Mexican forces were waging a guerrilla war against Emperor

Maximilian I with support from the U.S. government.[4] It continues with pictures of U.S. Army officers, government officials, and prominent merchants of the day, and the forts and buildings where they were based or had business, particularly as these related to their presence in the Southwest in connection to the Civil War and the American Indian Wars, specifically the Apache Wars (1851–1900) and the Navajo Wars (1846–1868).[5] Of the military installations photographed in New Mexico and Texas, most are of Fort Sumner—its buildings and troops and the Navajos and Apaches interned there between 1863, when the Mescalero Apaches, the first to be interned, arrived, and 1868, when the Navajos returned home.[6] It concludes with posed studio portraits of Native American warriors and women whose dress and demeanor express both defiance and the misery of their uprooted lives.

Until now, *Souvenir of New Mexico* had not been published in its entirety, though *some* of the images it contains have been broadly reproduced and circulated. This book represents the first systematic effort to identify the people who took the photographs and the person who gathered and organized them into a visual memoir of his time in New Mexico Territory. The historical research involved in this undertaking required collaboration with numerous museums and ultimately reconnected related photographs that were scattered among disparate and disassociated collections and archives. Among other things, it unearthed copies of a previously unidentified image of the famed

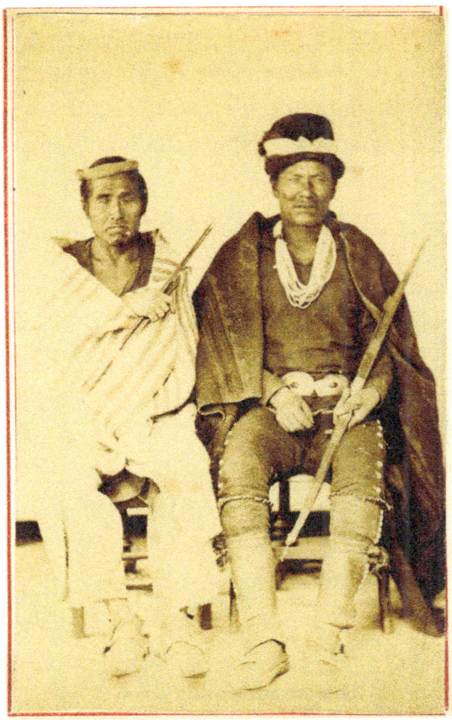

FIG. 1. Unidentified Navajo man (*left*) and Navajo headman Manuelito (*right*), New Mexico Territory, ca. 1866–1868. Photograph by Nicholas Brown é Hijo. Carte de visite mount; albumen print. The British Museum, William Blackmore Collection, Album 9, AM, A9.59. Photograph © The Trustees of the British Museum.

Copies of this photograph are found in both the British Museum and the Smithsonian Institution National Museum of the American Indian collections. In neither collection, at the time of research for this book, had the photograph been identified as portraying Manuelito. In the version at the Smithsonian Institution National Museum of the American Indian, the print is erroneously attributed to Edward F. Weed, who would have been the collector of the image (Smithsonian Institution, National Museum of the American Indian, P07353).

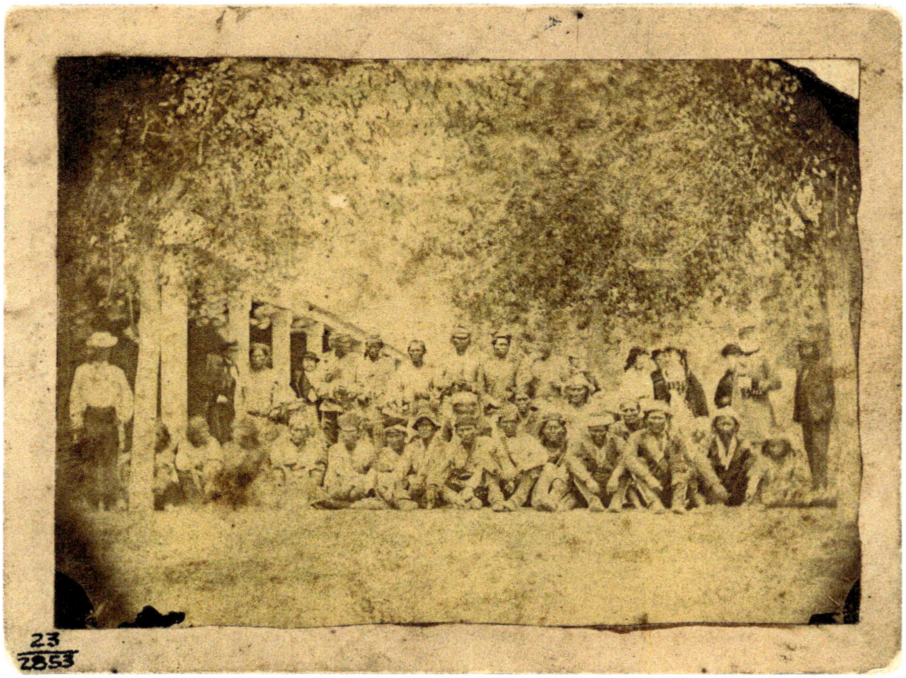

FIG. 2. Peace commission and the signing of the Navajo Treaty, Fort Sumner, New Mexico Territory, June 1, 1868. Photograph by Valentin Wolfenstein. The three male figures seated bottom right (*from left to right*) are Cayetanito, Manuelito, and Barboncito. Albumen print. Smithsonian Institution, National Museum of the American Indian, P20819.

The print was erroneously attributed to William N. Grier at the time of its donation to the National Museum of the American Indian by a descendant of Grier.

and prominent Navajo headman Manuelito (figure 1), and a long-lost 1868 photograph that depicts the signing of the treaty that allowed interned Navajos to return to their homeland (figure 2). While this book focuses on the photographs in this album, piecing together the story the images have to tell, there is a larger entanglement of connection between the *Souvenir* album photographs and other related photographic portraits of the era that, when taken together as a larger body of narrative and evidence, weave together a more complete picture of the era.

Beyond serving as a reminder of people and places, the album depicts associations and alliances that the compiler wished to remember, as well as ties he might not have recognized or that had not yet fully evolved, such as political and business affinities, cultural associations, and links between people and places. The individuals and places seen in the album are all joined, first and foremost, by their relationship with the person who assembled the images.

The interlaced themes of indigeneity, war, slavery, and colonialism weave through the silent narrative. The first image and last group of images portray indigenous peoples of the Americas at a time when the United States, fresh from its victory over the southern slavocracy, prepared to battle tribal nations that blocked its "Manifest Destiny" to control all lands between the Pacific and Atlantic coasts south of the Canadian border and north of Mexico. As a Zapotec from Oaxaca, Juárez, the subject of the first photograph in the album was the first indigenous person to rule in Mexico since the Spanish overthrew the Aztec confederation in the early sixteenth century.[7] His status contrasts starkly with that of the Navajo exiles whose photographs conclude the collection. War, or its consequences, is visible in nearly every image. Pictures of Civil War veterans stationed in the West to subdue the original inhabitants and enforce the eighteen-year-old boundary between the United States and Mexico follow photos of the Mexican president and his advisors, who were exiled by war and dependent on a former adversary for arms, ammunition, and espionage. Images of Native American prisoners of war follow pictures of the landscape they fought to keep and the forts and military installations built to protect and equip the soldiers determined to remove them from their homelands and imprison them in the name of U.S. imperialism.

Slavery is a subtext that runs throughout the album. Many of the army officers portrayed in it, who fought to end chattel slavery, themselves often facilitated the holding of indigenous peoples as captive slaves or peons before and after New Mexico's establishment as a U.S. territory. In some cases, the officers, too, held indigenous captives. Congress outlawed peonage in 1867 specifically to halt the practice of holding people in bondage in New Mexico Territory, either through the system of peonage or captive slavery, though even with the passage of this legislation these practices persisted into the twentieth century.[8] Peonage was the practice of holding people indebted to landlords or business owners in servitude until the debt was paid, while captive slavery was the outright capturing of Native Americans, often baptizing them and coercing their labor.[9] The album features people from communities who were to be found on all sides of the institution and the issue of peonage or captive slavery: those who tolerated and facilitated these practices, those who lost loved ones to peonage and slavery, and those who possibly were forced into prostitution by kidnappers and sex traffickers (see plates 51, 52, 54, 61, and 62).

Close examination of the images and research into their subjects reveal the social, cultural, and financial connections forged by colonialism and conquest. All the men in the second section of the collection had business dealings with one another at various points in their lives. Members of the Santa Fe Ring and other cabals appear. (The Santa Fe Ring of the late nineteenth century was an unofficial organization of powerful men who amassed great fortunes through speculation, fraud, and corruption).[10] Their presence in the album foreshadows the violence they would later incite in the Lincoln County War of 1878 and the El Paso Salt War of 1877 and 1878.[11] Despite whether it was the album compiler's intention to do so, his collection binds together the haves and have-nots of 1866 New Mexico—men enriched by the spoils of war and entire nations whose subjugation and captivity made that theft possible.

Before the research described in this book, no one had explored the deep and literal interconnections of all those portrayed in the album: soldiers and captives, exiled Mexican statesmen and the onetime enemy that smuggled arms to help them repel a foreign invasion. The events, people, and themes present here have been interrogated separately but have never been taken together as one integral story of a place and time. All the people portrayed in the album were bound together by commerce (above and below board), trade in food and flesh, a pursuit of autonomy (on national or factional levels), and the struggle to survive—as displaced indigenous tribes; disenfranchised Nuevomexicanos (New Mexicans of Spanish descent); or Anglos seeking treasure, opportunity, adventure, or battle—in a harsh environment. The people in these portraits lived at a time when national borders were being redrawn—including around indigenous nations inside the recently preserved union of the United States of America. Inside the *Souvenir* album, as in life, the story of those portrayed is a shared one, even though many of their names may never be known.

Photography in Mid-Nineteenth-Century New Mexico

To solve the puzzle of who took the pictures in *Souvenir of New Mexico*, the anthropological/historical sleuth looks first for forensic evidence in the images themselves and for hints of a consistent style or creative approach that would indicate the work of a single individual. It's not enough to simply accept the stamped name on a printed photograph, as negatives created by one photographer often ended up in another photographer's studio to be printed with that photographer's stamp. It seems unlikely, though not impossible, that one individual could have taken photographs of all the places and people depicted in this album in the space of one or two years.[12] Furthermore, stylistic presentations, production qualities, and contemporary accounts of when and where photographers were working suggest the possible handiwork of at least two people or two photographic partnerships, one for the portraits and one for the landscapes.

At the time these pictures were taken, photography was an emerging visual arts discipline, and the technology of capturing images was complicated and cumbersome. The daguerreotype of the early nineteenth century used a silver-plated copper sheet that was polished and then washed with iodine, which made the surface light-sensitive when placed in a camera. After twenty to thirty minutes of exposure, the sheet was treated with silver chloride to fix the image. The tintype, patented in 1856, most often used iron to mount the image, not tin as the name would indicate, and the process allowed pictures to be taken quicker and cheaper and resulted in a much lighter and more durable image than the daguerreotype, making it the most popular type of photograph during the Civil War.[13] The collodion wet-plate process, which was used to create the *Souvenir* album, emerged in the 1850s, mostly supplanting the daguerreotype and tintype by the early 1860s.[14] With this technique, a plate of glass is coated with a light-sensitive chemical mixture and placed into a camera while wet to capture an image as a negative.

Positive prints, higher-quality images with sharper details than the tintype, printed from the collodion wet-plate glass negatives, were made using paper treated with salt, silver nitrate, and other chemicals:

> The common silver-print is made on paper coated with egg albumen, which has been "salted" with chloride of sodium or ammonium, and sensitized by floating on a strong solution of silver nitrate. The dry paper is usually fumed with ammonia shortly before it is used. After proper exposure to sunlight under the negative, the print is fixed by immersion in hyposulphite of soda. In the fixing bath[,] the picture acquires an objectionable reddish tint, which is corrected . . . [with a] "toning" [bath]. After the prints are toned and fixed, all the soluble substances which they retain must be completely removed by thorough washing with water.[15]

In the mid- to late nineteenth century, albumen papers were popular, and by the end of the century, billions of eggs had been used to create these prints.[16] The collodian wet-plate technique, in addition to creating a sharper image than a tintype, was more lucrative than the daguerreotypes or tintypes, because a photographer could make multiple prints from a single negative.[17]

Some photographers in this era had studios, but most were itinerant photographers who traveled to battlefields and other sites using wagons as portable darkrooms and as a means to lug all the heavy equipment their craft demanded. The collodion wet-plate process required that the photographer carry the camera (90 pounds), the camera plate holder (25 pounds when holding a plate), the darkroom tent (about 13 pounds), glass plates for negatives, chemicals (approximately seventeen different kinds), a barrel of fresh water, and assorted other equipment and supplies. The total weight of equipment could be between 120 and 200 pounds.[18]

The westward movement of photography began shortly after Samuel Morse, inventor of the telegraph, imported the first daguerreotype camera in 1839, bringing the camera to New York City.[19] This westward migration of photography coincided with the settlement and expansion of the U.S. frontier—a phenomenon that many photographers wanted to experience and document. New Mexico was not yet a U.S. territory in 1847 when an anonymous photographer made the first known photograph in what became New Mexico Territory, a daguerreotype portrait of padre Antonio José Martínez (figure 3), a progressive proponent of

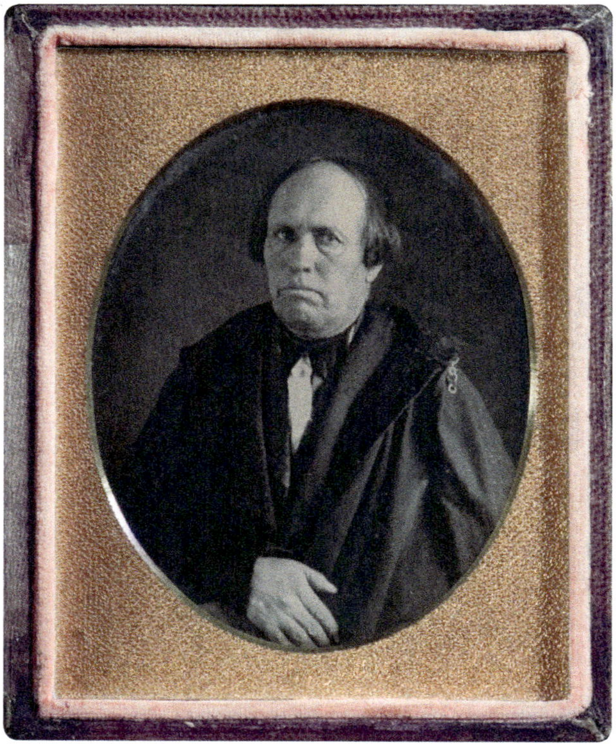

FIG. 3. Padre Antonio José Martínez, Taos, New Mexico Territory, ca. 1847. Photographer unknown. Daguerreotype, silver/copper, brass, glass, wood, leather, paper, velveteen; 4¾ × 3¾ × ¾ in. Photograph of the daguerreotype by Heugh Edmondson. The Albuquerque Museum, Ward Alan and Shirley Jolly Minge Collection. Museum purchase, 1995, PC1998.27.29.

This is the earliest known photograph taken in the New Mexico Territory.

land reform, first president of the upper house of New Mexico's first U.S. territorial legislature, and owner of the first printing press in New Mexico.[20]

Before 1870, when the railroad arrived in Denver (making Santa Fe more accessible), other daguerreotypists came to or moved through New Mexico only via overland trails.[21] The earliest *known* daguerreotypist in Santa Fe was Siegmund Seligman, a German Jewish immigrant who arrived in Santa Fe in 1851 and opened a daguerreotype studio in 1854, which he operated until 1856.[22] Another early photographer in New Mexico was Professor T. McEwen, who set up shop for a few months in Santa Fe; in 1859, he made two portraits of Kit Carson, whose portrait is absent from the *Souvenir* album, even though Carson's actions played a big part in the events it documents (figure 4).[23]

Although the Civil War was the first war to be extensively documented in photographs,[24] there are relatively few images of Civil War battles in the West and practically none from New Mexico, even though pivotal skirmishes happened there. In New Mexico, the most important battles happened at Valverde in February 1862 and Glorieta Pass in March 1862. A handful of photographs immortalize the Glorieta battle, including one image found in a collection at

FIG. 4. Kit Carson, 1859. Photograph by T. McEwen, Santa Fe, New Mexico Territory. Ambrotype portrait. The Newberry Library, Everett D. Graff Collection.

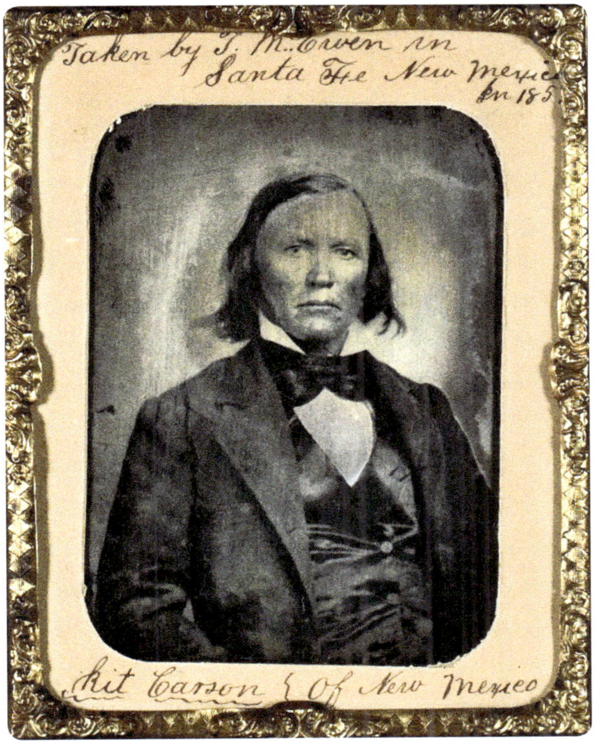

the National Anthropological Archive (NAA) of the Smithsonian Institution, in the *James E. Taylor Scrapbook of the American West*. This scrapbook is worth mentioning, as it becomes helpful in understanding the *Souvenir* album. Before the Civil War, "there had been little photography in the West,"[25] but after the Civil War, photography in the West burgeoned as a way to envision an America of "unending wonders, and limitless possibilities for the remaking of the American nation."[26] Among the earliest photographers to arrive in New Mexico were many who got their start during the Civil War, some having trained directly with Mathew Brady, a prolific American photographer most well known for his photographs of the Civil War, in his studio in New York.[27]

Many of the glass plate negatives of this era no longer exist, including (as far as is known) the negatives for this album. In the mid-nineteenth century, glass was scarce and plate negatives were often scraped clean so they could be reused. "Plate recycling" was the work of itinerate junk men who would collect unwanted negatives and sell the recycled glass to dry-plate manufacturers.[28]

The story of the photographs from the Souvenir Album that is about to unfold in the following pages brings mid-nineteenth-century New Mexico into sharper focus, making the times, places, and people more palpable and alive. Many of the questions that this album has begged, which have heretofore gone unanswered, are addressed. A dense interconnectedness of people and events is revealed even as new avenues of inquiry are opened up to be further explored. The violence of the time is not depicted directly in the images, but it is inferred: desperation and oppression sit just beyond the frame of the images. If in "reading" photographs we are apt to overinterpret, to project our own emotions onto people sitting before a camera long ago, the histories and networks revealed through research for this book do affirm that if we imagine we see on the faces of the people pictured here hardship, greed, and sorrow, we may not be wrong.

CHAPTER 1

FACES AND PLACES

Portraits and Landscapes in the *Souvenir* Album

PORTRAITS AND LANDSCAPES are the two main categories of photographs in the *Souvenir* album. The "landscapes," however, are perhaps more like "scenes." On the one hand, many of the landscapes, including many of the panoramic images of forts, are cut off from the actual terrain and physical features of the larger geography within which they sit and are strangely unpopulated. On the other hand, some scenes in forts or landscapes are incredibly populated with people, such that in either case, these "landscapes" do not appear to be what is typically thought of as a landscape (i.e., a vista with a view). The specific forts portrayed are clues to how the officer who compiled the photographs was associated with particular military installations. The views of officers' quarters at Fort Union (plates 13 and 14) and Fort Bliss, and specifically of reconstruction at Fort Bliss (plates 37 and 38), imply that the compiler was housed in those quarters and was present at Fort Bliss when they were being rebuilt.[1] If the fort photos are indeed souvenirs of personal assignments or tours of duty, the compiler would seem to have been stationed the longest at four of the forts: Fort Union, Fort Marcy, Fort Bliss, and Fort Sumner.

Details of various aspects of Fort Union (plates 13–20) show most of the fort, indicating perhaps that the compiler spent a long time there. Likewise, the compiler may have spent a fair amount of time at Fort Marcy and in Santa Fe (plates 21–28), since about half of the plates are of the Plaza, and the others are of Fort Marcy. The photo of General Carleton's quarters (plate 25) shows two men in a buggy, and the man closest to the viewer is perhaps Carleton himself. The images of Franklin, Texas, and Fort Bliss (plates 32–40), coupled with the portraits of Benito Juárez and his cabinet, point to the compiler being at Fort Bliss in the general time frame when the Mexican government was in exile in El Paso del Norte, just across the border (fall of 1865 until spring of 1866). The images of Fort Sumner and Bosque Redondo are directly connected to the portraits of Navajos at the end of the album. There are far fewer photographs of other forts, so it seems possible that the compiler may have only briefly been at those forts, including Los Pinos (plate 29) and Fort Craig (plates 30 and 31).[2] Pictures of Franklin, Texas (today's El Paso), and Santa Fe, New Mexico, suggest that the compiler also spent time in those towns (plates 21–24 and 32).[3]

In one 1866 photograph of Santa Fe (plate 23), two men lean on either side of the doorway of a bakery that is mentioned in James F. Meline's 1866 account of his journey across the Southwest: "Crossing the stony bed of the creek, and passing the alternating fields and adobes, we enter the Plaza. English and Spanish signs[,] intermingled, meet the eye. '*Vienta de las Vegas*,' '*Bakery*,' '*Effectos*,' &c."[4] This image also shows corn growing on the Plaza, barely visible on the edge of the photograph. One image of Franklin (plate 32) shows a business, "S. Schutz & Bro., Tienda Barata," with a horse-drawn carriage and four men standing in front. This general merchandise store on San Francisco Street belonged to Samuel Schutz and his brother Joseph, the first Jews to arrive in the city, having emigrated from Westphalia, Germany, in 1854 and 1859, respectively.[5] The various landscapes and the details they reveal surely had meaning for the compiler, and they help explicate the narratives of the *Souvenir* photographs. Whether or not the compiler intentionally selected these photographs for those details is hard to say, though it is difficult to imagine spending time in those towns and not patronizing or being familiar with the bakery in Santa Fe or the largest purveyor of goods in Franklin.

The portraits are assembled in three sets, each taken at different times and places, with the contexts of each appearing seemingly unrelated. It's not a given that one person was responsible for taking the photographs in all three of the sets. Additionally, at first glance, the portraits of Juárez and his cabinet, of U.S. Army officers and Anglo civilians, and of Navajos seem to reflect the creative tastes and perspectives of more than one photographer. However, in visiting this more thoroughly, the notion of more than one photographer, or one team of photographers, for the portraits is drawn into question.

Beginning at the front of the album, the set of portraits of Juárez and his cabinet (plates 1–5) show a consistency among them that suggests one person took all these portraits. All the sitters pose before the same clumsily painted backdrop—an outdoor garden with a Romanesque pillar—that is most visible in the portrait of Sebastián Lerdo de Tejada, minister of foreign affairs (plate 2). Each sits with his right arm leaning on a table that has a book or books. The table has the same damask cloth in each image, except for the image of Señor Gotien (this is likely a misspelling of his name, though research has not unearthed his real name; plate 5), identified as the "Steward of the Household"; the table in his portrait is covered with a plain dark cloth. Each sitter poses with a different book, and only Juárez poses with two books on the table, the

Romanesque backdrop and the placement of the books representing the "cultural capital" of the sitter and reflecting the high status of those portrayed.[6]

More variability is seen in the second set of portraits featuring seven men, five army officers and two civilians (plates 6–12): Henry Cuniffe, a businessman and U.S. foreign consul in Mexico, based in El Paso del Norte; General James H. Carleton, leader of the California Column and commander of the Department of New Mexico; Captain David Hammett Brotherton, who had studied at the U.S. military academy, enlisted in the army in 1854, and served in Texas, Kentucky, Utah, New Mexico, Kansas, Minnesota, and ultimately at Fort Buford in what is now North Dakota, where he received the surrender of Sitting Bull, on July 20, 1881; Major Cyrus Curtis Clark, army paymaster at Franklin, Texas; Captain Emil Fritz, captain of Company B of the First Regiment California Volunteer Cavalry (part of the California Column), later assigned to Fort Sumner, ultimately becoming a ranch and business owner in Lincoln County, New Mexico; Major William McCleave (misspelled "McClave" on the inscription in figure 33c), who escaped famine in Ireland, came to America, and joined the mounted infantry (Dragoons), subsequently organizing the First California Cavalry under the command of Carleton, and later becoming the commander of Fort Sumner; and Nathan Webb, a business associate of Cuniffe's.

Six of the portraits in this set have plain backgrounds. In four, the background is darker and might be the wall of a room (plates 6, 7, 9, and 12: Cuniffe, Carleton, Clark, and Webb). The remaining two portraits have lighter backgrounds with no discernible details (plates 10 and 11: Fritz and McCleave). The remaining portrait, that of Brotherton (plate 8), has the same painted backdrop found in *all* the Juárez pictures, and he sits at a table with a plain dark cover, the same table cover as seen in the portrait of Gotien (plate 5); this offers the first real indication that these first two sets of portraits, that of Juárez and his cabinet and the set of the army officers and merchants, could be related. As for the props in this second set of portraits, three of the men sit at tables, two with the same damask cover seen in most of the Juárez photos (plates 6 and 9: Cuniffe and Clark). Clark also poses with two books as props (plate 9), just as Benito Juárez does.

The presence of similar props and backdrops in this second set of portraits (employed variably in plates 6–12) implies that one photographer took all or most of the photographs in this set and probably also took the portraits of Juárez and his fellow exiles. The portrait of Brotherton, which shares the same painted backdrop with the Juárez cabinet photographs, makes it almost certain that the same photographer or photographic team took all of these first twelve portraits (the first two sets) in the album (plates 1–12).

The set of Navajo portraits, consisting of thirteen images (plates 47, 48, 50–57b, 61, and 62), could be sorted into at least three groupings within the set, broken down into groups based on the commonalities of backdrops, carpeting, and props consistent within the groupings. Although the subjects are staged differently within each of the three groupings, *all* the portraits in the Navajo set were taken during the Navajo internment at Fort Sumner/ Bosque Redondo. In the first grouping within the set, nine portraits have been taken against a plain backdrop that sags slightly at the bottom. A plain carpet adorns the floor, and the sitters are wrapped in stylistically similar blankets in this grouping as well. All the men in this grouping sit in chairs, while most of the women in this grouping sit much lower to the ground, sitting either on the carpet or just slightly above it on a shallow platform covered by a blanket (plates 47, 48, 50, 52, 53, 55, 56, 57b, and 62), though in three of the portraits, women are seen sitting a bit higher, on either a covered stool, a box, or a chair (plates 52, 56 and 62). In the second grouping in this set, three portraits feature a patterned carpet (plates 51, 54, and 57a), as opposed to the plain carpet of the first set.

The last grouping consists of a single image, a group portrait, which is different in its backdrop from the rest of the portraits in this set. In that group portrait of five women and one girl (plate 61), the subjects are posed against a painted backdrop, with a plain carpet on the floor—the backdrop is the same sloppily painted backdrop seen in the Juárez cabinet set and the Brotherton portrait. Seemingly, the Navajo portraits might have been taken by a different photographer from the photographer or team of photographers that took the first two sets of portraits *but* for the backdrop that appears in the group portrait of the women. This one badly painted but unquestionably unique backdrop draws all three sets of portraits in the album together, strongly intimating that one photographer took all the portraits in all three sets. If more than one photographer was involved, they were associates—perhaps a team of photographers who worked together or shared props and equipment.[7]

The thirty-eight landscape photographs (plates 13–46, 49, 58–60) show the greatest variation by displaying variation of place, featuring different forts or towns, which makes sense given the nature and purpose of landscape photography. Photographic style varies little among the landscape images; there is nothing dramatic enough to indicate that more than one photographer took the landscapes or, for that matter, that the landscape photographer was someone other than the photographer who might have taken all the portraits. The album and its photos are alike enough that it's possible one person created them all. However, it is the sheer volume of photographs taken in a relatively short time span, the landscapes and portraits together, that make it a distinct possibility that one photographer took the portraits and another photographer took the landscapes, even though it is not impossible to say that one photographer took all the images.

Eye of the Beholder: Who Compiled the Album and Why?

The order and grouping of the images say something about the person who compiled the album and hint at his intended audience. A chronology or hierarchy is evident in the intentional manner in which groups of images are arranged.

The compiler would have almost certainly been a Union officer, even possibly one portrayed in the album. As such, he was likely involved with resistance to the French Intervention in Mexico and likely would have been part of U.S. efforts to support the Juaristas (followers of the Juárez government) in El Paso del Norte during or immediately after the U.S. Civil War. Comparatively little has been written and researched about this part of American-Mexican history, allowing the research undertaken for this book, which investigates the relationships between the first two sets of portraits, to deeply illuminate this specific history.[8] The album compiler was likely an army officer stationed at Franklin or Fort Bliss (plates 32–40) near El Paso del Norte, where Juárez and his cabinet made their headquarters during their exile. There he would have worked with the army officers pictured in the album, and he would have served at Fort Sumner during the Navajo internment there, specifically during the surrender of Manuelito and the small group of holdouts who surrendered with him (plates 41–62).

Perhaps by amassing these photos in this order and barely annotating what is pictured, the compiler hoped to express the narrative embedded in the images by recounting it orally to his intended audience with every viewing. Or the sparse annotation might be a sign that the compiler hoped to sell the collection to someone interested in its themes and left the door open for somebody else's narrative. However slight the annotations are on the photographs, they do, however, offer clues, with sometimes the slightest caption opening a window onto the time the photograph was taken or the attitude or context of the compiler or person who made the annotations.[9]

While the landscapes and forts that figure in the album offer some insight into the compiler's identity, many are found in other collections, publications, and archives, including in the U.S. Army Signal Corps collection of the National Archives. That collection contains many of the landscape photographs in this album—certainly almost all of the images of Fort Sumner and Bosque Redondo—as well as many of the photographs of other forts. The only landscape/fort image that is not found in other collections and appears to be singular to this collection is plate 44, which depicts soldiers and Navajos. While collected and retained by the Army Signal Corps, the photographs of forts in that collection were not commissioned by the organization; the photographic unit of the Army Signal Corps was only established in 1917.[10] The impetus for the numerous photographs of forts from this era would actually have been the

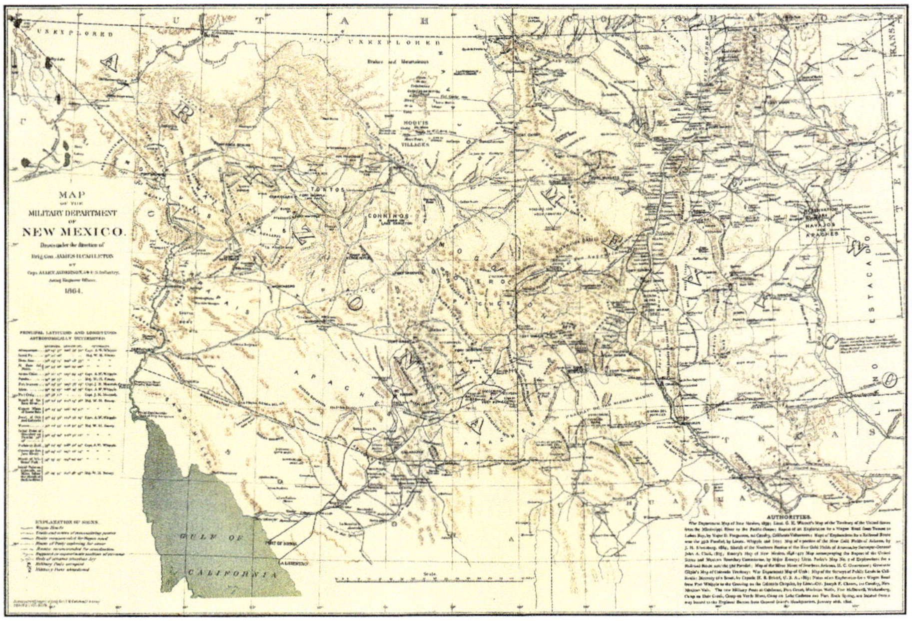

FIG. 5. Map of the Military Department of New Mexico, 1864. Drawn under the direction of Brigadier General James H. Carleton by Captain Allen Anderson. Fray Angélico Chávez History Library, Palace of the Governors Photo Archives, New Mexico History Museum, Santa Fe, 650512.

This map depicting U.S. Army forts in New Mexico was originally published by Julius Bien and Co., Lithographers, New York.

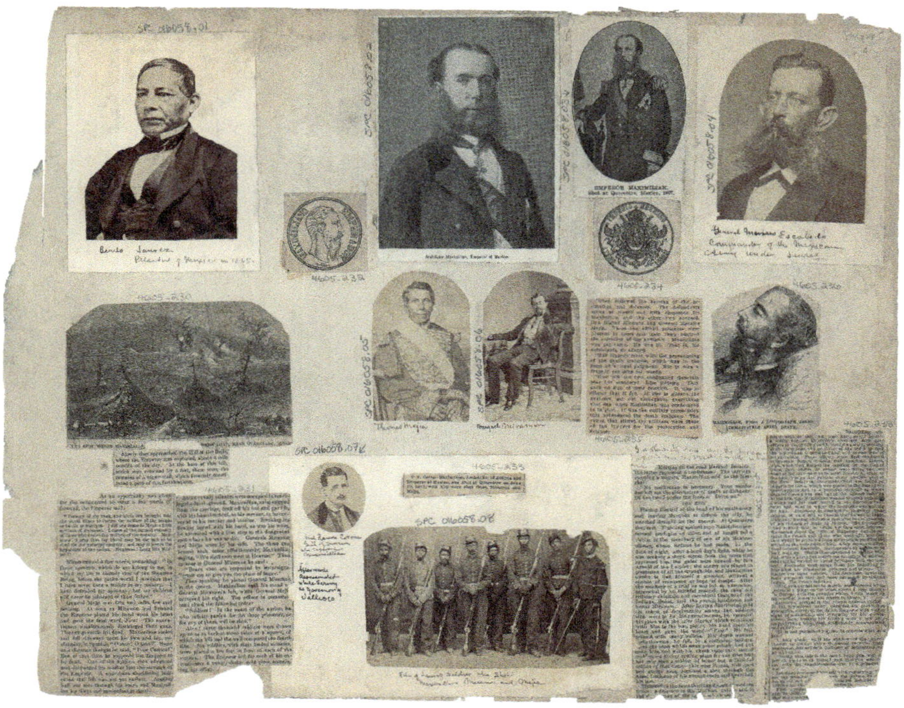

FIG. 6. James E. Taylor scrapbook of the American West, page 117. Benito Juárez, (*upper left*). Photographer unknown (possibly C. Duhem and Bro. or Gaige). Smithsonian Institution, National Museum of Natural History, National Anthropological Archives, Photo Lot 24 SPC BAE 4605 01605801.

issue of General Order No. 3, established by the quartermaster general in 1864, requiring each military district to document, with photographs or drawings, the condition of each structure built by the army.[11] The purpose of the order was to achieve accountability regarding structures owned or occupied by the U.S. military. With the issue of General Order No. 3 in 1864, it is reasonable to suppose that the dates for the photographs of forts in the album are not earlier than 1865, as it took time to organize the photographic documentation that this order required. The photographs of the forts alone do avail information about the compiler, or at least about the individuals portrayed in the album. Every U.S. Army officer portrayed in the album, as well as the Anglo merchants portrayed, was stationed at or had some business with many if not all of the forts represented. However, it is when the photographs are taken in relationship to one another that a larger picture emerges, which becomes even clearer when considering how these locations were mapped out (figure 5).

As opposed to the landscapes, which, again, are to be found in numerous collections and archives as original-era prints, most of the portraits are so rare and have so little documentation that it is hard to assess the driving impetus for or the original contexts in which they were taken. The portraits of Juárez and Carleton are the most widely circulated of the portrait images, but most are circulated as reproductions, with the *Souvenir* album serving as the original source for them. The Juárez portrait as an original-era print is found, however, in three other archives in the United States, including in the National Anthropological Archive of the Smithsonian Institution in the Smithsonian's James E. Taylor Scrapbook of the American West (figure 6), as well as two other archives, and this becomes very revelatory. The Navajo portraits are the least circulated of all the images but nevertheless offer the greatest insights into the photographer and compiler.

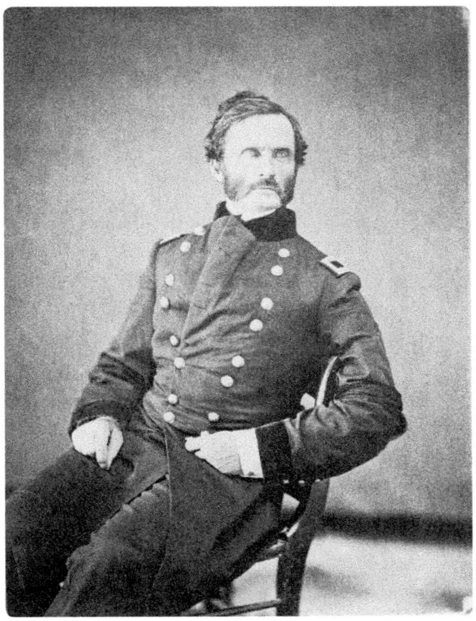

FIG. 7. James H. Carleton, 1st California Infantry, ca. 1866. Photographer unknown (possibly C. Duhem and Bro. or Gaige). Glass, wet collodion negative. Library of Congress, Prints and Photographs Divison, LC-DIG-cwpb-07381.

As far as is known, no original negatives for any of the portraits survive, though there may be a related original negative from the army officer series. The Library of Congress has a collodion glass negative, which is to say mid-nineteenth-century negative, of a Carleton portrait (figure 7) that appears to be from the same sitting as the Carleton portrait in the *Souvenir* album (plate 7). In the Library of Congress negative, Carleton's pose is slightly different, but all the other details in the portrait are the same: the same chair, same background, and same uniform. Since the negative is a collodion glass negative, it is clearly from the original era, but it may nevertheless be a copy negative, and not an original one; that is unclear.

Of the Navajo portraits, a few of the exact images, or related images, are found in other archives as prints original to the era they were taken but perhaps are reprints. "Navajo Girl" (plate 51) depicts a girl in a *biil*, a traditional Navajo dress; she wears moccasins, and a blanket is draped around her shoulders. She sits on a shallow platform of some sort, covered in a blanket, and leans against a blanket-covered chair. One elbow rests on the box and her head rests against her hand. The Blackmore Collection at the British Museum has a portrait of the same girl, in an *almost* identical pose, though with a different carpet and different background (figure 8).[12] The backdrop in the Blackmore Collection portrait is the same as found in *Souvenir* album portraits of Juárez and his cabinet, of Brotherton, and of the Navajo women at Fort Sumner (plates 1–5, 8, and 61)—the poorly rendered outdoor garden with Romanesque pillars. This backdrop, again, is the link that connects all the *Souvenir* album portraits and all but proves they were taken by one photographer or group of photographic associates.

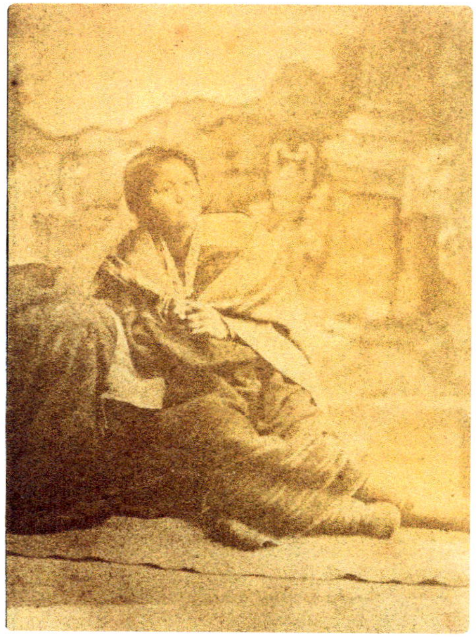

FIG. 8. Unidentified Navajo woman (Doña Jesús or her sister), New Mexico Territory, 1866. Photographer unknown (possibly C. Duhem and Bro. or Gaige). Carte de visite mount; albumen print. The British Museum, William Blackmore Collection, Album 9, AM, A9.91. Photograph © The Trustees of the British Museum.

The subject of "Navajo Girl" (plate 51) reappears yet again, this time in a photo with her sister, which is found only as a photocopy in the files of "J. G. Gaige" at the Palace of the Governors Photo Archives.[13] The photocopy is accompanied by a June 12, 1995, letter from a Joanna Blyth to Joanna Pace, project director for the Bosque Redondo Memorial at Fort Sumner, which opened in 1991 to commemorate the tragic episode in New Mexico history of the internment of the Navajos. Blyth writes that her family's photo collection includes one image not found in the Meem album photos that were reproduced for the memorial. An inscription on the back of this photocopied Blyth family photo identifies the subjects as "Doña Jesus & sister." The other girl in the photocopied double portrait could be the same girl seen in plate 54 in the *Souvenir* album, though the quality of the photocopy makes it difficult to say so conclusively.[14]

Another Navajo portrait from the album (plate 57a) is found as an original-era photographic print, which may or may not be a copy print, in various formats, in five separate archives: the American Philosophical Society collection; the James E. Taylor scrapbook of the American West, circa 1863–1900, in the National Anthropological Archives of the Smithsonian Institution; and, separately, as a copy negative in the National Anthropological Archives of the Smithsonian Institution, the Peabody Museum of Archaeology and Ethnology at Harvard University, and the Netherlands Photo Museum. In each instance where the image is found in these other archives, the subject, a Navajo man, is misidentified, with both his name and tribal affiliation labeled incorrectly, though *consistently* incorrect in almost every instance, except for in the Peabody Museum collection and the Netherlands Photo Museum, where the portrait is identified correctly as depicting a Navajo man. This is a classic example of the problems encountered when trying to trace the history of a 150-year-old photograph, its creator, and

FIG. 9. Ute and Jicarilla Indians, including agent W. F. M. Arny, New Mexico Territory, 1868. Photograph by Nicholas Brown. Palace of the Governors Photo Archives, New Mexico History Museum, Santa Fe, 045814.

This photograph was taken in the studio of Nicholas Brown, Santa Fe, New Mexico Territory. Sobita is standing just right of center in the back row, behind Arny, who stands dead center, back row. The photograph offers an opportunity to see a portion of Brown's studio and backdrop setup.

its collector. It also reflects how insignificant it was for colonizers, occupiers, and Anglos in general to name Native American individuals and recognize their autonomy and humanity. Subsequently, it has also opened the door for these images to later be commercialized and circulated devoid of their context.[15]

This particular portrait (plate 57a) depicts a Navajo man seated on a blanket-covered box or low stool, holding a bow and arrow, and is found, as mentioned, in numerous different collections. In most instances, the Navajo man is misidentified as Capote Ute chief Sobita. The numerous substantiated portraits of Sobita, an important scout and ally of the U.S. Army (instrumental in capturing large numbers of Navajos for the Army), show him attired in the manner of a Ute chief (figure 9), whereas the man in plate 57a is clearly dressed as a Navajo: his hair is tied in a *tsiiyéél*, and he wears a fur hunting cap, bandolier bag, cotton shirt and trousers, and footwear.

The American Philosophical Society Library's A. Zeno Shindler American Indian Photograph Collection labeled this portrait of a Navajo man as "Sobita (Head Chief of the Capote Utes and Brother of Carrisa, Head Chief of the

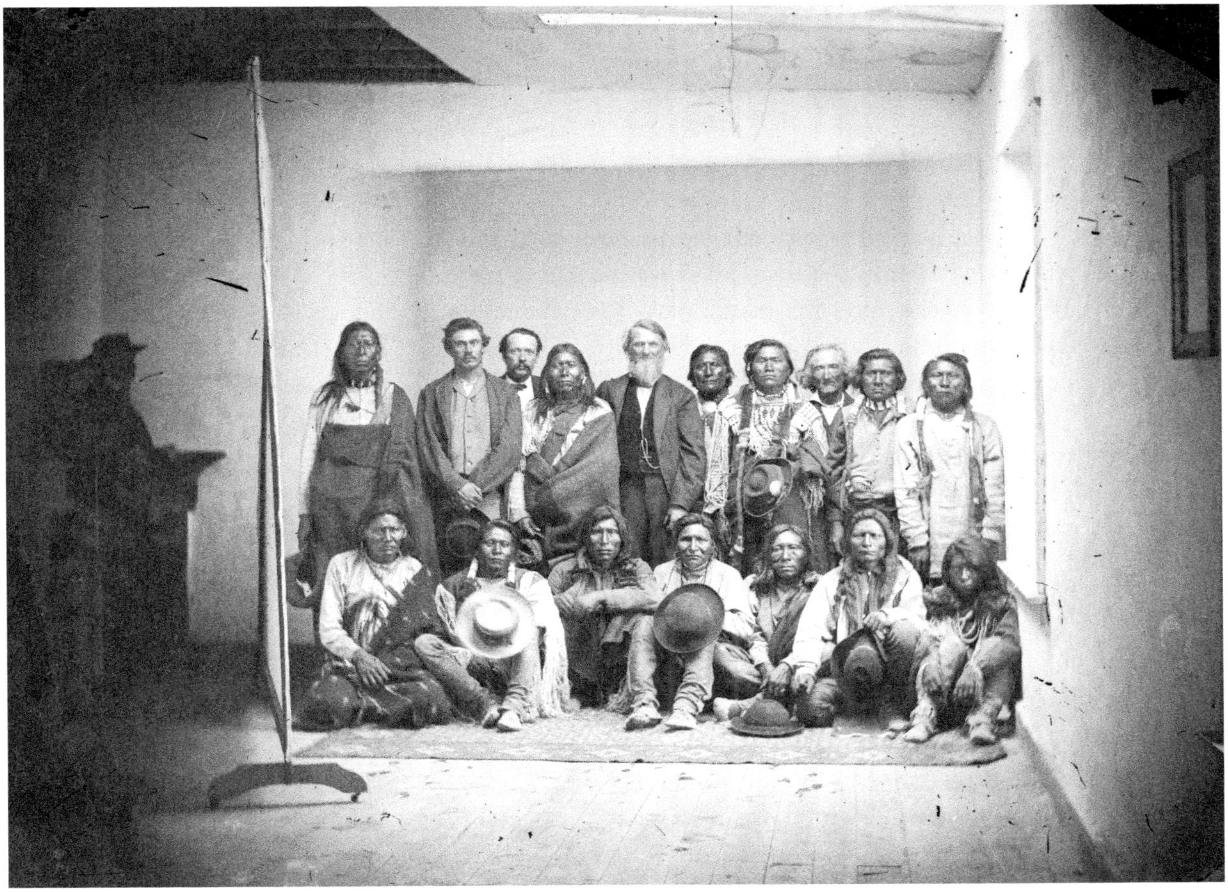

Utas, Colorado Territory, New Mexico)."[16] The photo is attributed to Antonio Zeno Shindler, a photographer who worked for the Smithsonian Institution from the end of the Civil War until his death in 1899. Shindler's main task for the Smithsonian was to copy early photographs of Native Americans at the encouragement of Ferdinand V. Hayden, head of the U.S. Geological Survey, and William Henry Blackmore, an English philanthropist, collector of Native American photographs and objects, and founder of the Blackmore Museum in Salisbury, England.[17] The Blackmore Museum was initially founded in 1864 to house the Squier and Davis collection of American archaeological finds from the earthwork mounds in Ohio.[18] With the suicide of William Blackmore in 1878, some of his papers and collections were dispersed, and beginning in the 1930s, the Blackmore Museum began a decades-long process of dispersing all of its holdings, with his papers on his work in New Mexico notably coming to the Historical Society of New Mexico.[19] Most of Blackmore's photograph collection came to the Smithsonian and to the British Museum.[20]

The National Anthropological Archives of the Smithsonian also has the same Navajo portrait mislabeled as "Sobita" in its James E. Taylor scrapbook of the American West (figure 10, upper left).[21] Taylor, an artist and correspondent for *Leslie's Illustrated Weekly Newspaper* from 1863 to 1883, amassed more than seven hundred images in his scrapbook, an astounding resource portraying the last decades of the nineteenth century in the American West, and he likely used it as a source for his own illustrations, many of which relate to the photographs of the *Souvenir* album, as seen, for example, on the page with the portrait mislabeled "Sobita." The scrapbook page also contains accounts of praise for Sobita, the praise being offered by Col. Albert H. Pfeiffer, a trapper and guide, agent of the Southern Ute, and a close friend of Kit Carson.[22] Additionally, the scrapbook page has a portrait of Pfeiffer affixed on the page next to the misnamed Navajo man (figure 10, center top). The page is clearly meant to recount events related to both Pfeiffer and Sobita. The page also has a letter written by Pfeiffer, in which he recounts how Sobita helped him pursue a group of Navajos or Apaches after they had burned down his house at the base of the Nacimiento Formation.[23] When selecting this image for the scrapbook, Taylor may have found the image of the Navajo man (plate 57a) already mislabeled as "Sobita." Written in ink on the page, the caption below the portrait reads "Sobita Ute Sub Chief Col Pfeiffer's friend." The Smithsonian National Anthropological Archives electronic record for that image in the scrapbook does, however, identify the image in the following manner: "Portrait of Barboncito (Little Beard) with Bow and Arrows, n.d." It should be noted, however, that the man in the portrait is not the well-known headman Barboncito, but a different and seemingly younger man (see the group portrait, figure 2, for an image of the headman Barboncito).

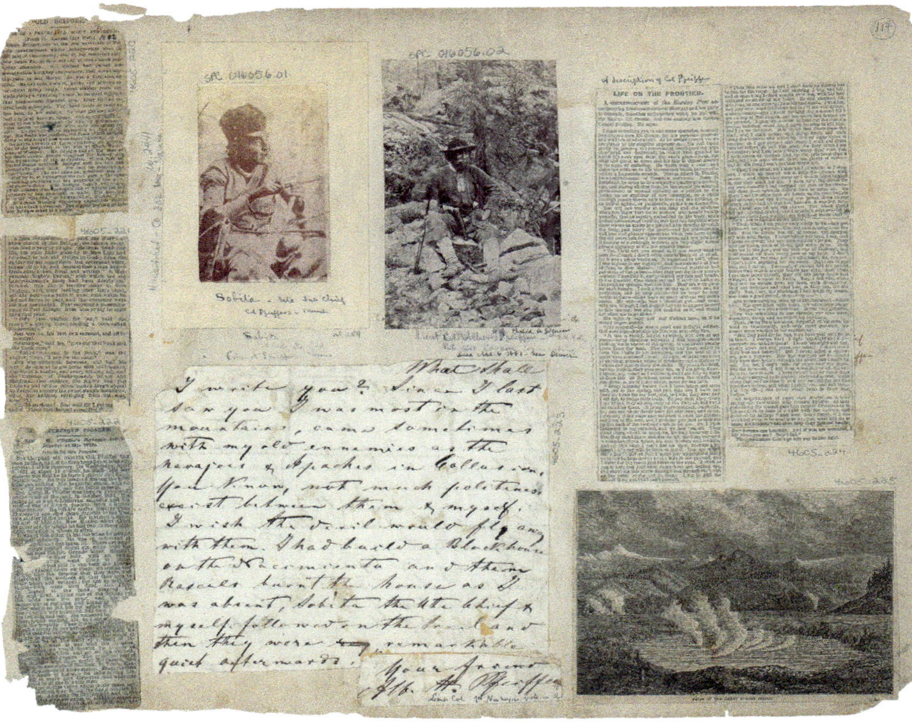

FIG. 10. James E. Taylor scrapbook of the American West, page 114. Photograph of a Navajo Man (*upper left*), and Colonel Albert Pfeiffer (*center top*). Smithsonian Institution, National Museum of Natural History, National Anthropological Archives, Photo Lot 24 SPC BAE 4605 0160560.

The photograph of Col. Pfeiffer was taken by Constant Duhem (1869), upon Duhem's rescue of Pfeiffer when he was lost in the woods near Denver, Colorado (no. 01605602). The photograph of the Navajo man, mislabeled "Sobita," which is the same image as plate 57a of the Souvenir album, bears the inscription "Sobita—Ute Sub Chief, Col Pfeiffer's Friend" (no. 01605601).

The Smithsonian National Anthropological Archives has a glass plate copy negative of the image of the Navajo man, for which the creator is listed as Antonio Zeno Shindler, and the date given is 1869, the year Shindler would have copied the original portrait. The electronic record for this image reflects that the subject is Navajo, stating: "Portrait (Profile) of Barboncito? (Little Beard) or (Full-Bearded Man) in Native Dress with Ornaments and Holding Bow and Arrows 1869." On the negative itself, photochemically embedded, the word "Navajo" and the number "786" are visible.

Another original-era copy of this print is found in the Peabody Museum of Archaeology and Ethnology at Harvard University.[24] To add yet another layer of confusion to the story, that image is attributed to William Henry Jackson, a painter who, in 1867, opened a photography studio in Omaha, Nebraska. In 1869, he became a photographer for the Union Pacific Railroad, taking photographs for promotional use. In 1870, he joined Hayden's geological survey and became a survey photographer for the geological and geographical surveys of that decade. In the early 1870s, Jackson picked up where Shindler left off by creating an ongoing catalog of more than one thousand images of North American Indians, which included most of the three hundred images Shindler had created either by taking them himself or, as we have seen, by copying them from the photographs of others, which included, once again, this portrait of a

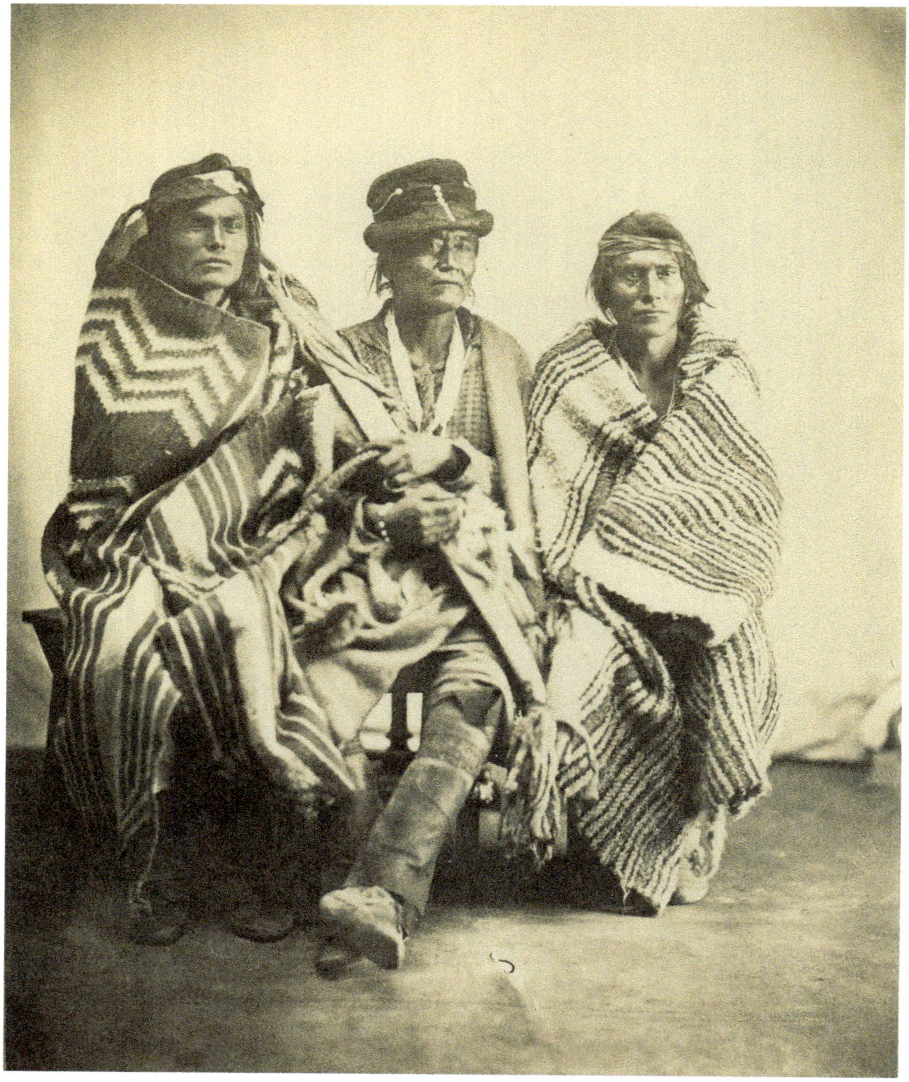

FIG. 11. Navajo men at or on their way to Fort Sumner, New Mexico Territory, 1866. Photographer unknown (possibly C. Duhem and Bro.). Albumen print adhered to paperboard, 7½ × 9½ in. (19.05 × 24.13 cm). Peabody Museum of Archaeology and Ethnology at Harvard University, 2004.29.4244.

The man on the left is likely Manuelito's brother El Ciego, and the man in the center is possibly his brother Cayetanito.

Navajo man (plate 57a).[25] In 1877, Jackson created his "Descriptive Catalogue of the Photographs of North American Indians," which offers a listing of the photographs that he assembled. It would seem, then, that Shindler made a copy of the portrait from an original 1866 print, and this in turn was copied by Jackson, finding its way into the Peabody collection.

Of additional note at the Peabody museum is an original-era print that is clearly from the same sitting as the set of Navajo portraits found in the *Souvenir* album, but like the photocopy of the image of "Doña Jesus & sister" found in the Gaige file at the Palace of the Governors, this specific image is not in the album (figure 11).[26] In the Peabody portrait, three Navajo men are seated. The man on the left-hand side, who is very likely Manuelito's brother, El Ciego (The Blind Man), is seen in two of the *Souvenir* album portraits (plates 53 and 57b), and the man in the center is possibly Manuelito's brother Cayetanito (also seen in plate 53). In the *Souvenir* group portrait depicting five men (plate 53), the man who may be El Ciego is seated on the left, and the man seated in the center of the Peabody portrait is also in the center of this *Souvenir* group portrait. The man who may be El Ciego is also seated on the right in the group portrait that bears the inscription "Navajo Thieves" (plate 57b) from the *Souvenir* album. It is not completely clear if the man on the right in the Peabody portrait appears in any of the other portraits of Navajo men in the *Souvenir* album, though it seems not. How this portrait came to be in the Peabody collection is not entirely clear, though it can be said that some of the photographs of Navajos in the Peabody collection came from Washington Matthews either directly or indirectly, through a donation by Lucy Kluckhohn, with this portrait likely being collected by Matthews. Washington Matthews was a U.S. Army surgeon and an ethnographer and a linguist, known particularly for his studies of the Navajo in the 1880s. He began these studies when he was appointed Post Surgeon to Fort Wingate in 1880.[27] The reason Matthews proves interesting is that it appears that some of the photographs he collected he obtained in August of 1883 from Herman F. C. ten Kate, a Dutch physical anthropologist. This proves relevant when considering the last original-era print of the Navajo man (plate 57a) found in circulation.

The portrait of the Navajo man is also, perhaps most compellingly, found in the archive of the Netherlands Photo Museum (see, for example, figure 19) along with four other portraits of Navajos, with writing on the reverse of the image that reads "Apache/or Navajo?," clearly indicating that when this specific print of the portrait was collected, it was not mislabeled as being an image of the Ute chief Sobita.[28] The other images in the Netherlands Photo Museum that are also found in the *Souvenir* album, in addition to the portrait that matches Plate 57a of the *Souvenir* album, are portraits that match Plates 47, 50, 56, and 62. All the prints in the Netherlands Photo Museum collection are attributed to Alfredo Laurent, a French photographer who was active in Mexico, and the collector of Laurent's photos is identified in the records of the Netherlands Photo Museum as Herman F. C. ten Kate, who donated the prints to the museum. The presence of the group portrait of three Navajo men found in the collection at the Peabody, and the connection between Matthews, ten Kate, and Laurent, though inconclusive, may be part of how these earliest of Navajo portraits, as found in the *Souvenir* album and in limited fashion elsewhere, circulated in the nineteenth century, as it seems highly likely that ten Kate was the source of the 1866 Navajo portraits for both Matthews and Laurent, but how did ten Kate acquire them? More is revealed about this set of photographs as found in the Netherlands further down the line, and this question will, at least in part, be answered.

Circulation of additional images from the group of Navajo portraits is found at the Library of Congress, which has a collection of copy prints of five of the Navajo portraits from the *Souvenir* album, which further illuminate aspects of the *Souvenir* collection. The Library of Congress records for the five copy prints (plates 47, 48, 55, 56, and 62) attribute the photographs to "John Gaw Meem," with birth/death dates for Meem being given as 1833–1908. The records go on to declare the copyright holder of the copy print images to be "Cyrus P. Jennings." On the back of these images themselves, inscribed in pencil, is "Cyrus P. Jennings, Macedon, N.Y. © claimant," as well as the names "Jim, a Navajo Indian" (plate 47); "Manuelito" (plate 48); "Harririo, a Navajo Chief" (plate 55); "A Navajo Squaw and Papoose" (plate 56); and "Notrossia and Pattia, 2 Navajo girls" (plate 62). A copyright date is stamped on the verso as well: January 19, 1914. The Library of Congress card catalog notes read, "Original images attributed to Meem by Denver Museum of Art. Possibly taken from U.S. Army Signal Corps during period of Navajo incarceration at Bosque Redondo or Fort Sumner. . . . Penciled captions on versos transcribed from U.S. Copyright Office records."

Further investigation reveals that Cyrus P. Jennings was the son of Charles T. Jennings, a lieutenant and quartermaster in the First Regiment California Volunteer Cavalry during the Civil War.[29] The elder Jennings was quartermaster at Fort Sumner until the summer of 1866, with a special assignment of "superintending Indian issues." He later served at Fort Bascom on the Canadian River in San Miguel County, and after mustering out in August of 1866, he went into business with other officers, ultimately opening his own trading post at Hatch's Ranch, not far from the Gallinas River.[30] The author of the letter in the Gaige file, Joanna Blyth, that discussed the photograph of "Doña Jesus & sister" is the granddaughter of Cyrus P. Jennings and the great-granddaughter of Charles T. Jennings. Apparently, the elder Jennings, Charles, had original prints of these Navajo portraits that his son, Cyrus, later made copy prints of, copyrighted the copy prints, and then gave those copy prints to the Library of Congress in 1914.[31] The Denver Art Museum's misattribution of John Gaw Meem as the photographer in the Library of Congress records is a confusing sidetrack; the museum, in supplying this information to the library, referred not to the architect John Gaw Meem, whose descendants donated the *Souvenir* album to the Palace of the Governors Photo Archives, but rather to Meem's grandfather of the same name, a lieutenant in the Confederate Army.[32]

It's unclear why somebody at the Denver Art Museum misattributed the name of the photographer, but it likely happened after Frederic H. Douglas, curator of Indian Art at the Denver Museum of Art, wrote his notes about the *Souvenir* album at the request of the younger Meem. Copyright concerns might have arisen in 1970 when Dee Brown used the portrait of "Jim," as the portrait of the Navajo man from the *Souvenir* album (plate 47) is labeled at the Library of Congress, for the cover and inside illustration of his classic *Bury My Heart at Wounded Knee*.[33] Dee credits the Denver Art Museum for the photo, and the image on the book cover was likely taken from a copy print that the Denver Art Museum would have made from the *Souvenir* album in the 1930s.

Narrowing the Field: Who Took the Photographs in the Album?

A surprising number of people could have been the photographer behind the *Souvenir* album. But of all the people known to have photographed subjects similar to those found in this album, not all could have been present at the photo sites at the appropriate time—a fact that narrows the list considerably.

Charles Roscoe Savage and William Abraham Bell both worked in the area at the time, but Savage, a Mormon photographer from England, worked mostly in Utah, and his Navajo portraits were taken after the pictures in *Souvenir*.[34] Bell was a homeopathic doctor and amateur photographer, also from England, who took pictures for the Kansas Pacific Railway survey in the New Mexico Territory at roughly the right dates. But he is disqualified by the low quality of his work, which led railway officials to hire Alexander Gardner to replace him as the survey photographer.[35] A closer look at Bell's years of activity additionally show that they postdate 1866.

Bell originally joined the list of candidates for the *Souvenir* album photographer because his surname appears in a biographical file of photographer J. G. Gaige at the Palace of the Governors Photo Archives. In that file is a letter dated 1866 from William Bell to General A. B. Eaton; the letter indicates that Bell had photographs from Fort Sumner, including images of rations being issued to "captive Indians." He offers Eaton an opportunity to "procure for $23.00 a series of photographs of Fort Sumner and groups of Indians." Bell's description of the photo album matches the *Souvenir* album in basic ways, but the author of this letter, after further investigation, turns out to be William Hemphill Bell, a captain in the U.S. Army who served in New Mexico as chief of the Commissariat of the Department of New Mexico at Fort Sumner from June 24, 1864, to July 27, 1865, making William Hemphill Bell's collection of photographs mentioned in *his* letter too early to be those of the *Souvenir* album.[36] William Hemphill Bell's letter, nevertheless, might offer an indication in a general sense about why the *Souvenir* album was assembled in the first place. His letter suggests and lends credence to the idea that a collection of photographs in that era could have been assembled for eventual sale rather than for nostalgic reasons, as clearly William Hemphill Bell was in possession of a photo album that he desired to sell, and other army officers might have had the same notion.

In his book *Navajo and Photography: A Critical History of the Representation of an American People*, James Faris notes that the Swedish-born photographer Valentin Wolfenstein took portraits of Navajos in the Bosque Redondo era, making Wolfenstein a possible candidate for the *Souvenir* portraits, at least of Navajos.[37] But the only known photographs of Navajos that Wolfenstein took were at Fort Sumner, on March 30 and June 1, 1868, during the Peace Commission and signing of the Navajo Treaty, rather than 1866, when the *Souvenir* album photos were taken, as Wolfenstein only made it out that far west by 1868. Wolfenstein's photos of that event are in the archives of the National Museum of the American Indian and the St. Louis Museum of Art. Confirmation of Wolfenstein's dates come through translated diary excerpts (his original diary would have been written in Swedish) at the Palace of the Governors Photo Archives, though it was through digging to find whether Wolfenstein could have been "the" or "a" photographer for the *Souvenir* album that the long-lost group photo of the signing of the Navajo Treaty was recovered (see figure 2). Other photos Faris mistakenly attributes as possibly by Wolfenstein,[38] related in time period and subject matter to the *Souvenir* album, are most likely taken before Wolfenstein even arrived out west and are probably by Nicholas Brown, J. G. Gaige, or the Duhem brothers, all of whom also happen to be the best possible candidates for the *Souvenir* photographer.

Nicholas Brown moved to Santa Fe in 1866, although chances are he visited Santa Fe in 1864 and 1865.[39] Before the Civil War, he worked in the New York studio of the renowned Civil War photographer Mathew Brady. After a stint as an operator in John H. Fitzgibbon's St. Louis studio (Fitzgibbon, like Brady, was another of the most distinguished American photographers of the mid-nineteenth century), Brown opened his own studio, the Great Western Photographic Gallery, in St. Louis.[40] Brown is mistakenly credited for the iconic Civil War photo of Confederate Col. William P. Rogers and his fallen comrades at Corinth, Mississippi, in October 1862; George Armstead actually took the picture.[41] Part of that misappropriation is Brown's doing: he made and sold second-generation copies without crediting Armstead as the original photographer, a common practice at the time and an early indicator that Brown was willing to put his name on photographs that others had taken (figure 12). After the Civil War, Brown left the East Coast and came to New Mexico. On August 11, 1866, Brown and his son Henry announced the opening of a gallery in New Mexico, Nicholas Brown and Son, in the *Santa Fe New Mexican*. A month later, one of the Browns went to Fort Union while the other stayed in Santa Fe. Father and son traveled to Chihuahua in April 1867 to set up a gallery and returned to Santa Fe the following February.[42]

The Browns can be placed at the sites photographed in the album at roughly the time the pictures were taken. Given their professional skills, they might well have taken some of the portraits and landscapes in the *Souvenir* album. As well,

FIG. 12. Confederate dead (Colonel William P. Rogers and his comrades) in front of Fort Robinette, Corinth, Mississippi, October 4, 1862 (printed 1880–89). Photograph by George Armstead, printed by Nicholas N. Brown. Library of Congress, Prints and Photographs Division, LC-DIG-ppmsca-35455.

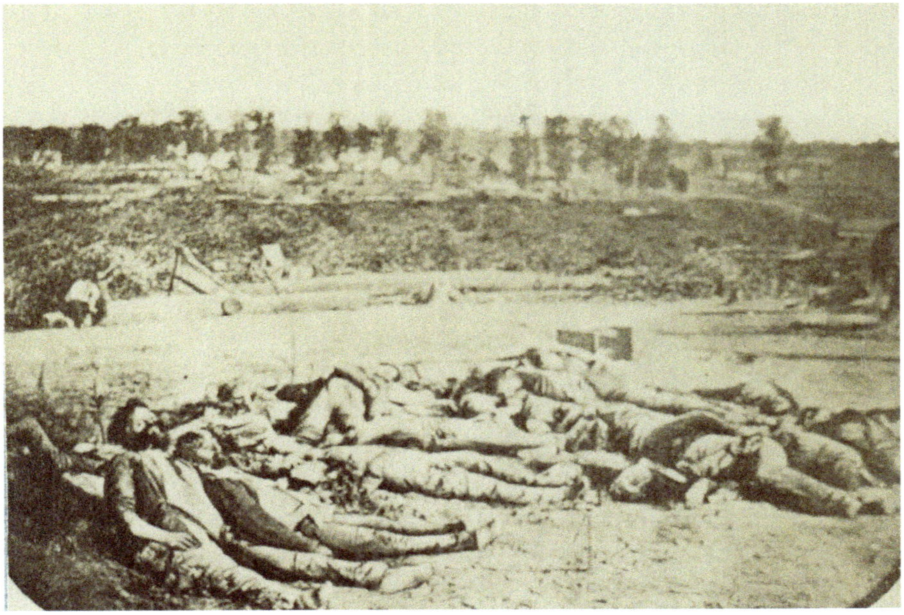

"Nicholas Brown and Son" (sometimes with a mark in Spanish, "Nicholas Brown e Hijo") is stamped on the backs of Navajo portraits from the same era found in the Blackmore Collection at the British Museum and the Department of Rare Books and Special Collections at the Princeton University Library (see figures 1, 31, and 32 as examples). However, the Browns can't be placed in El Paso del Norte in February 1866, when, as will be discussed in detail further on, specifically, the portrait of Juárez was taken, as it's very likely the portraits of his cabinet were as well. The Browns arrived in Santa Fe, probably coming directly from St. Louis in August of 1866, many months after the portrait of Juárez was taken. The Browns only traveled in the direction of El Paso del Norte in April of 1867, when they left for Chihuahua, and by then, Juárez and his cabinet were en route back to Mexico City. The absence of a mark on the photos in the *Souvenir* album also casts doubt on a Brown provenance, given the penchant of Nicholas Brown and his son Henry for marking work they printed and distributed with their names, even when they didn't create it. Furthermore, in Navajo portraits that the Browns distributed under their name, and likely did take, the poses of the sitters are quite different in style and affect than the *Souvenir* album Navajo portraits.

Another candidate for photographer is Gaige, who had a studio on the Santa Fe Plaza in 1862, judging by an ad in the *Santa Fe Gazette*.[43] Little is known about Gaige, and it doesn't help that several photographs taken in the geographic area at that time were attributed to people with similar names who might well have been the same individual: "J. G. Gaige," "A. G. Gaige," and "George A. Gaige."[44] It is known specifically of George A. Gaige that he was born in Vermont and worked in Brady's New York gallery at the same time Brown did before heading west.[45] George Gaige was also active in Kansas City, Missouri, from 1859 until 1861, as indicated by advertisements in the newspapers there. One ad calls him "A. G. Gaige," so it does seem these two "Gaiges" are one and the same. In 1861, the *Western Journal of Commerce* announced: "Something New. Gaige is going to New Mexico in the Spring. Parties wishing Pictures now is the time. Pictures at Half Price."[46] In 1865, under Army Signal Corps General Order No. 3, a "Gaige" obtained a commission from the U.S. Army Quartermaster's Department to photograph military posts in the New Mexico Territory, including Fort Sumner and Bosque Redondo.[47] This "Gaige" was at Fort Sumner from February to March 1866, where he shot landscapes and portraits.[48] Gaige turned down an invitation from his associate William A. Smith to operate a gallery in Franklin, Texas, but Gaige visited the city in mid-July 1866, before traveling to Chihuahua.[49] Gaige later worked in Arizona and died at Camp Goodwin on July 2, 1869.[50] An A. J. Gaige, photographer, born in New York, is listed in a Tucson mortality schedule of the 1870 U.S. Census as dying in 1869 at age thirty-eight of delirium tremens; so even in death, it is hard to say if all the Gaiges in consideration are one and the same, though it seems highly probable.[51]

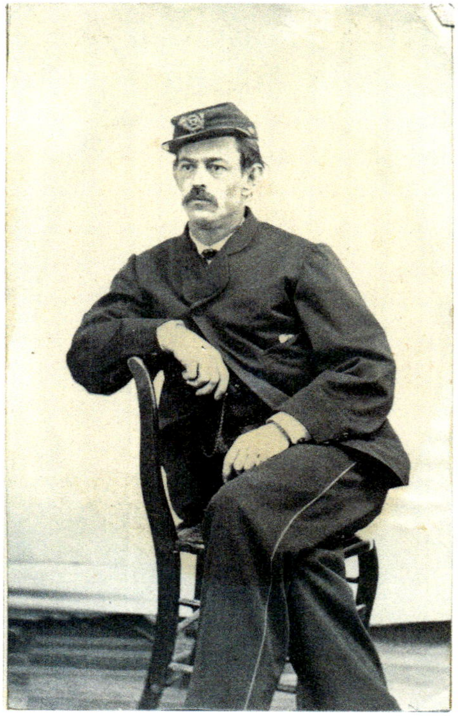

FIG. 13. Lieutenant Shepard, 1869. Photograph attributed to J. G. Gaige. Arizona State Library, Archives and Public Records, History and Archives Division, Phoenix, MG121_B06_F19_I006.

This photograph was probably taken at Camp Goodwin in 1869.

Nevertheless, attributing the *Souvenir* album photographs to Gaige is complicated in numerous ways. First by the fact that there are very few known photographs, portrait or landscape, that bear his mark. A few portraits attributable to Gaige, one with his stamp on the back, are at the Arizona State Library. A portrait of an officer, probably one who was stationed at Camp Goodwin, labeled simply "Lt. Shepard," bears some similarities to Navajo portraits in the *Souvenir* album: the backdrop, a slightly drooping plain canvas, the chair in which the officer sits, as well as the full body pose (figure 13). But the dates when Gaige was in both El Paso del Norte and Fort Sumner, while generally proximate, are slightly off. Gaige probably wasn't in El Paso del Norte at the right time to have taken the portraits of Juárez and the army officers and civilians, or at Fort Sumner when the *Souvenir* Navajo portraits were taken there, though it is not impossible. He is documented as having been at Fort Sumner in February 1866, and he could have traveled to El Paso del Norte to photograph Juárez and to Franklin to shoot portraits of army officers and the citizens who interacted with them, though he would have had a small window of time in which to do that. It also cannot be completely ruled out that he took the portraits of the Navajos, but it is unlikely. Manuelito and the Navajos who surrendered with him would not have been at Fort Sumner when Gaige returned there that summer, because that surrender happened on September 1, 1866, after Gaige had left Fort Sumner; Gaige would have had to make a later trip to Fort Sumner to take the Navajo portraits, and there is no record of such a trip. So while matching dates is not completely impossible, further assessment of the Navajo *Souvenir* portraits argue more for their being taken in Santa Fe or, more likely, in Albuquerque, on the way to Fort Sumner rather than *at* Fort Sumner, but more on that later. All in all, though it is not impossible that Gaige made all the portraits in this album, it is hard to make a clear case for that.

Some have suggested that Gaige's associate William A. Smith took the photos in the *Souvenir* album. Smith was the photographic assistant to the special commission led by Julius K. Graves, special agent of the Office of Indian Affairs, sent to investigate the conditions at Bosque Redondo.[52] Smith kept a diary, which had long been lost, which kept Smith as a candidate for the *Souvenir* photographer. However, his diary was found in the course of research for this book, and it sheds some light on the question.[53] While Smith was at Fort Sumner in the spring of 1866, his diary notes that Fort Marcy was the only fort he photographed during his work with the commission. After that assignment ended, Smith partnered with photographer George W. Wertz in Santa Fe, and on June 15, 1866, Smith's name appears in a Santa Fe newspaper, which reports the photographic partners' plans to visit Fort Union the following week, the third week of June 1866.[54] This places Smith at Fort Union before the surrender

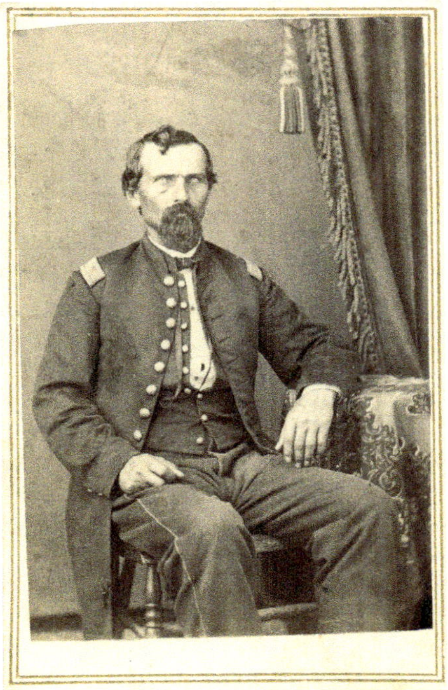

FIG. 14A. Unidentified member of the Eleventh Kansas Volunteer Cavalry, Kansas City, Missouri, ca. 1863–64. Photograph by George W. Wertz. Kansas State Historical Society.

This photograph is one of the few known photographs by George. W. Wertz.

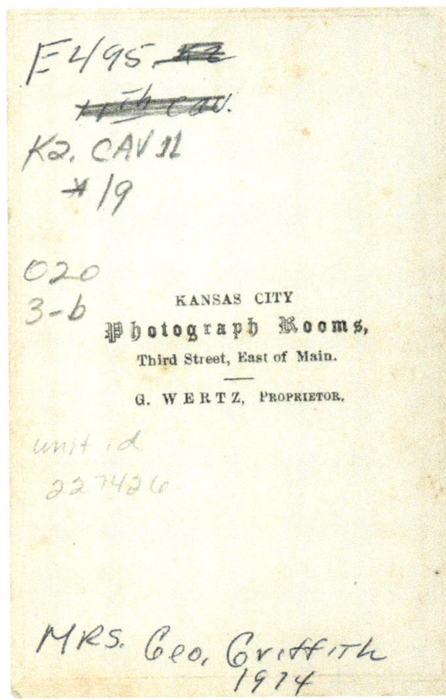

FIG. 14B. The stamp on the reverse.

and arrival of Manuelito and his band in September of 1866. If anything, Smith could have taken the *Souvenir* photographs of Fort Marcy and Santa Fe (plates 21–28) but not any of the other photographs. No known photographs of Smith's survive, and it is not clear if he is the same Smith of Smith and Company Photographers, active in Santa Fe by May 1864. However, a few photographs by George W. Wertz from the Civil War do survive (figure 14).[55] Wertz was active in Kansas City between 1863 and 1868, but he was also in New Mexico, perhaps about 1866, having sold his gallery in Kansas City that year.[56] Given the dates and places, it is possible Wertz and Gaige crossed paths in either Kansas City, Missouri, or in New Mexico.

Last in the list of possible photographers are the brothers Constant Benjamin Louis Duhem and Victor Marie Duhem, who operated as C. Duhem and Bro. They were born in Paris and likely immigrated to the United States in 1852, ending up in San Francisco.[57] Both brothers enlisted as privates in the Fifth California Infantry Regiment, Company G—Constant on October 14, 1861, and Victor on January 24, 1862. Constant would have joined the California Column's march across New Mexico in 1862 before being stationed at Fort Bliss and finally mustering out on November 27, 1864, in Las Cruces.[58] On April 16, 1865, he reenlisted at Franklin, Texas, joining Company K of the Fifth California Infantry Regiment. He transferred from fort to fort in Texas, New Mexico, and Kansas from October 1865 until his discharge in November 1867 as duties required. (An uncorroborated report says Constant Duhem traveled to Mexico as part of a select group from Company K to attend the capture and execution of Maximilian on June 19, 1867.) Victor saw much of the same country during his service, and he left the army at the same time as Constant but at Fort Harker, Kansas.[59]

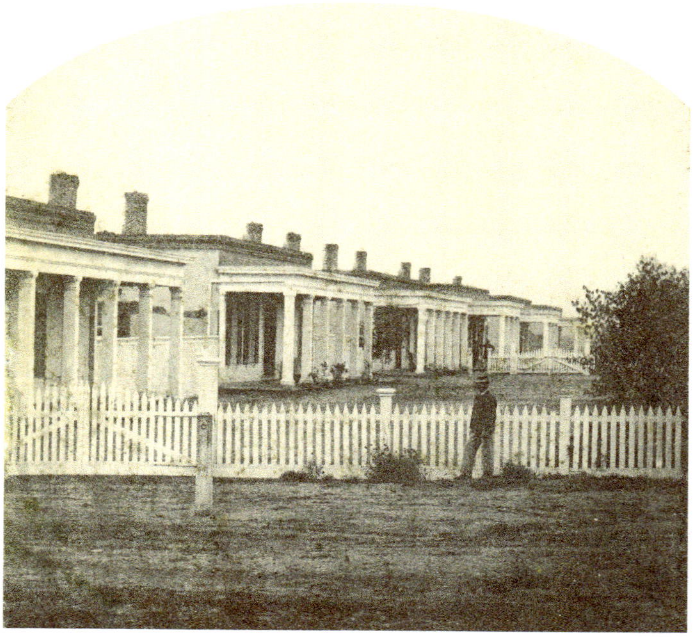

FIG. 15. Officers' quarters, Fort Union, New Mexico Territory, ca. 1864–86. Photograph by C. Duhem and Bro. Palace of the Governors Photo Archives, New Mexico History Museum, Santa Fe, 138014.

This photograph is one of the few known photographs, in addition to the portrait of Kit Carson (figure 17a) and Brotherton (figure 18a), by the Duhems from their time in the U.S. Army.

It is unclear exactly when the Duhem brothers began taking photographs, though certainly they began while they were in the army, between 1862 and 1867. On July 17, 1867, Victor Duhem applied for a tax license for a photography studio in Santa Fe for C. Duhem and Bro., making it clear they were an established presence as photographers at least by that date.[60] Given the dates of the brothers' various service postings, they were in the right place at the right time to have photographed Juárez and his cabinet and the U.S. Army officers and Anglo civilians in *Souvenir.* Their dates also match up well for the Navajo

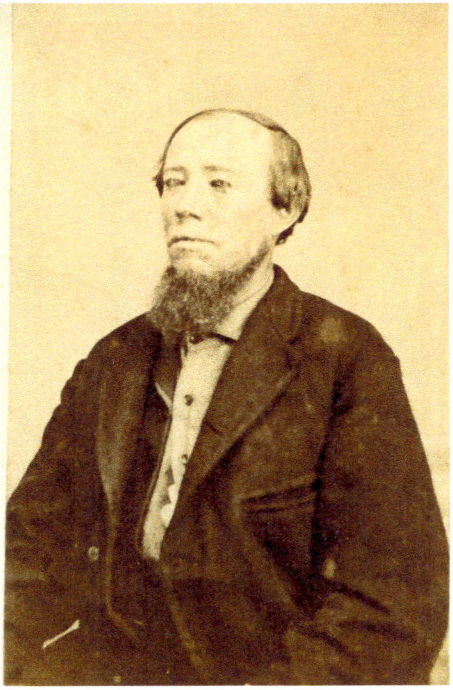

FIG. 16. Colonel Albert Pfeiffer, Denver, Colorado, 1969. Photograph by C. Duhem and Bro. Carte de visite mount; albumen print. The British Museum, William Blackmore Collection, Album 9, AM, A9.186. Photograph © The Trustees of the British Museum.

photographs, because they had a studio in Albuquerque when the recently surrendered Manuelito and his remaining followers came through on their way to Fort Sumner, after having left Fort Wingate on September 9th with Captain Montoya escorting the group.

Few photographs taken by the Duhems from their time in the army can be located, though a stereoscope of officers' quarters at Fort Union, taken between 1864 and 1869, resides in the Palace of the Governors Photo Archives (figure 15). In addition to the image of Pfeiffer in the Taylor scrapbook (see figure 10), and another portrait of Pfeiffer found in the British Museum's Blackmore Collection (figure 16), a few more of their portraits can be found in the Blackmore Collection, including a portrait of Kit Carson, in Album 9. That carte de visite (CDV; the nineteenth-century version of a postcard) of Carson does not have a stamp, though an inscription on the reverse indicating that it was taken in Albuquerque in 1866 and other versions of the same image confirm that they took this portrait (see, for example, figure 17a).

Additional versions of this same photograph of Carson, mounted variably on different carte de visite backs, have shown up in the last ten years for auction or on the internet. One is circulated on a card from the studio of Mathew Brady. Brady, or possibly Levin C. Handy, did indeed take a portrait of Carson, though not this one, but Brady was known to circulate the work of other photographers. Another version that was up for auction in 2007 was framed, so the back was not available. Two additional versions up for auction have C. Duhem and Bro. stamps and inscriptions that date the image in 1867, though one on April 15 and the other on July 11, as near as can be ascertained from the writing (figure 17). These CDVs of Carson make it fairly certain that one or both of the Duhem brothers were taking studio portraits in Albuquerque in 1866 or 1867. However, related to the *Souvenir* album, the most compelling of the Duhems' images from their time in the army is a portrait of Brotherton very similar to the one in the *Souvenir* album—a carte de visite marked "C. Duhem & Bro., Photographers on the Rio Grande" and inscribed "June 5, 1867" (figure 18).[61]

An incident that occurred while the Duhems were stationed in Texas further positions them as photographers, albeit daguerreotypists at the time, and connects them to another U.S. Army officer pictured in the album—Paymaster Clark (plate 9). Victor Duhem was a witness in the trial of three men charged with stealing almost $16,000 in government funds from a safe in Clark's quarters on April 6, 1865. Duhem's September 3, 1865, testimony mentions his being in his daguerreotype studio on the day of the crime. This incident places some of the *Souvenir* players in the same place at the same time, and it indicates that the

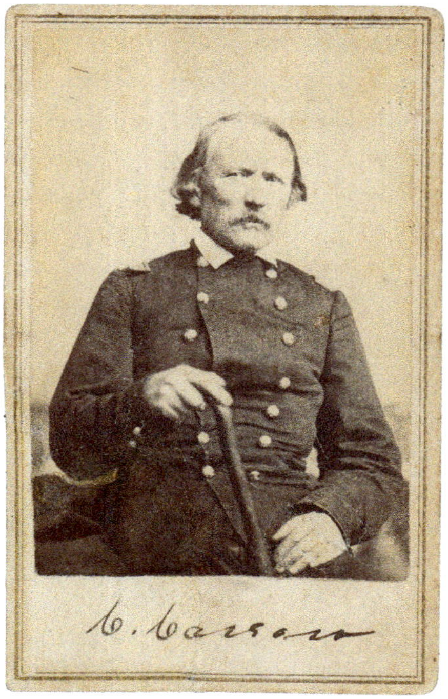

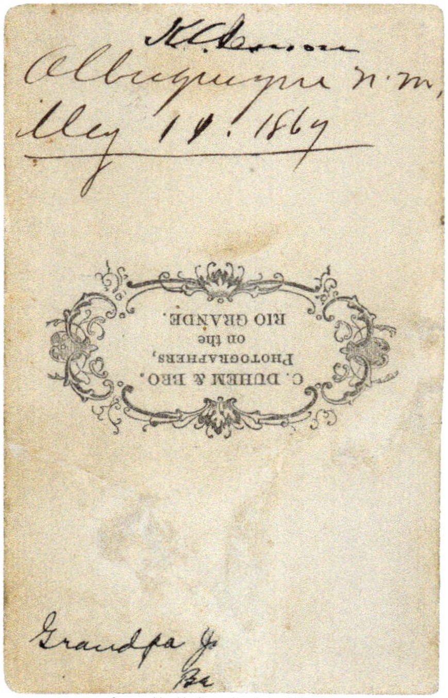

FIG. 17A. Brevet Brigadier General Christopher "Kit" Carson, July 11, 1867, Albuquerque, New Mexico Territory. Photograph by C. Duhem and Bro. Carte de visite mount; albumen print. Courtesy of Heritage Auctions, HA.com.

FIG. 17B. The stamp in combination with the ink inscription indicate that the Duhem brothers were operating out of Albuquerque in 1867. It is possible to read the year of the inscription as "1869," except for the fact that Carson died on May 23, 1868, lending to the reading of the year in the inscription as "1867," less than a year before Carson's death.

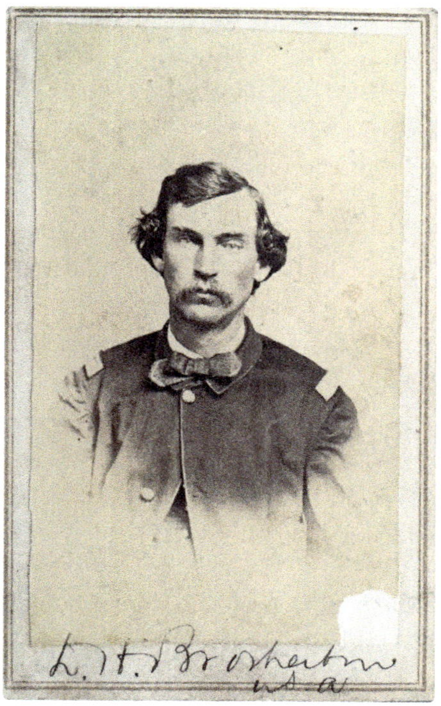

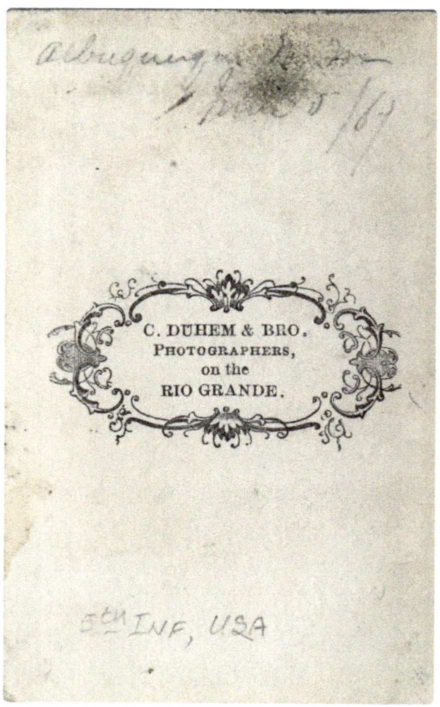

FIG. 18A. Captain David Hammett Brotherton, Albuquerque, New Mexico Territory, June 5, 1867. Photograph by C. Duhem and Bro. Carte de visite mount; albumen print. Courtesy of J. Dale West

FIG. 18B. Stamp of photographer C. Duhem and Bro., Photographers on the Rio Grande, and pencil inscription "Albuquerque. June 5, 1867."

The stamp in combination with the pencil inscription indicate that the Duhem brothers were operating out of Albuquerque in 1867, confirming that they photographed at least one of the sitters in the Souvenir album, David Hammett Brotherton.

Duhem brothers had a photography studio in Franklin.[62] In addition to associating the Duhems with Clark, the account offers insight into Clark's character and how an officer stationed in Texas at that time might have lived. It reveals that Clark was living with a Mexican prostitute and that officers involved with the case attempted to coerce testimony by threatening to lynch a potential witness, a civilian Mexican.[63] While Clark may have been implicated in the crime, he was never charged, and the two men ultimately convicted of the crime may well have been innocent, but they spent fifteen years of hard labor at Fort Craig, each wearing a twenty-five-pound iron ball attached to his leg with a five-foot chain.[64]

In 1869, the Duhem brothers, now civilians, opened a photography studio at 448 Larimer Street in Denver.[65] On January 3, 1877, a notice in the *Rocky Mountain News* reported that the Duhem brothers were to appear in court for bankruptcy proceedings.[66] They continued to work as professional photographers on and off into the 1880s, when Constant moved to Tucson, Arizona, to work as a photographer and prospector with other artistic sidelines.[67] In May 1883, according to the *Arizona Daily Star* of Tucson, he was preparing to present a panorama of Tucson, including "magnificent dissolving views."[68] On June 14, 1898, Victor reenlisted in the army in Denver.[69] The brothers' ongoing money troubles, which included a number of bankruptcies, might explain how several of the *Souvenir* album's Navajo portraits ended up, as mentioned earlier, in the archive of the Netherlands Photo Museum. Those photos are attributed to the French photographer Alfredo Laurent and were collected by Dutchman Herman F. C. ten Kate, better known as Ten Kate (plates 47, 50, 56, and 62).

Ten Kate traveled to the American Southwest and Mexico in 1882, sponsored by the Dutch government and the Société d'Anthropologie de Paris, to study the indigenous people of the area. On March 24, 1883, after failing in attempts to take his own photos, he hired Laurent, who lived and worked in Guaymas, Mexico, from 1882 to 1883, to help him photograph the local Yaquis. Ten Kate returned to Arizona on March 9, 1883, and on June 14 engaged Constant Duhem—through General George Crook—to take pictures during his two-week study among the Apaches.[70] In addition to taking photographs for Ten Kate on the expedition, apparently Duhem brought along a magic lantern slide show to show the Apaches, who responded with delight.[71]

Ten Kate's connections with both Duhem and Laurent might explain how images from the *Souvenir* album at the Netherlands Photo Museum came to bear Laurent's mark (figure 19). Laurent, like the Duhem brothers, was born in France, likely in Meurthe-et-Moselle, Lorraine, in 1840.[72] He lived and worked in Guaymas in 1882–83.[73] Not much is known about Laurent, other than that he was mostly active in Sonora, Mexico, with some presence in Tucson, Arizona.[74] Laurent might have obtained the Duhem borthers' negatives through trade or sale.[75] With the Duhem brothers often short of cash, it's conceivable that they

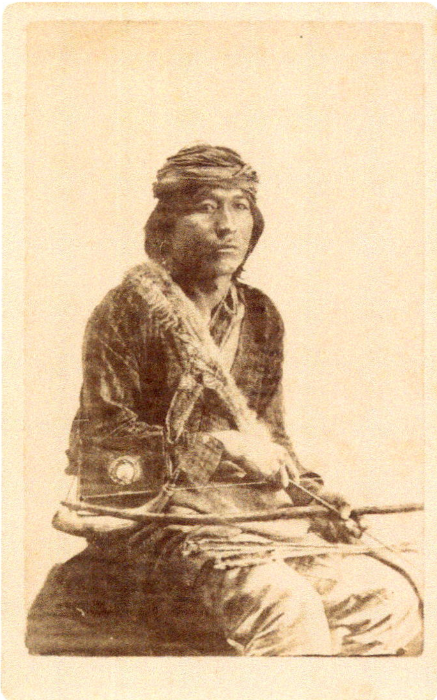

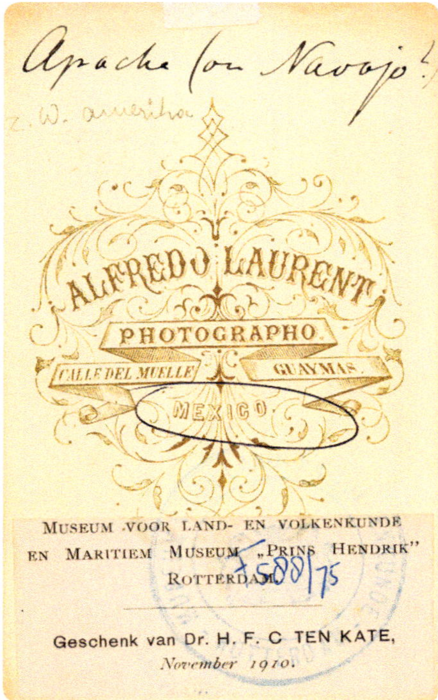

FIG. 19A. Unidentified Navajo man, New Mexico Territory, 1866. Photograph printed by Alfredo Laurent (possibly C. Duhem and Bro. or Gaige). Nederlands Fotomuseum, Rotterdam, WMR-900588_NB.

See also plate 47, page 114.

FIG. 19B. Stamp of photographer Alfredo Laurent, with various inscriptions and a sticker from the Museum voor Land en Volkenkunde en Maritiem Museum indicating that the print was a gift to the museum from H. F. C. ten Kate in November of 1910.

sold their negatives to Laurent. This might also explain why, if the negatives weren't recycled, no negatives from the *Souvenir* photos, with the possible exception of the one Carleton negative (see figure 7), have ever been found, because the negatives could have ended up in Mexico with Laurent. It was not uncommon in the nineteenth century for photographers to sell their negatives to another photographer, who would then be free to make prints, often under his own name, such as we've seen with Nicholas Brown's Civil War photo of Confederate dead at Corinth, Mississippi, in October 1862.

The most likely supposition is that the Duhem brothers took the photographs in the *Souvenir* album and distributed them in a limited fashion, including providing prints to both the compiler of the *Souvenir* album and to Charles T. Jennings. The Duhem brothers then probably sold the negatives of those prints—at least the negatives of the Navajo portraits—years later to Laurent, who made prints of a few of the images (plates 48, 50, 56, 57a, and 62) that he sold to Ten Kate, which would explain their presence in the archive in the Netherlands with Laurent's stamp. With no evidence that Laurent was ever in the New Mexico Territory or any part of the United States, and with his active dates later than the *Souvenir* album photographs, he is not a possible candidate as the actual photographer for the album.

CHAPTER 2

GOVERNMENT IN EXILE

Portraits of Benito Juárez and His Cabinet

THE PROMINENCE OF BENITO JUÁREZ and his cabinet in the *Souvenir* album says something about its origins. The first clue appears in an original-era print of the portrait of Juárez (plate 1) found in the collection of the American Heritage Center at the University of Wyoming with the date "February 1866" inscribed on the verso. The photograph is with the papers of Ichabod Sargent Bartlett, who served with the Tenth New Hampshire Volunteer Infantry Regiment during the Civil War and remained in the U.S. Army until 1868.[1] Bartlett was a paymaster in New Mexico, Arizona, and Texas; while in Franklin, Texas, he was introduced to Juárez by Juan N. Zubirán, a wealthy El Paso del Norte merchant who served as the Mexican consul in Franklin in the 1850s and was customs collector in El Paso del Norte during and after the Civil War.[2] Bartlett later recounted his friendship with Juárez in the *Bulletin of the Pan American Union*, recalling how Juárez arrived in El Paso de Norte with his cabinet, staff, and about five hundred soldiers (and, "mysteriously," ten pieces of American artillery) when Bartlett was U.S. collector of customs at Franklin. In that article, Bartlett calls El Paso del Norte "'the last ditch' of the Mexican Republic" and calls Franklin a slumbering, idyllic place (figure 20 and plate 32).[3]

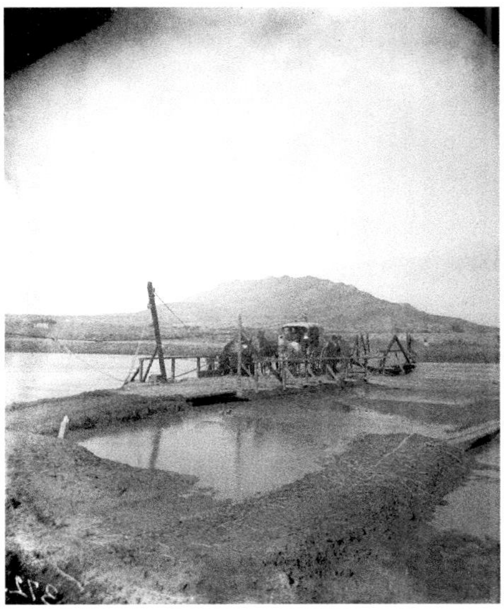

FIG. 20. Rio Grande crossing at El Paso del Norte, Mexico, ca. 1881–84. Photograph by Ben Wittick. Stereo glass negative. Palace of the Governors Photo Archives, New Mexico History Museum, Santa Fe, 015666.

This photograph portrays the U.S.-Mexico border between Franklin, Texas, and El Paso del Norte, Mexico.

The date on the Juárez portrait in Bartlett's collection might indicate

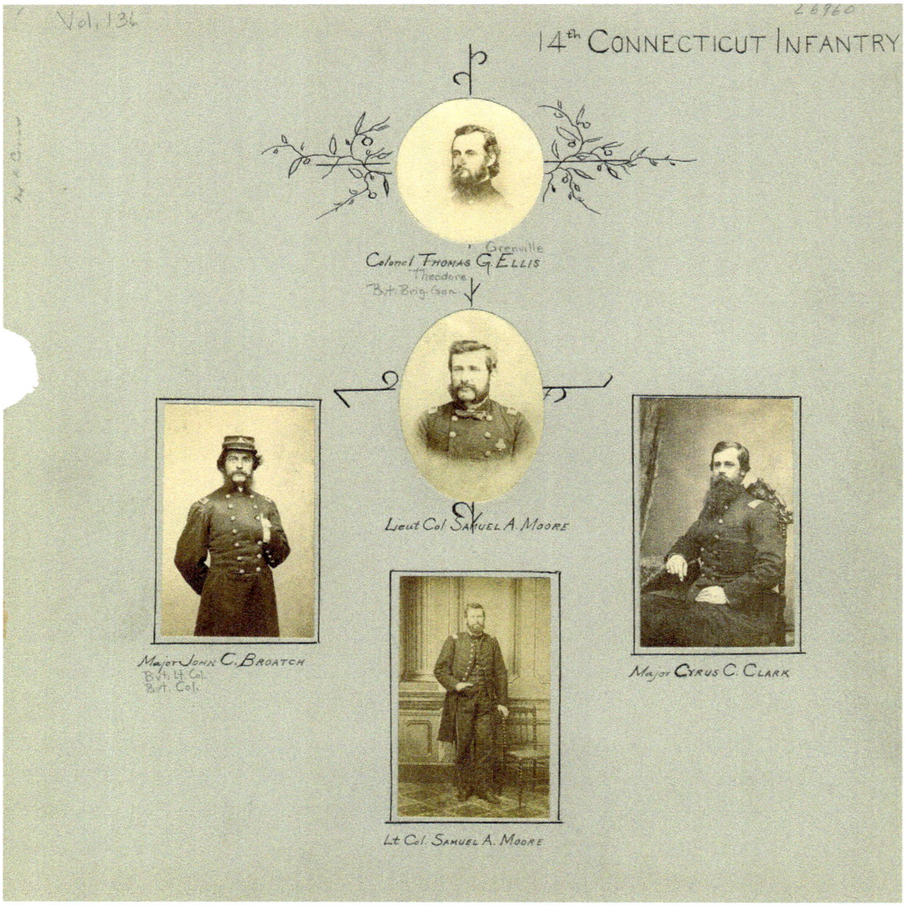

FIG. 21. Major Cyrus C. Clark (*lower right*), ca. 1861. MOLLUS Mass, United States Army Heritage and Education Center, Carlisle, Pennsylvania.

Many of the members of MOLLUS *had their portraits compiled in such volumes. The same series of volumes has the same portrait of Carleton as the one in the Library of Congress glass negative (figure 7), which is so similar to the portrait in the Souvenir album (plate 7).*

when the photo was taken or when Bartlett obtained it. In either case, it helps narrow the date for the portrait of the president and his cabinet, as it clearly could not have been taken after February of 1866. On February 7, 1866, Juárez was named a 3rd Class (honorary) Companion of the Pennsylvania Commandery of the Military Order of the Loyal Legion of the United States (also known as MOLLUS), an organization for Civil War veteran officers and their descendants, as well as civilians who provided exceptional service to the Union during the war.[4] Carleton, Clark (figure 21), McCleave (plates 7, 9, and 11), and other MOLLUS members of the California regiments stationed at Fort Bliss probably supported this election and perhaps arranged for the portraits of Juárez and his cabinet that are found in the *Souvenir* album in commemoration of Juárez's induction.[5]

Another clue about the context of these portraits surfaces in the memoirs of Mary Dowell Phillips, housed in the special collections at the University of

Texas, El Paso, Library.[6] Phillips, then Dowell, was the daughter of Benjamin Shacklett Dowell, who owned a saloon, general store, and post office in Franklin, Texas, before joining the Confederate Army.[7] Dowell fled with his family for Mexico when the Union Army assumed control in Texas, though they returned when the war ended. Dowell would become the first mayor of El Paso after its incorporation under that name in 1873.[8] In the general time frame when the Juárez portrait was taken, eleven-year-old Mary Dowell attended a ball at Fort Bliss on February 22, 1866, to honor Juárez and his government—and possibly also to honor the conferring of the MOLLUS status. Her memories of the occasion were cited in a 1973 article in the *El Paso Herald-Post* that also included excerpts from Bartlett's papers as well, as Bartlett, too, had attended the ball. Juárez did not leave Mexico during the French Intervention and skipped the ball, but his son and members of his cabinet and staff joined U.S. Army officers and "all the best families" of Franklin and El Paso del Norte at the event.[9] The ball, according to Bartlett, was an event of "bowing and elegance," with the "Mexican officers and their waxed mustaches" and the "ladies of [El Paso del Norte] with their fine silks and jewelry, and low cut dresses."[10] The dance was held at the quartermaster's storeroom at the freshly reconstructed fort (plates 33–38).[11] Large Chinese lanterns illuminated portions of the space, and portraits of Washington, Lincoln, and Juárez were hung for the occasion.[12] "Ice had been carried overland all the way from New Mexico for the occasion," Bartlett recalled, and the orchestra played until dawn.[13]

Bartlett also relays in the *Bulletin of the Pan American Union* that the ball was attended by prominent Mexicans, Nuevomexicanos, Tejanos (Texans of Spanish descent), and Anglos. Guests included Mexican and American government officials, merchants and traders, U.S. Army officers and former Confederates, judges, and landowners.[14] Also present were members of Texas monopolies, or rings, unofficial organizations and affiliations that dominated trade and commerce between private entities and businesses, and between businesses and the U.S. Army.[15] Specifically, the Custom House Ring, named for New Mexico Territory customs collector W. (William) W. Mills and his allies (who controlled the movement of goods, and by which the ring granted or denied favors to local merchants), was well represented at the Fort Bliss ball, as were those who would become a part of the Salt Ring.[16] This latter group, which formed after the demise of the Custom House Ring, was later involved in the twelve-year-long El Paso Salt War, a range war during which various factions struggled for control of salt lakes at the base of the Guadalupe Mountains in Texas.[17]

International alliances and business relationships between former Civil War rivals reflect the changes in the region that recent wars and their aftermaths had brought to the city. Both Confederate and Union soldiers mingled with one another and with Mexican government exiles in El Paso del Norte and Franklin after the Civil War. Even before the American Civil War, after the 1848 Treaty of Guadalupe Hidalgo severed existing north-south trade routes, many Mexicans living north of the redrawn border moved farther south to maintain their Mexican citizenship, and El Paso del Norte remade itself as an east-west route for a more diverse group of California-bound treasure seekers.[18] These mixed social circles created the basis for much of the social and economic life on both sides of the border. It would seem, for example, that Juárez counted Alexandre Daguerre, a cross-border wagon-train-shipping owner, as a friend and attended card games at his El Paso del Norte home.[19] Card games were one manner of socializing at which businessmen and politicians would sit down together and solidify relationships or business deals. The social season in 1866 in Franklin and El Paso del Norte revolved around Juárez and his cabinet members.[20] In another account that reflects the diversity in social mixing and networking at the border at this time, Mexican officers and local talent produced a piece of open-air theater and performed it on the plaza of El Paso del Norte, surrounded by ancient, high adobe walls. The audience extended beyond the more elite social scene and included "all classes of Indians, Mexicans, Americans, German Jew traders, mule packers, vaqueros and soldiers of both nations" from both sides of the border.[21]

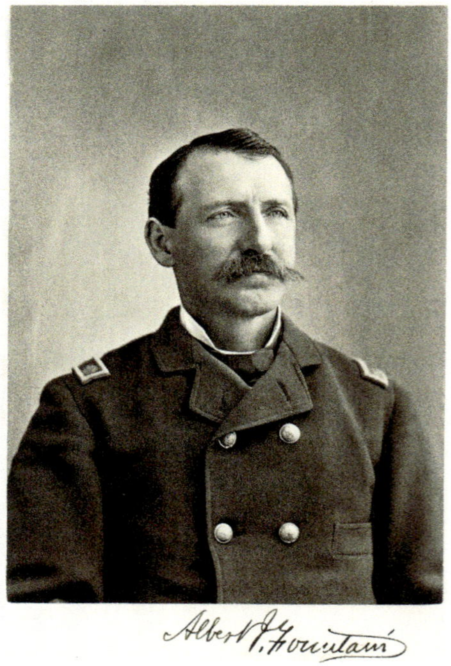

FIG. 22. Major Albert J. Fountain, 1883. Photograph by Francis Parker. Palace of the Governors Photo Archives, New Mexico History Museum, Santa Fe, 077788.

Broadening the picture of cross-border relations in this era and bringing even greater clarity to the reasons Juárez and his cabinet are included in the *Souvenir* album is the discovery of another original-era print of the portrait of Juárez, which appears in the archive of the New Mexico State University Library Archives and Special Collections. That portrait is found in the collection of Mary Alexander, a descendant of Albert J. Fountain (figure 22), from whom she inherited the print. Albert J. Fountain joined the Union Army in 1861 in California during the Civil War, serving as captain of the New Mexico Volunteers, and winding up at Fort Bliss, where he initially went to be treated for wounds received fighting Apaches. While convalescing at Fort Bliss, Fountain became a protégé of W. W. Mills.[22] According to Alexander, Fountain received the portrait from Juárez when Fountain was himself a customs agent at the border in Franklin (1865–67), a position he obtained through his connection to Mills. In 1867, Fountain took a leave of absence from his customs position and joined Juárez's army to fight the French Army in Mexico, like some, if not all, of the other officers in the *Souvenir* album—including, reportedly, Constant Duhem.[23] Fountain was made a colonel in the Mexican Army and organized the artillery, helping Juárez's forces take Chihuahua.[24] Later in life Fountain would serve in the Texas Senate and the New Mexico House of Representatives and become embroiled in the El Paso Salt Wars. Ultimately, Fountain and his eight-year-old son, Henry, would disappear near White Sands, New Mexico, in February of 1896, presumed murdered in relation to his prosecution of corrupt cattle ranchers in Lincoln County, New Mexico.

Though the Juárez portrait is widely circulated and appears in numerous archives and books and on the internet (the sources for which, as far as can be deduced, being any one of the three archives in the United States named here, where the original-era print is found), a photographer is never identified, though all the portraits of the Juárez cabinet appear to be made by the same photographer, likely the Duhem Brothers, Gaige, or Nicholas Brown and his son. The setting in all the portraits seems to be the same, almost certainly El Paso del Norte in 1866, as extrapolated from the date of the album, the inscription on the Juárez photographs found in the American Heritage Center at the University of Wyoming and the New Mexico State University Archives and Special Collections, and the portrait subjects themselves. Juárez and his cabinet lived in exile during this part of the French Intervention in Mexico, locating to El Paso del Norte from August 14, 1865, until April 1866, when they began their return journey to Mexico City.[25]

Benito Juárez was born in the village of San Pablo Guelatao, Oaxaca, where his parents died when he was just four years old, and he was then raised by relatives. He worked in the fields until he was twelve years old, at which time he went to live with his sister in the city of Oaxaca, where he began his formal education.[26] His education in Oaxaca is an often overlooked but significant part of his story, as it is for *this* story, because it was in Oaxaca where he, and those who would later become his political allies, including Ignacio Mejía, developed their early liberalism. This liberalism was certainly central to an idea of Mexican autonomy and in keeping with the Monroe Doctrine (an American doctrine that opposed further European colonization in the Americas), and it would be, on the face of it, one of the main reasons the United States and Union supporters during the American Civil War would politically support Juárez and oppose Maximilian.[27] Juárez's liberalism was born of the regional politics of Oaxaca and specifically through his studies at the newly founded Instituto de Ciencias y Artes.[28] There is some debate as to exactly how liberal, as well as how anticlerical, the Instituto de Ciencias y Artes was.[29] However, there can be no doubt that many of the liberal ideals Juárez would ultimately come to embrace, including an anticlerical stance, began in some way while he studied in Oaxaca. In the portrait of Juárez in the *Souvenir* album, he wears the "black frock coat and the bow tie [of] his deliberately chosen alternative uniform," which he saw as emblematic of his embodiment of the liberal, lay—which is to say, anticlerical—state.[30] At the age of twenty-five in 1831, Juárez was elected to the City Council of Oaxaca, and over the course of many years, he would hold numerous political positions, sometimes in the majority party, sometimes as a member of the opposition, and on occasion holding his position from a place of exile.

Juárez's rapidly changing position from insider to outsider and back again was due to the swift changes in leadership in Mexico in the nineteenth century. At one time he was even arrested by President Ignacio Comonfort, just ten days after he took the oath to be president of the Supreme Court, to which Comonfort *himself* had appointed him. In early 1858, Comonfort was overthrown as president by a military coup that declared Félix Zuloaga president. However, Juárez succeeded Comonfort in the presidency, in accordance with the Constitution of 1857. He took the oath of office on January 19, 1858, in Guanajuato, and Mexico subsequently had two presidents and a civil war on its hands.[31] During the Mexican War of Reform, as it is called in Mexico, Juárez turned to the United States, as he would during the French Intervention, for help to restore his liberal government, ultimately declaring victory in 1860. With the Mexican War of Reform over, Juárez was elected president in 1861, but due to the fiscal damage caused by the civil war, he suspended payments of debt to foreign powers, including Spain, Great Britain, and France. Thus were set in motion the events that predicated the French Intervention in Mexico when the British, Spanish, and French fleets arrived at Veracruz between December 8 and 17, 1861, demanding payment on their debts.[32]

Much is known about Juárez's foreign affairs minister Sebastián Lerdo de Tejada (plate 2); General Ignacio Mejía, minister of war (plate 3); and José María Iglesias, minister of public instruction (plate 4), as these were the most important cabinet members who accompanied the president into exile. Less is known about Gotien (plate 5), whose name is probably misspelled as written on the page his portrait is mounted on, except that he likely managed household affairs. He was important enough to be photographed, so he must have mattered to the larger political cause or to the rest of the group portrayed.

José María Iglesias, labeled "Senor Yglesias" in the album (plate 4), was a historian, jurist, liberal politician, and former editor of the liberal newspaper *El Siglo*, which opposed the policies of military and political leader Antonio López de Santa Anna and the Treaty of Guadalupe Hidalgo. Before joining Juárez's cabinet, he was minister of justice for Santa Anna's successor, President Ignacio Comonfort, who held power from December 1855 until January 1858.[33] Under Comonfort, Iglesias promulgated the "Ley Iglesias," a law that sought to limit the power of the Catholic Church and prevent impoverishment by prohibiting excessive church fees for the poor.[34] Iglesias held a number of positions in Juárez's government, though the *Souvenir* caption calls him minister of public instruction, which was part of the appointment he received in 1863, when he was named minister of justice, public improvement, and public instruction.[35]

Ignacio Mejía, like Juárez, was born in Oaxaca and studied at the Instituto de Ciencias y Artes, a liberal alternative to the Seminary of Santa Cruz, which was the only secondary school in Oaxaca before the Instituto was founded.[36] When war with Spain seemed imminent in 1829, he joined the army in opposition to the National Church Party in 1833. Among his various government positions, he was military governor of Tehuantepec and interim governor of Oaxaca. In 1855, he became chief of staff in a brigade commanded by Juárez, serving until his capture at the second Battle of Puebla in 1863. Sent to France as a prisoner, he was liberated in 1864 and traveled to the United States via England. Juárez summoned him to El Paso del Norte on September 15, 1865.[37] This portrait of Mejía in the *Souvenir* album, then, was made only a few months after his arrival in El Paso del Norte.

Sebastián Lerdo de Tejada was a lawyer who held public office starting in 1855, holding various positions, including serving as president until his overthrow in 1876.[38] His older brother, Miguel Lerdo de Tejada, was a member of Mexico's Liberal Party, leader of the Revolution of Ayutla—the beginning of liberal reform in Mexico—and author of the Lerdo Law (1856), which prohibited land ownership by corporations, including the Catholic Church and indigenous communities (the annexation of indigenous lands was a disaster for campesinos [small farmers] and had the opposite effect of its goal to build a rural middle class).[39] Lerdo de Tejada served in Comonfort's cabinet as minister of foreign affairs, the same role he played in Juárez's cabinet.[40] On November 8, 1865, Lerdo de Tejada wrote the decree that extended Juárez's term as president and voided General Jesús González Ortega's attempt to succeed Juárez as president by claiming that Juárez's presidency had expired during the war, a thing Ortega had been advocating for since November 30, 1864.[41] When Juárez returned to Mexico City in 1867, recapturing the city and putting Maximilian and his generals on trial, according to some sources, it was Lerdo de Tejada who convinced Juárez not to pardon Maximilian when he and the others were found guilty of treason, but rather to have him executed.[42] Lerdo de Tejada was elected vice president after Juárez regained the presidency, and when Juárez died in 1872, Lerdo de Tejada inherited the presidency and was subsequently elected president later that year. Although he would be reelected one more time in 1876, he ultimately fled into exile when his government was overthrown in an armed revolt led by General Porfirio Díaz.[43]

Lerdo de Tejada, Mejia, Iglesias, and Gotien accompanied Juárez when in 1866, during his exile along the U.S. border, he asked the United States for assistance—though this wasn't the first time he had asked for help from his country's northern neighbor and recent adversary. After becoming president by default in 1858, he sought and won recognition of his government from the United States in 1859 during the War of Reform between liberals and conservatives.[44]

Juárez was elected to the presidency in 1861. With the United States distracted by its own Civil War starting that same year, Spain, France, and Britain saw an opportunity to invade Mexico in December 1861 to recover unpaid debts and establish a client state.[45] Despite their heroic resistance, Mexicans lost the second Battle of Puebla, and Juárez and his government fled Mexico City on May 31, 1863.[46] They moved ever northward, establishing and reestablishing new centers from which the government in exile would operate, including San Luis Potosí, Saltillo, Monterrey, Chihuahua, and El Paso del Norte.[47]

Juárez and U.S. Army officers who appear in the *Souvenir* album forged a years-long alliance in opposition to French encroachment in the Americas, even before the U.S. Civil War ended. The Americans surreptitiously shipped arms to the Juaristas, and sympathetic civilians worked, covertly and overtly, to aid the expulsion of French forces from Mexico. Neither President Abraham Lincoln nor Secretary of State William H. Seward supported France's ambitions in Mexico and, as previously addressed, they decried the incursion as a violation of the Monroe Doctrine.[48] But Lincoln's public posture was one of neutrality to avoid antagonizing the French, fearing that such antagonism would encourage them to support the Confederacy.[49]

Covertly, however, Mexican diplomat Matías Romero and other Mexican operatives pressed the United States to aid the Juaristas.[50] After the Civil War, in May 1865, General Ulysses S. Grant, commander of the Union Army, sent 50,000 troops to the Texas-Mexico border under the command of General Philip Sheridan.[51] Rebel forces in Texas remained a threat despite the Confederate surrender, and U.S. military leaders worried that they might attract compatriots who weren't ready to quit fighting. Likewise, they feared Confederates might join Maximilian's forces in Mexico.[52] The deployment of troops mirrored the smuggling of arms and other types of assistance from the United States to Mexico, both during and after the American Civil War, with the journey of arms being by turns circuitous, dangerous, and creative: one shipment of arms was even concealed in barrels of pickles.[53] The officers portrayed in the *Souvenir* album would have been stationed at Fort Bliss at this time and unquestionably played some part in smuggling arms to the Juaristas in exile in El Paso del Norte.

CHAPTER 3

HARDSHIP AND GREED

Portraits of U.S. Army Officers and Prominent Merchants

WHEN GENERAL JAMES H. CARLETON (plate 7) and his California Column reoccupied West Texas on the heels of the retreating Confederates, the general established a command center in Mesilla (Doña Ana County, New Mexico) on August 15, 1862.[1] Mesilla presented multiple problems of "disease and demoralization" that led district commander Brigadier General Joseph R. West, in February 1863, to reevaluate its usefulness.[2] Chief medical officer Dr. O. M. Bryan cited malaria, scurvy, and the proximity of prostitution and "grog shops" in Mesilla as reasons why Franklin, Texas, some forty miles south, might be a better headquarters.[3] The post first moved to Hart's Mill, north of Franklin, and in 1864 to Franklin itself.[4] In general, the troops who served in the Southwest endured "privations, toil and hardships," with alcohol and women serving as outlets for the boredom and loneliness that many experienced.[5]

Drinking and prostitution remained a problem, even with the relocation to Franklin, with "lewd women" even living on post. *A Civil War History of the New Mexico Volunteers and Militia*, Jerry Thompson's study of military life in New Mexico before and after the Civil War (with subheadings like "Drunkenness and Disorder at Cubero," "Chronic Inebriation," "A Vile and Immoral Place," "Alcohol and Fisticuffs at Fort Wingate," "Beastly Intoxication," "Pugilistic and Undisciplined," and "A Bestiality State of Intoxication"), paints a picture of drunkenness, both on duty and off, that is staggering.[6] Prostitution and sex trafficking thrived in a setting where women were often without other options to survive or, in the case of indigenous and Mexican women, were slaves and peons with no choice in their fate.[7]

Brigadier General West was tasked with controlling vice as part of his responsibility for enforcing martial law.[8] But plenty of vice was of the financial kind. Under martial law, the army leased property at low rates, especially the property of Confederate-sympathizing business owners who had abandoned properties when they fled the Union Army's advance.[9] Republican businessmen and property owners benefited from the army's presence, and Union officers shared in the profiteering. In 1864, for example, Republican businessman W. W. Mills owned six of the ten properties leased by the Union Army. Two years earlier, he had secured an appointment from President Lincoln as a county customs collector, which put him in a prime position to do business with the Union Army officers who arrived later that year.[10] "The military posts in northwest Texas and southern New Mexico were supplied with corn, flour, beef, hay, fuel, etc., by El Paso [Franklin] merchants and contractors," Mills noted. "The products of the mines, crudely worked, in northern Mexico, were brought to El Paso and exchanged for merchandise and money."[11]

After the Civil War ended, exchanges of goods increased, and the once surreptitious shipments of arms and other supplies to Mexico in support of the Juaristas could now be sent more openly. On a local level, supporters of Mexico in the United States established pro-Mexican organizations to raise awareness, support, and money. A leading architect of American arms shipments to the Juaristas was General Lew Wallace (figure 23), who became the territorial governor of New Mexico in 1878.[12] One of the largest movements of American arms to the Juaristas happened in early 1865. At that time, an unnamed "confidential" agent of the Mexican republic visited Carleton at his headquarters in Santa

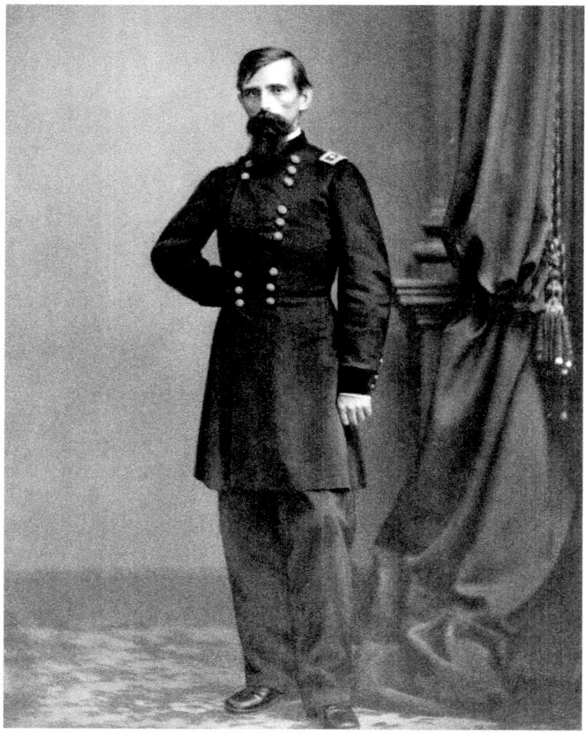

FIG. 23. General Lew Wallace, ca. 1860s. Photographer unknown. Palace of the Governors Photo Archives, New Mexico History Museum, Santa Fe, 077788.

This photograph shows Wallace when he was a Union general.

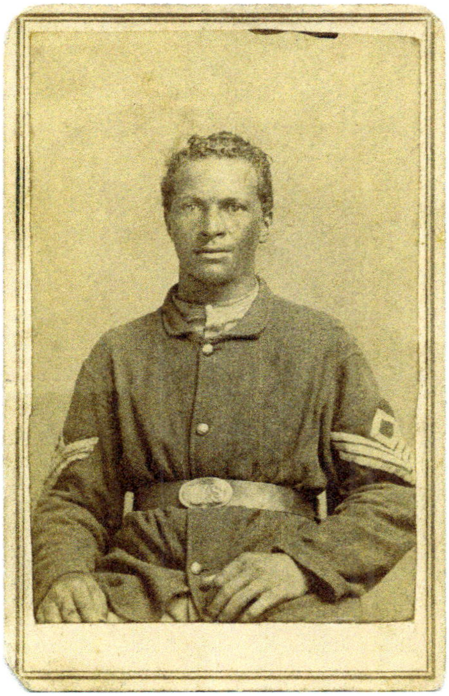

FIG. 24. First Sergeant William Messley, Company C of the Sixty-Second U.S. Colored Infantry, ca. 1864–66. Photographer unknown. Carte de visite mount. Wilson's Creek National Battlefield, U.S. National Park Service; WICR 11510.

Messley, a former slave from Glasgow, Missouri, was twenty-two when he enlisted and was part of the deployment of 50,000 troops sent to the border by General Grant in late spring of 1865.

Fe, stopping at Franklin on the way, as Ichabod Bartlett recounted years later.[13] After meeting with Carleton, the agent went to Washington, D.C. Soon after that meeting in D.C., and as no matter of coincidence, the U.S. War Department declared thousands of rifles unserviceable and sold them at Las Cruces. They were sold at a deep discount, along with a large supply of ammunition, to Mexican customs collector Juan N. Zubirán, the wealthy El Paso del Norte merchant who, as previously mentioned, introduced Bartlett to Juárez.[14] This sale would have been part of General Grant's larger scheme of late spring 1865 for the Union Army to "lose" 30,000 rifles near the border with El Paso del Norte for the Juarista troops.[15] The movement of arms also coincided with Grant's previously mentioned large deployment of troops to the border, 50,000 of them, most of them from regiments of the United States Colored Troops, later referred to as "Buffalo Soldiers" (figure 24).[16]

Further pertinent to exchanges and tensions at the border, in 1863, Carleton had developed a local strategy aimed at thwarting Confederates who had begun operating in Mexico.[17] The two-pronged plan intended to build better regional ties in Mexico, beginning with Chihuahua, and to use that foundation to improve the Union intelligence network, a network of spies.[18] Carleton's more localized efforts were in concert with the later concerns of Grant and Sheridan to keep the Confederates from regaining any part of the Southwest. And those concerns were justified. For example, in early May of 1865, while on a scouting expedition, Captain Brotherton (plate 8) encountered nineteen Confederate deserters making their way to Franklin. The deserters reported that Confederates and Confederate sympathizers who had fled south of the border were planning a "marauding" attack on New Mexico in an attempt to take back the territory.[19] When Carleton heard this news, it affirmed his belief that the Confederate Texans had not given up on the idea of marching back into New Mexico Territory, and his network of spies were directed to be on the lookout "for any suspicious persons or organized forces," as recommended by Assistant Inspector General N. H. Davis.[20]

One member of Carleton's network of spies was Henry J. Cuniffe (plate 6), who also thrived from doing business with the U.S. Army.[21] Born in Ireland,[22] Cuniffe came to Las Cruces, New Mexico, as a young man and opened a store there in 1850. In 1854 and 1857, he also held the position of postmaster. After marrying Francisca Lujan, who came from an important New Mexico family, in 1857 (figure 25) the couple moved to Franklin, Texas, just before the outbreak of the Civil War.[23] Cuniffe, who was thirty-eight years old when his *Souvenir* album portrait was taken and already a very successful businessman, had developed deep roots in Franklin.[24] In 1862, Cuniffe began his service as American consul at El Paso del Norte, and in 1863, he partnered with Nathan Webb (plate 12), who had just opened a sutler store at Fort West with William H. Moore (H. Moore and Co.), who himself had just served as sutler at Fort Union.[25] Fort West was founded by Major William McCleave (plate 11) in February of 1863 to house the California volunteers, who were in turn charged with protecting Pinos Altos miners from attack by the Apaches.[26] In early 1863, Webb and Moore also opened a store at Fort Bliss in Franklin.[27]

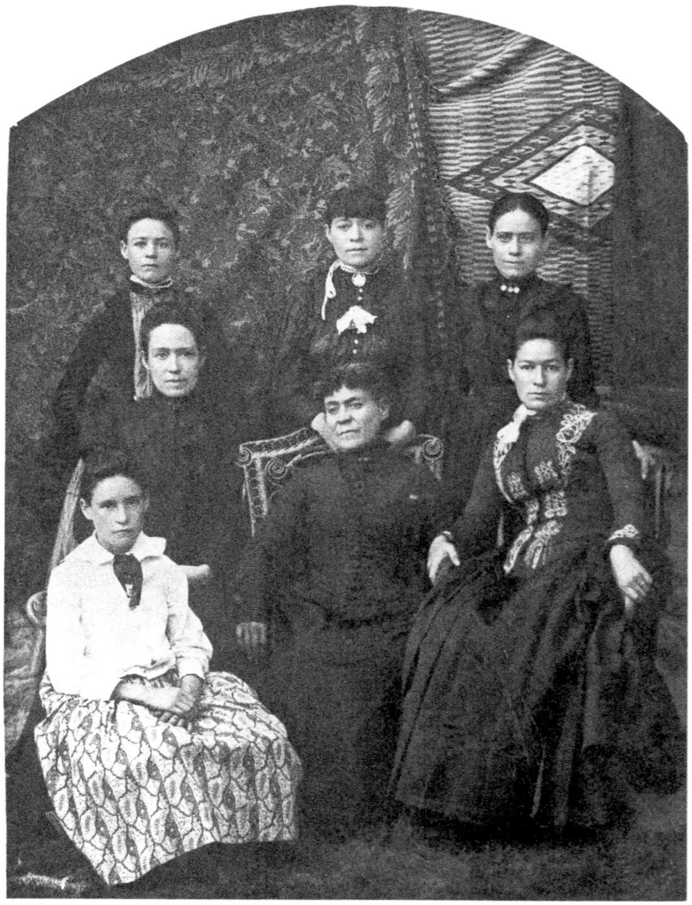

FIG. 25. Cuniffe family women, presumably with Francesca Lujan seated at the center, 1890s. Photographer unknown. Amador Family Papers D, Collection MS004, New Mexico State University Library, Archives and Special Collections, Las Cruces, 00040579.

Webb became post sutler at Fort Bliss, managing both of the partners' concerns under the name of N. Webb and Co. In the same year, 1863, Webb and Moore took on a third partner, William Kroenig, and together they built a flour mill near the junction of the Mora and Sapello Rivers, nine miles from Fort Union. The mill was profitable during the war years, running without stop to fill government contracts for flour and wheat meal.[28] The Cuniffe-Webb partnership included a contract to supply flour and bran to the military, grain that they ground themselves, having leased Hart's Mill for that purpose.[29] Cuniffe and Webb also sold flour in Mexico, securing a contract with Zubirán in El Paso del Norte.[30] Indicative of the network Cuniffe and Webb had been building in Franklin, another photograph from roughly the same time as the *Souvenir* portrait shows Cuniffe playing cards with other prominent businessmen and politicians from both sides of the border, including W. W. Mills (or possibly

FIG. 26. (*From left to right*) Henry Cuniffe, W. W. Mills (or possibly his brother, Anson Mills), José María Uranga (possibly), Nathanial Webb, and Juan Zubirán (possibly), ca. 1866. Photographer unknown. Courtesy Evelyn Rosen and Carl Hertzog.

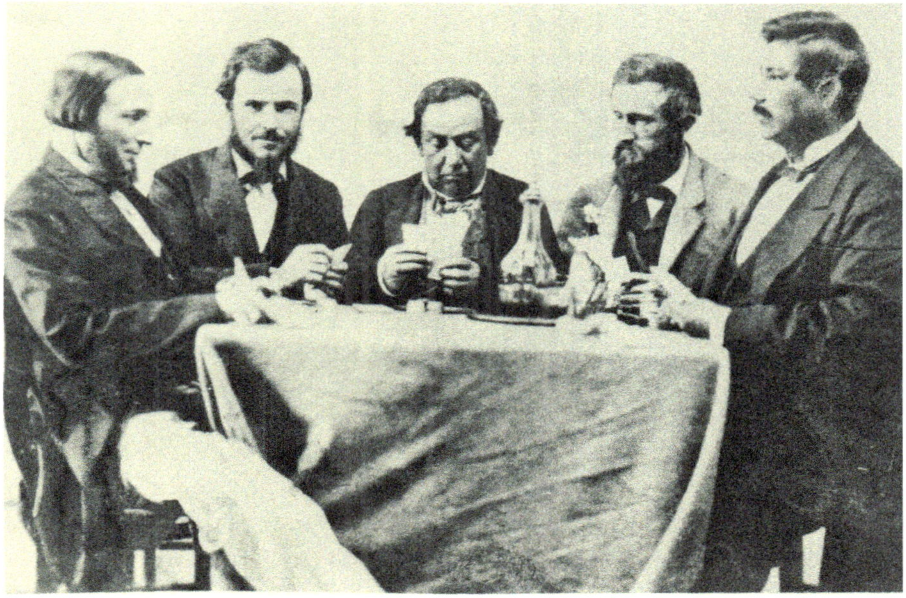

his brother, Anson Mills), possibly *José María Uranga*, Nathanial Webb, and possibly Juan Zubirán (figure 26)[31]—another example of associations and networks present in the *Souvenir* album, which were manifest and made through the real-life socializing of those pictured, including playing cards.

Further examples of commerce exchanges and the intrigue of gunrunning and politics as facilitated and bolstered by the social and economic engagements of local power brokers are numerous. For example, on January 30, 1864, Mariano Samaniego, El Paso del Norte politician and merchant, held a ball in Carleton's honor at his home. The *Santa Fe Weekly Gazette* of February 27, 1864, reported that Colonel James Bowie's brass band from Franklin played, and that "the ball . . . was one of the most brilliant and recherché displays of the kind ever seen on these frontiers . . . The table was mounted with the purest wines, choicest fruits, and all the varieties of sweetmeats. In the center was a pyramid cake of an enormous size; from the top floated the colors of the United States and Mexico, beautifully comingling."[32] In another instance, after an arms sale on November 11, 1865, officers at Fort Bliss held a reception honoring Juárez at the El Paso del Norte home of Rafael Velarde.[33] It was an elegant affair, according to Bartlett, who was in attendance, with officers of both armies in uniform and music by the Fifth Infantry band from Fort Bliss.[34] And on Christmas Eve 1865, Cuniffe held an open house in Franklin, entertaining large numbers of people from both sides of the border with cake and wine.[35] These social engagements were often the basis on which financial and social contracts were set in motion among those who attended them.

While Brotherton (plate 8) does not seem to figure in the international social scene and business dealings of elite officers and businessmen at the border, he appears to have been involved in the supply of American arms to the Juaristas. He was commander at Fort Bliss when the *Souvenir* photographs were taken.[36] In correspondence with Lerdo de Tejada (plate 2) in January and February 1866, Brotherton asked permission to pursue Apaches on the Mexican side of the border.[37] It was common at the time to use such pretexts, very specifically that of pursuing hostile Indians, to rationalize the deployment of American soldiers in Mexico who were actually there to help oust Maximilian.[38] The Brotherton-Lerdo letters were mentioned in correspondence between Secretary of State William H. Seward and the Mexican diplomat Matías Romero, which suggests that Brotherton was among the thirteen elite troops from Fort Bliss who served in the American Legion of Honor recruited from Texas to serve under Major George William McNulty to help expel Maximilian. The date of those letters approximates the time when Juárez's cabinet was likely photographed, which could explain why Brotherton's portrait shares the same background as those of the Juárez cabinet portraits and the same table covering of the Gotien portrait. It could be that Brotherton (plate 8) actually had his portrait taken in El Paso del Norte at the same time the portrait of Gotien was taken (plate 5).

Captain Emil Fritz (plate 10), like Brotherton, also does not appear in the social correspondence of the day in Franklin, though he looms large in the story of New Mexico. Fritz was an immigrant from Germany who probably came to California as part of the California gold rush, and served several tours of duty in the U.S. Army in California and New Mexico.[39] He served with Lawrence G. Murphy, an Irish immigrant, who was stationed with Fritz in the 1860s at Fort Sumner and Fort Stanton, the latter of which was established in 1855 and located in Lincoln County in south-central New Mexico (figure 27).[40] In 1866, while Fritz was post commander at Fort Stanton, he and Murphy opened a brewery and store, L. G. Murphy and Co., through which they secured grain and cattle from local ranchers to sell to the U.S. Army, and at the same time, obtained bacon, beans, and coffee from the army to sell to ranchers.[41] Fritz and Murphy's company, which would earn the nickname "The House," took on additional business partners and increasingly was known for its tough business deals in which the owners were scamming and skimming off the top and creating a monopoly through coercion and control (figure 28). Reflective of how such monopolies were constituted, Fritz and Murphy were associated with the Santa Fe Ring, as well as being Freemasons (most if not all members of the Santa Fe Ring were members of a Masonic Lodge).[42] When Fritz died on a visit home to Germany on June 26, 1874, disputes about the settlement of his insurance policy set into motion one of the most tumultuous conflicts in New Mexico in the late nineteenth century, the Lincoln County War. That war was a long-standing

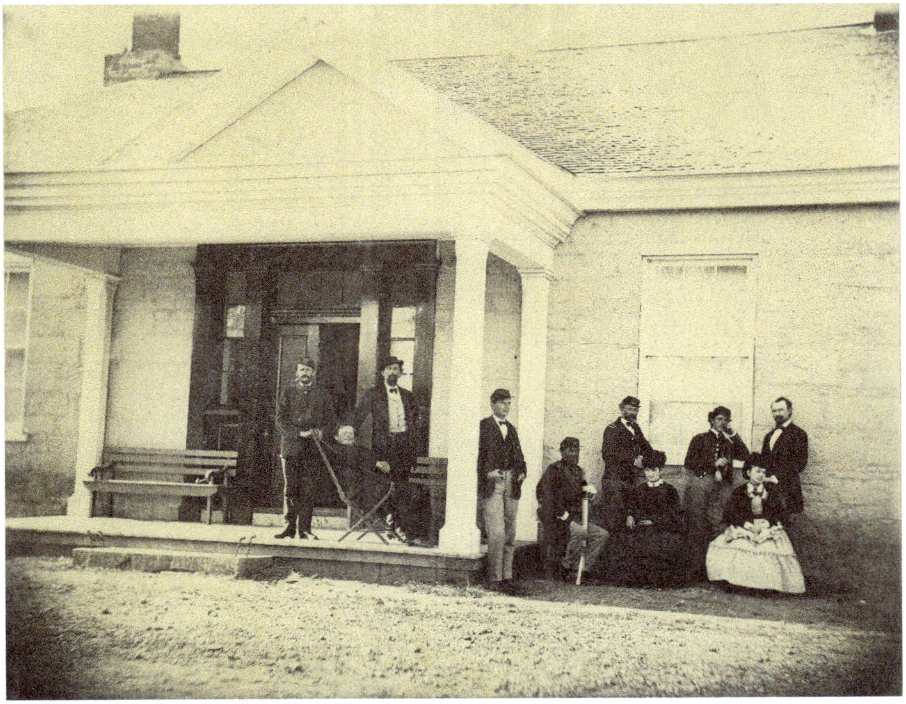

FIG. 27. (*From left to right*) Dr. Charles Styer, Lieutenant Orsemus Bronson (*seated*), Captain Emil Fritz, Lieutenant Casper Hauser Conrad, Lieutenant Colonel August Valentine Kautz (*seated*), Captain Chambers McKibbin, Mrs. Mary McKibbin (*seated*), Captain William McCleave, Mrs. Anne Boyd (*seated*), and Major L. G. Murphy, at Post Headquarters, Fort Stanton, New Mexico Territory, ca. 1871. Photograph by Nicholas Brown. Palace of the Governors Photo Archives, New Mexico History Museum, Santa Fe, 101417.

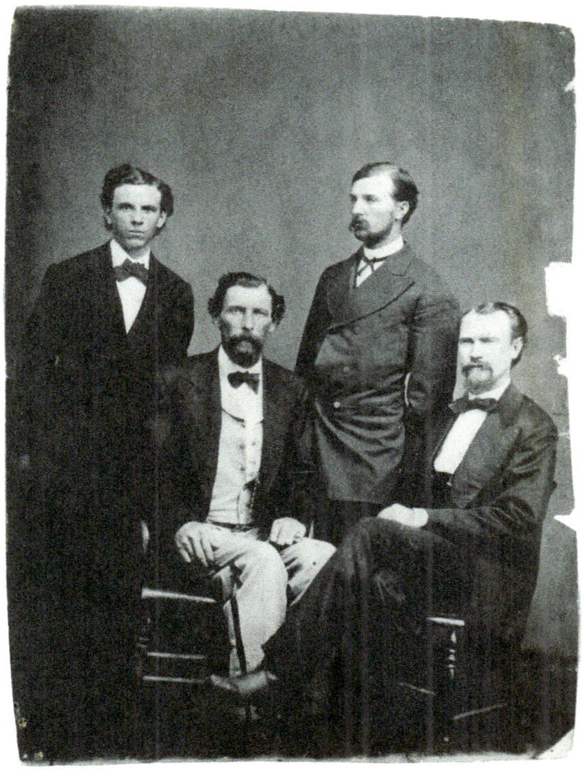

FIG. 28. Personnel of L. G. Murphy and Company. (*Seated, left to right*) Captain Emil Fritz and Major L. G. Murphy; (*standing*) J. G. Dolan (bookkeeper) and W. J. Marin (clerk), Lincoln County, New Mexico Territory, 1871. Photograph by Nicholas Brown. Palace of the Governors Photo Archives, New Mexico History Museum, Santa Fe, 104912.

feud that in its fame placed the names of many involved in the historical canon of New Mexico, including Fritz, Murphy, cattle rancher John Chisum, Sheriff William J. Brady, lawyer Alexander McSween, businessman James Dolan, and, most famous of all, the outlaw Billy the Kid.[43]

These monopolies, built by Anglos who were relative newcomers to New Mexico, challenged the dominance of the local Comancheros, longtime New Mexican farmers and ranchers who traded with Plains tribes, especially the Comanches and Kiowas, after the annexation of the New Mexico Territory.[44] The U.S. government was intent upon stopping the business between the Comancheros and the Southern Plains Indians, in order to overtly destroy the military might of the Comanches and Kiowas, as well as, perhaps more covertly, to allow American economic interests, above or below board, to prevail. And the government's efforts were effective, as even businessmen who are not thought of as being in the middle of these monopolies benefited from the changing political landscape. At the end of the Lincoln County War, after the death of Billy the Kid, Henry Cuniffe invested with some of those who had been embroiled in that conflict, and founded the Tularosa Land and Cattle Company with heads of cattle in the tens of thousands.[45] The impact of these corrupt monopolies and rings, which existed to maximize profit at all costs, is manifest in extreme form in the last group of photographs.

CHAPTER 4

SORROW

Portraits of Navajos at Bosque Redondo

THE LAST GROUP OF PHOTOGRAPHS, mostly portraits with a few landscapes, are of Navajos and of Fort Sumner and the surrounding Bosque Redondo in southeastern New Mexico. This is where Navajos and Apaches were imprisoned between 1863, when five hundred Mescalero Apaches (N'de) were forcibly relocated there, and 1868, when the Navajos returned to their homelands after four years of internment.[1] These images specifically depict the final destination of the Long Walk of the Navajos, when approximately 9,000 to 11,000 Navajos (Diné) were forcibly removed from their homelands and compelled to walk hundreds of miles to internment at Hweéldi, or the Place of Suffering, as the Navajos call it.[2] On the journey, the Navajos endured "hunger, disease, rape, slave raids by Comanche[s] and Kiowas, extreme weather, grief and despair."[3] Hundreds died en route, and hundreds if not thousands more Navajos died from smallpox in the first year of imprisonment.[4]

General Edward Canby initially proposed removing the Navajos from their lands, but it was Carleton who conceived the specific removal plan, which began with the Mescalero Apaches.[5] Carleton had witnessed firsthand the operation of an Indian reservation when, in 1858, he was stationed at Fort Tejon, next to the Sebastian Indian Reservation in California. There he observed Superintendent Edward F. Beale's "experiment" with the Kitanemuk, Native Americans of Southern California, who were placed on a reservation to become farmers.[6] As an indication of what was to come at Bosque Redondo, the Fort Tejon Sebastian Indian Reservation was a logistical and moral failure, whose residents suffered from widespread disease and food shortages.[7]

Carleton lays out his argument for removal of the "barbarians," as he referred to the Navajos, in a pamphlet in 1865, titled "To the People of New Mexico":

> At the Bosque Redondo there is arable land enough for all the Indians of this family (the Navajoes [*sic*] and Apaches . . .) and I would respectfully

> recommend that now the war is vigorously prosecuted against the Navajoes [*sic*], that the only peace that can ever be made with them must rest on the basis that they move on to these lands [Bosque Redondo], and, like the Pueblos, become an agricultural people, and cease to be nomads.[8]

The pamphlet was Carleton's public relations response to a December 1864 editorial in the Santa Fe *Weekly New Mexican* that attacked him and the contractors and merchants who were profiting from the internment at Bosque Redondo and Fort Sumner, labeling the whole arrangement as "nothing more than a contractor's scheme."[9] An earlier letter of Carleton's outlines his interest in "arable lands in other parts of the Territory," in "a country evidently teaming with millions on millions of wealth." The letter establishes Carleton's rationale for wanting to keep the land from the "rebels," as well as establishing the foundation for what would later be revealed as his personal greed for land occupied by Native people in the territory. On May 10, 1863, in a letter to Major General Henry W. Halleck, Carleton writes:

> My Dear General:
>
> I am aware that every moment of your time is of value to the country, and I would not presume to ask you even to read this note did I not believe that what is herewith enclosed would be of interest to you as a general, and, therefore, as a statesman. Among all my endeavors since my arrival here, there has been an effort to brush back the Indians, as you have seen from official correspondence, so that the people could get out of the valley of the Rio Grande, and not only possess themselves of the arable lands in other parts of the Territory, but, if the country contained veins and deposits of the precious metals, that they might be found. So I re-establish Fort Stanton, and at least a hundred families have gone to that vicinity to open farms, and they are commencing to find gold there.
>
> I established Fort West, and have driven the Indians away from the head of the Gila, and they are finding gold and silver and cinnabar there. There is no doubt in my mind that one of the richest gold countries in the world is along the affluents [tributaries] to the Gila, which enter it from the north along its whole course. Thus you can see one reason why the rebels want, and why we may not permit them ever to have, a country evidently teaming with millions on millions of wealth.[10]

Carleton and the former miners in his California Column had searched for gold and silver deposits en route to the New Mexico Territory, and the general had secretly been investing in mines where his troops were prospecting as they went.[11] His plan to remove Native Americans from areas that held rich mineral deposits is no coincidence and was not only about subduing and controlling

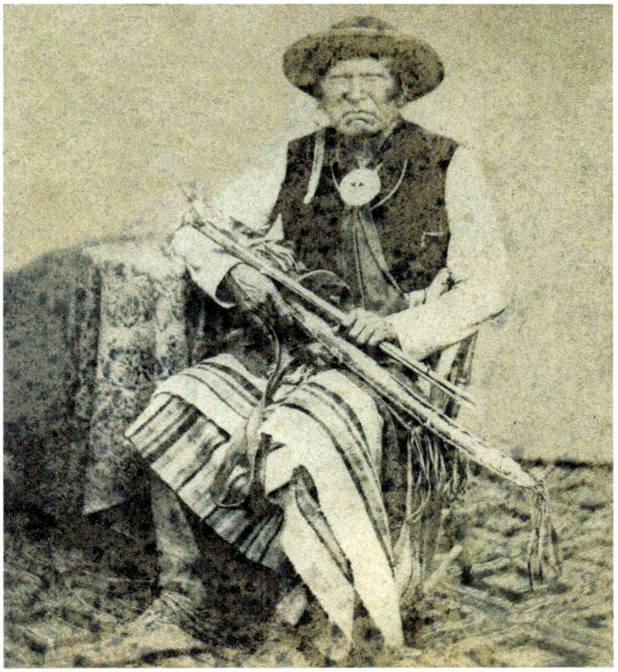

FIG. 29. Coetta (Cadete), Chief of the Apache Nation, 1872–78. Photograph by Henry T. Hiester. Palace of the Governors Photo Archives, New Mexico History Museum, Santa Fe, HP.1974.25.34.

indigenous peoples; it was also motivated by his personal investments and avarice.[12] In October 1862, Carleton ordered Colonel Kit Carson with the First Regiment, New Mexico Cavalry, to reoccupy Fort Stanton and use it as a base from which to wage war on the Mescaleros, with orders that all Mescalero men were to be killed "whenever and wherever" Carson's troops found them.[13] When the leading Mescalero chief, Cadete, surrendered in December (figure 29), the tribe's survivors were moved to Fort Sumner and put to work expanding the fort in anticipation of the arrival of the Navajos.[14]

The campaign against the Navajos began in 1863 with Carleton's brutal scorched-earth policy—carried out by Kit Carson and his troops—in which homes of Navajos, along with their crops of corn, wheat, beans, melons, and peaches, were destroyed in order to force them to surrender.[15] The enormity of the destruction is hard to envisage. Ultimately, more than four thousand peach trees were destroyed, as well as acres upon acres of crops: "The systematic destruction of the orchards was one of the most vengeful acts inflicted upon the Navajo," and it is the thing Navajos today mention the most when they talk about the Carleton campaign.[16] Many Navajos refused to leave, and Carson was ordered to invade Canyon de Chelly on January 12, 1864, to chase down the holdouts. Hounded by soldiers and starved from their lands, many Navajos surrendered at various forts in New Mexico Territory. On March 4, 1864, the Long Walk began, with more than two thousand Navajos leaving from Fort Canby (earlier called Fort Defiance), in Apache County, Arizona, to walk 450 miles to Fort Sumner, commencing the most devastating time in Navajo history.[17] As more groups of Navajos surrendered, they were forced to walk various routes. The longest route, beginning at Fort Canby, went southeast by Ojo del Oso and Fort Wingate; turned north at Los Pinos, arriving at Albuquerque; continued north by Santo Domingo and Fort Marcy/Santa Fe; headed even farther north to Fort Union; before turning south along the Pecos River, arriving at Fort Sumner after a 498-mile journey. The shortest of the routes, and also the roughest and least used was 375 miles long.[18]

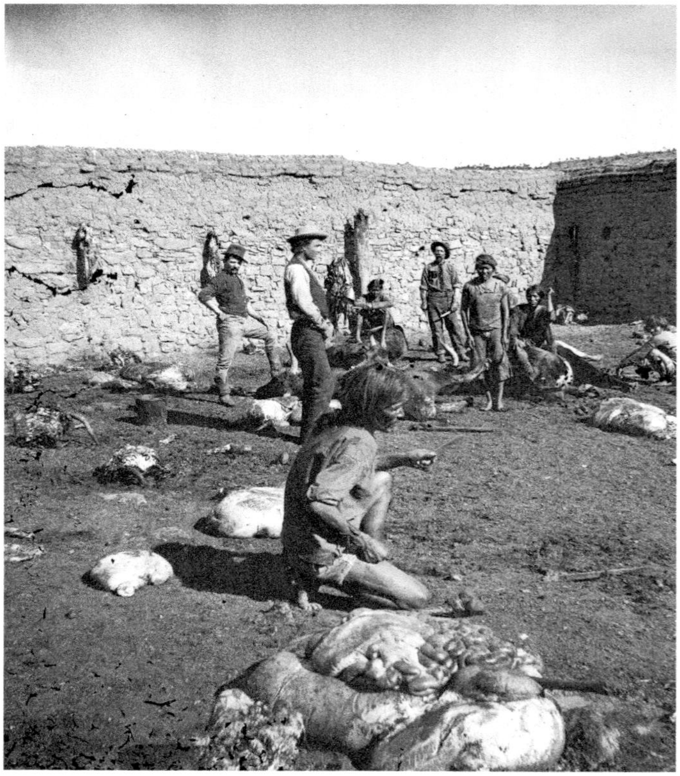

FIG. 30. Indians butchering cattle, 1872–78. Photograph by Henry T. Hiester. Stereo glass negative. Palace of the Governors Photo Archives, New Mexico History Museum, Santa Fe, 037968.

While this image of butchering and distribution of rations was taken some years after Jennings's description of that activity at Fort Sumner, it likely depicts a similar scene: Navajo butchering cattle for rations at a fort in New Mexico Territory, most likely Fort Defiance.

Survivors of the Long Walk arrived at a place with poor soil, alkaline water, and sparse trees.[19] The internees endured years of crop failures; in their final year in captivity, they were compelled to work the unproductive fields at the points of bayonets, by some reports.[20] The government was ultimately forced to supply food, clothing, and other necessities to the internees, which was carried out by distributing rations, which were often insufficient, rancid, and inedible, with supplies of clothing and blankets likewise inadequate to meet the captives' needs.[21] The barren land with so few trees made it difficult for the Navajos to build hogans for shelter (plate 41). Nevertheless, they were constantly at work at Bosque Redondo, as they were responsible for irrigation, farming, and the butchering and dispersal of livestock, all under army supervision (plate 60). Lieutenant Charles T. Jennings wrote an account of the butchering of cattle by Navajos, which happened on alternate days, with twenty to thirty head of cattle being butchered and then divided into meager portions (figure 30). Jennings was responsible for the weighing of the beef, noting that it was not "easy to chop thirty head of cattle into six thousand six hundred pieces and have all equally large."[22]

While the Navajos and Apaches starved, traders and merchants who contracted with the government prospered, making money even when supplies were deficient or spoiled. Moore, the one-time partner of Nathan Webb (plate 12), supplied bad flour that contained "bits of stale, broken bread and something that resembles plaster of paris," and yet he received further contracts to supply Hweéldi.[23] Rationing was implemented in response to the shortages, and cardboard tickets were used to trade for provisions. When the Navajos began forging cardboard ration tickets, a system of stamped metal discs was introduced. These, too, were duplicated by the skilled Navajo metalsmiths.[24] Finally the army asked Washington for metal coupons that were too intricate to counterfeit.[25] The desperate captives were labeled "thieves" for forging ration tickets and tokens to stay alive (plates 57b and 60), as seen in one widely circulated photo (plate 60) that bears the caption "Navajo chiefs accused of counterfeiting ration tickets at Bosque Redondo." The constant deprivation and near-starvation conditions that the Navajos endured for years required fortitude, endurance, and creativity to survive, making the label "thieves" in this context both inaccurate and hypocritical.

Compounding their misery, Navajos were the targets of slave raids by their traditional adversaries, the Kiowas, Comanches, and Utes. Kidnapping and slavery were practiced by all parties in the New Mexico Territory, including Anglos, Mexicans, and various tribes. While Native Americans did have slaves—often adopting those they had captured or bought—the number of slaves held by indigenous people in New Mexico was substantially less than the number of slaves held by Nuevomexicanos and Anglos. Spanish colonists, in addition to forcing indigenous people to work as laborers and household servants, also required them to become Christians.[26] The number of Navajo baptisms was far fewer than one hundred in the decades before and after the 1860s, but they reached almost eight hundred in that decade alone, during the time of their internment at Bosque Redondo.[27] It was the Navajos who suffered the most from the practice of captive slavery and peonage, particularly once removed from their homelands. In January 1864, Superintendent of Indian Affairs Michael Steck estimated that at least two thousand Navajos lived as slaves in the New Mexico Territory.[28] In August 1864, he reported that in one ten-day period, a band of Utes brought sixty captive Navajo children into Abiquiú, a center for trafficking in Navajo slaves, after killing thirty other Navajo adults.[29]

Many army officers were indifferent toward slavery in New Mexico. In 1851, General Carleton brought the first black slaves, known to history as "Hannah" and "Benjamin," into New Mexico and sold them to Governor William Carr Lane.[30] It was not uncommon for army officers, including Kit Carson and Col. Pfeiffer, to own Native American slaves, specifically Navajo slaves, as did Henry Connelly, governor of the New Mexico Territory from 1861 until 1866.[31] The capture and enslavement of Navajos was the main reason the Navajos waged war with the Nuevomexicanos and Anglos of the territory. Indeed, Carleton was warned by Carson and Captain Asa Bacon Carey that lasting peace with the Navajos would never be reached if slave traders were allowed to persist.[32]

When Congress passed the Peonage Abolition Act of 1867, it was designed to shore up the Thirteenth Amendment and specifically address the torment of slavery and peonage in the New Mexico Territory.[33] During the Bosque Redondo era, officers' reports featured frequent accounts of soldiers encountering Navajo slaves fleeing their owners. A February 20, 1864, letter from Fritz to Brotherton contains one such account:

> Sir, I have the honor to state that I have sent to your post a Captive Boy named Jesus Garcia, who says that he is the son of Miguel Garcia who lives in la Candelaria, below Albuquerque, N.M.[34]

In another letter, from August 4, 1865, Fritz writes from Fort Sumner to Lieutenant B. Taylor about the mistreatment of a Cebolleta Navajo woman named Trinidad, who was owned by Juan Armijo and reported being so mistreated that she preferred to go to the Bosque Redondo reservation rather than return to her owner.[35]

Slavery was such an ordeal for captive Navajos that they often preferred to join other Navajos at Bosque Redondo. However, the adversity of life at Bosque Redondo, coupled with the ongoing conflicts between the Mescalero Apaches and the Navajos, age-old enemies, compelled the Mescaleros to make their exodus from the Bosque Redondo reservation on the night of November 3, 1865, never to return.[36] To evade being recaptured, the Mescaleros scattered, some even going to Mexico, and remained in large part elusive to the U.S Army until 1871.[37] While the number of Mescaleros at Bosque Redondo was large, initially five hundred, it was still manageable enough to devise an escape, compared to the thousands of Navajos interned there. The large number of Navajos at Bosque Redondo made it practically logistically impossible for them to slip away in the manner the Mescaleros had. It would be well over two more years before the Navajos returned home, though some Navajo captives also escaped before the negotiation of the 1868 Navajo Treaty.

The landscape photos in this last group from the album offer a small glimpse of the hardships endured by Native captives, but the Navajo portraits are the most riveting. There are thirteen portraits in all, and five are group shots. All but one has a plain canvas backdrop, presumably a canvas tent or photographer's canvas backdrop. The one portrait that has something other than the plain backdrop is a group portrait of six women and girls, which has the same painted backdrop seen in the Juárez cabinet portraits, the Brotherton portrait, and the "Navajo Girl" portrait in the Blackmore Collection (see figure 8). The subjects in all the portraits wear clothing typical of the time, the men often in the canvas split three-quarter pants or, in the case of Manuelito, Mexican-style pants with silver coin buttons up the side. The men also wear cotton shirts, plain or with patterns. One wears a military jacket. Many wear headbands, two wear hats, and at least one wears his hair in a *tsiiyéél*. The women all wear *biil*, a woven wool dress, and all wear typical Navajo buffalo-hide moccasins that would have had red ochre pigment applied, though the color is not visible in the sepia-toned prints. Many have blankets wrapped around them, or such blankets cover props in the portraits. Some are Navajo woven blankets, and some are army-issue "Mackinaw" blankets.[38]

The first Navajo portrait is of a young man holding a bow and arrow (plate 47), as many of the Navajo men are posed in the portraits. This is the image found on the cover of *Bury My Heart at Wounded Knee*, which is labeled "Jim, a Navajo Indian" in the Library of Congress copy prints. He also wears a typical pouch used to carry basic everyday items.[39]

The second portrait (plate 48) is of Manuelito, who, along with Barboncito, remains one of the most significant and eminent headmen of the Navajos. Manuelito resisted American and Mexican invasions and American expansion,[40] and he led many Navajos into hiding for more than two years in order to avoid the move to the Bosque Redondo reservation. Carleton sent delegation after delegation of Navajo captives to try to persuade Manuelito to surrender, but Manuelito and his band continued to hold out, causing Carleton to become increasingly enraged. Occasionally Carleton would hear reports from surrendering band members as to the disposition of Manuelitio and his band. One such report dates from March 20, 1865, when a large Navajo delegation led by headman Herrero Grande returned with news that Manuelito's band, who were actually under the command of Manuelito's older brother, according to the conversation Herrero Grande recounted, consisted by now of about one hundred people, twenty-five of whom were warriors, with the rest being women, children, and the elderly. Manuelito said that they refused to surrender even though they were starving, living in hiding, and sustaining themselves on roots.[41] Apparently, according to Herrero Grande, about seventy-five of his band wished to turn themselves in, but Manuelito and about twenty-five members of his band wished to remain in hiding. Carleton, writing to Major Shaw at Fort Wingate three days after hearing this report, had this to say:

> I understand that if Manuelito, the Navajo chief, could be captured his band would doubtless come in . . . Send runners to tell all Navajoes [*sic*] who want to come in to get to Fort Wingate as soon as possible . . . Try hard to get Manuelito. Have him securely ironed and carefully guarded. It will be a mercy to others whom he controls to capture or kill him at once. I prefer he should be captured. If he attempts to escape when again in our power, as he did from Fort Canby, he will be shot down.[42]

One later report, from January 18, 1866, offered by someone recorded as "Cabellado Chino" who came into Fort Wingate, said that Manuelito's followers had been dispersed by a Ute attack and were living along the Little Colorado River.[43] Chino said the only people left with Manuelito were his brother El

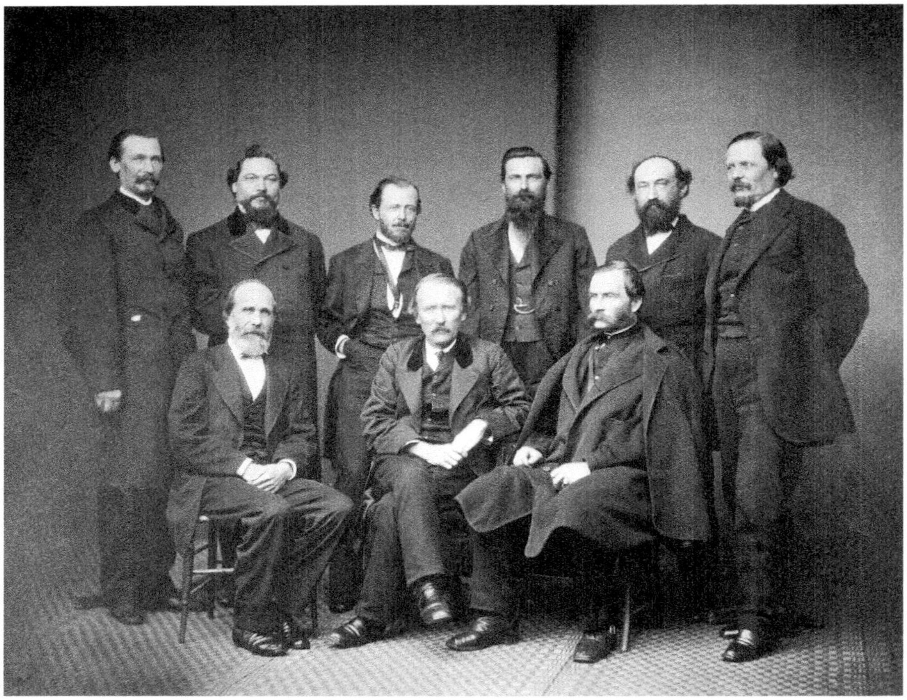

FIG. 31. Military personnel in Masonic group portrait, December 26, 1866, Masonic Temple, Santa Fe, New Mexico Territory. Photograph by Nicholas Brown. Palace of the Governors Photo Archives, New Mexico History Museum, Santa Fe, 009826.

(Seated, left to right) *Daniel H. Rucker, Kit Carson, and James H. Carleton.* (Standing, left to right) *E. H. Bergmann, Charles P. Cleaver, Nelson H. Davis, Herbert M. Enos, Basil K. Norris, and John C. McFerran. Cleaver was adjutant general of the New Mexico Territory, but all the others in this photo were army officers serving in New Mexico—all had served at Fort Union as either commander, quartermaster, or, in the case of Norris, as surgeon, and in the case of Davis, as inspector. Bergmann had been commander of Fort Bascom (Santa Fe Trail Research Site). This portrait was taken just over three months after Carleton was relieved of command.*

Ciego (plates 53 and 57b) and their families, El Ciego apparently being the older brother Manuelito referred to as commanding the band he was with. On September 1, 1866, Captain Edmond Butler received word that a group of Navajos were approaching Fort Wingate. When he rode to meet them, Butler accepted the surrender of Manuelito and twenty-three others.[44] Just over a month later, on November 7, 1866, Barboncito and a band of twenty-one others surrendered to Butler at Fort Wingate.[45] News of Barboncito's surrender was published in the *Santa Fe Gazette:* "Barboncito is reported as the last chief of influence that was left to the tribe, and his surrender may be said to be the surrender of the last of the Navajo Chiefs."[46] By then, hardships at Bosque Redondo were so atrocious that Carleton (figure 31) was relieved of command on September 19, 1866, and replaced by General George W. Getty.[47]

The portrait of Manuelito and other Navajos in the *Souvenir* album, which must have been taken after the September surrender, appear to have been taken in roughly the same time frame by the same photographer, though sometimes using different backdrops and props. Judging by the historical record, and most specifically by Cabellado Chino's account, the people in the thirteen portraits probably were members of Manuelito's and El Ciego's families and are among the twenty-four people who surrendered that September day. An article in the September 29, 1866, issue of the *Santa Fe Gazette* claimed that Manuelito's group had been brought through Santa Fe; given that this would not have been the direct route to Fort Sumner, this might have been done to make a public display of the group and to humiliate the captive Navajos:

> Manuelito, the Navajo Chief, and quite a large party of his band were brought to Santa Fe last week. They are to be taken to the Bosque Redondo Reservation and furnished with a new home where they will have less of the cares of State on their minds and more bread and meat to eat. Manuelito was the most stubborn of all the Navajo Chiefs and was the most difficult to be brought to terms.[48]

The portrait of Manuelito (plate 48) bears the caption "Pistol Bullet"—an Anglo nickname—and gives his height as "6 ft. 4 in." The origin of that nickname is recounted in, among other written accounts, *Bury My Heart at Wounded Knee* and *Red Shirt: The Life and Times of Henry Lafayette Dodge*, the latter of which lists three additional monikers (Manuelito had at least five names, nicknames, and monikers).[49] The nickname "Pistol Bullet," as well as the related nickname "Bullet Hole," referred to a scar under Manuelito's right breast from a wound he received in a raid on the Comanches.[50] Manuelito is bare-chested in the *Souvenir* portrait, most likely to show the scar for which he was famous. It is doubtful he posed this way gladly or willingly.

The third portrait in this set (plate 50), labeled in pencil "Apache Boy," invites the question of whether this Apache boy would have been adopted into Manuelito's group of followers and family—though apparently as late as July of 1866, many Apaches were with Manuelito's group of hold-outs.[51]

The girl or young woman in the portrait that follows (plate 51) appears in a slightly different portrait in the Blackmore Collection (see figure 8) and in the photocopy of the portrait where she appears with her sister that originally belonged to Charles T. Jennings. Presumably she is related to Manuelito and is either "Doña Jesus" or her sister. In general, less is known about the women in the other portraits (plates 52, 56, 61, and 62), as indigenous women, even more than indigenous men, were often photographed not as individuals with names, but as anonymous figures, meant to typify the collective. The picture of the woman with a baby on her back in a cradleboard and the double portrait of the two girls or young women that closes the album are also found at the Library of Congress with the Cyrus P. Jennings copy prints, but only the double portrait (plate 62) has names associated with the subjects in the Library of Congress record, "Notrossia and Pattia," though these are not Navajo names. Portrait photographs of indigenous women in the nineteenth century, such as the ones in this album, were often arranged in standard and repeated poses and often coupled with patronizing and standard captions.[52] For example, plate 56 portrays a woman with a baby on her back, the pose of mother and child a very standard one for Native American women in photographs of this time, the pose often related to earlier European traditions in painting of the same theme.[53] In other portraits of women, the label "belle" is sometimes used, as is the case with the portrait titled "The Belle of the Navajos" (plate 54). The girl in this photo is in a semireclining pose, as is "Navajo Girl" (plate 51). The employment of these conventional poses, such as the reclining pose, was meant to visually convey one of numerous tropes of the era about indigenous women, often meaning to suggest that they were sexually available or promiscuous, when in truth many indigenous women were forced into captive slavery or peonage and in this manner, sex trafficked.[54] At the very least, it can be said that indigenous women were repeatedly required to pose for photographs in a manner that was not of their choosing.

Navajo men appear in six portraits. In one group portrait of five men (plate 53), at least one of the men is identifiable. Three men sit on a bench in front of two men who stand. The man seated on the right is Mariano Martínez, a headman. The man seated on the left, whose right eye is missing, is likely Manuelito's brother El Ciego.[55] The high status of the unidentified man in the middle, possibly Manuelito's brother Cayetanito, is evident in his pearl button–studded top hat, bracelet, shell disk (*heishi*) necklace, and braided leather crop.

The man in plate 55 also appears to be high ranking judging by his outward appearance: He wears a shell button–embellished felted cap in the shape of a cat, perhaps emulating warrior helmets made from the skinned heads of mountain lions. In the Jennings series at the Library of Congress, this man is named "Harririo," a name that doesn't correlate to any known Navajo man. The Spanish word "Herrero" was given to some Navajo men, and two men so named, who were active at this time and named in written record, are Herrero Delgado (also known as Atsidi Sani), a famous silversmith, and Herrero Grande, a blacksmith and the man Carleton sent to meet with Manuelito on March 20, 1865, in an attempt to win his surrender. The man in the photo may be neither of these Herreros, though if he is, he is likely Herrero Grande, as Herrero Delgado, at age thirty-six when the portrait was taken, seems too young to be the man portrayed.

The man in plate 57a is seen in the same print in numerous other archives, covered extensively earlier in the book, and the man is Navajo and likely part of Manuelito and El Ciego's extended family. "Navajo Thieves" (plate 57b) shows two men close together, one seated and one kneeling, and holding hands; the man on the left is unidentified, and the man on the right most likely is El Ciego and is the same man sitting on the left in the group portrait (plate 53), and on the left in the triple portrait from the Peabody collection (see figure 11). The tragic irony of the photo's title is that, throughout their centuries of resistance to imperialist encroachment, indigenous people were demonized for acting to protect, sustain, or avenge themselves, and were called "thieves" when they defied the theft of their lands, language, livelihoods, and culture. More recently, in the circulating of this image in books and film, some have erroneously interpreted the men's physical intimacy in this specific portrait as an example of "two spirited," pan-Indian, homosexual expression, but that is a Eurocentric reading. Navajo concepts of gender and sexual variation, described as they would be in this instance by the term *nádleehí*,[56] are not on display in this portrait, and positing this portrait as "two spirited" is an example of outsiders projecting their own cultural assumptions onto something they don't understand.[57]

Although the thirteen portraits of Navajos in the *Souvenir* album are the first known portraits of Navajos, they are closely linked in time and topic—the captivity at Bosque Redondo—to another set of Navajo portraits by Nicholas Brown and Son, found in a few different archives, mostly the British Museum William Blackmore Collection, albums nine and seventeen, and the Princeton University Library Western Americana collection (figure 32). Given the mostly anonymous photographs and sparse accounts of indigenous people of the era and in this album, highlighting the interconnectedness of Navajo portraits of this era, if only in brief, seems particularly important in relation to the thirteen portraits at the end of this album. A print of one Nicholas Brown photo (figure 33), circa 1866–68, a copy of which is also found in the British Museum Blackmore Collection, was offered at auction in 2015. The front bears the

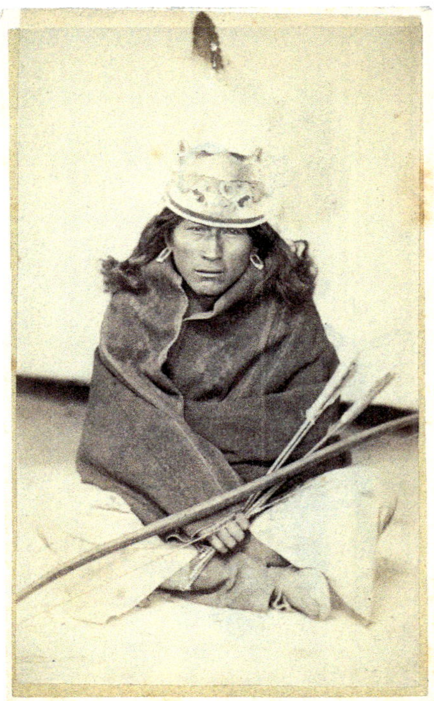

Fig. 32a. Navajo man, possibly at Fort Sumner, Bosque Redondo, New Mexico Territory, ca. 1866–68. Photograph by N. Brown é Hijo. Princeton University Library, Department of Rare Books and Special Collections, Western Americana Collection, WC064.

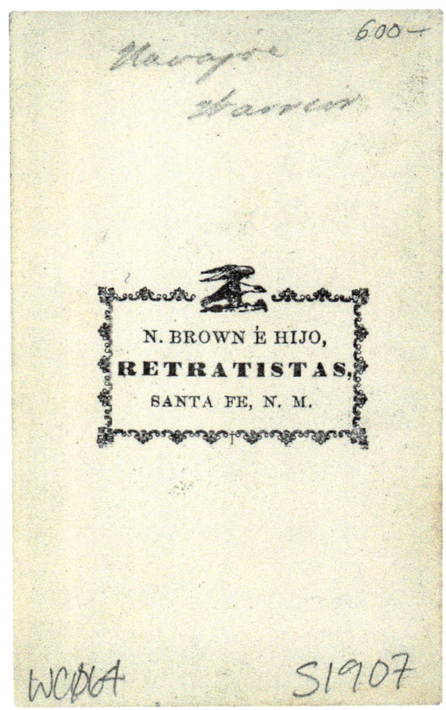

Fig. 32b. The back of this photographs shows the stamp for "Brown É Hijo."

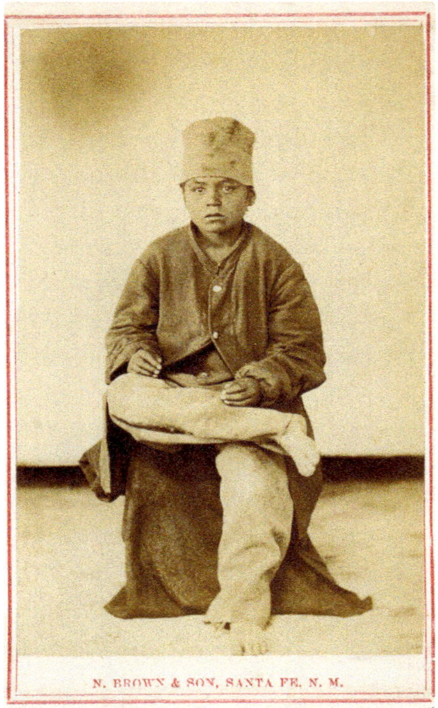

FIG. 33A. Unidentified Navajo boy, ca. 1866–68. Photograph by N. Brown and Son. The British Museum, William Blackmore Collection, Album 9, AM, A9.52. Photograph © The Trustees of the British Museum.

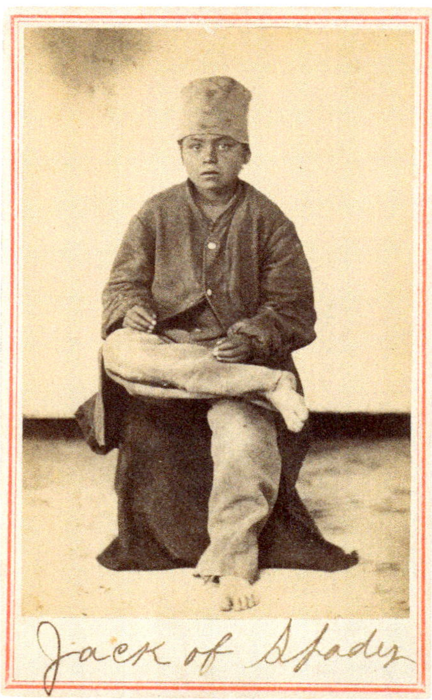

FIG. 33B. Unidentified Navajo boy, "Jack of Spades," n.d. Courtesy Cowan's Auctions.

FIG. 33C. The back of this photograph has various inscriptions, including "Jack of Spades, Navajo Boy, Pet of Col. McClave [McCleave]." Another inscription says "1862," but this date is incorrect; it likely dates to 1866–68.

label "Jack of Spades"; on the rear is inscribed "Jack of Spades Navajo Boy Pet of Col. McCleave." This would be a reference to the McCleave (plate 11) who commanded Fort Sumner and Bosque Redondo at the time of the Navajo internment.

In 1882, the Carlisle Indian School in Carlisle, Pennsylvania, had photographs of Henry Chee Dodge, interpreter; Major Dennis Riordan, the U.S. agent assigned to work with the Navajos; and two "Navajo Chiefs," including a twenty-seven-year-old young man referred to as "Navajo Jack," who may be the same "Jack" as the boy depicted in the portrait with the inscription "Jack of Spades," taken roughly sixteen years earlier. The "Navajo Jack" photographed at the Carlisle Indian School was also known as "John Bitzclay," as he was registered in the records of Carlisle (figure 34). John Bitzclay/Navajo Jack, a nephew of Manuelito, died of tuberculosis on March 10, 1883, less than five months after arriving at Carlisle. "Jack" had arrived at Carlisle on October 21, 1982, along with two of Manuelito's son's, Manuelito Chou and Manuelito Chiquito, and eight other Navajo young men and women or boys and girls. Manuelito's sons also died of tuberculosis, which they had likewise contracted at the school shortly after "Jack" had contracted the fatal disease. Manuelito Chou was fifteen when he arrived at the school, and he was sent home sick seven months after he arrived and died in July of 1883. After his death, Manuelito wanted all Navajo children sent home from the school. His older son, Manuelito

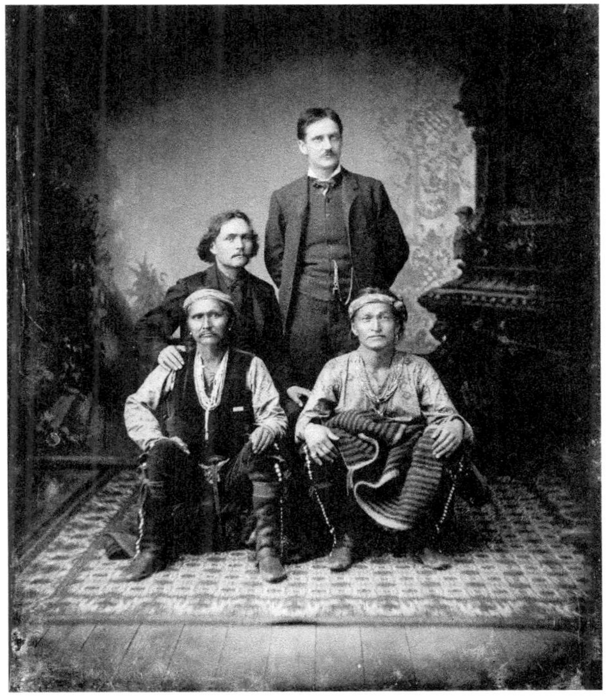

FIG. 34. *(Back row, left to right)* Henry Chee Dodge, interpreter, and Major Riordan, U.S. agent of the Navajo. *(Front row, left to right)* two "Navajo Chiefs," an unidentified Navajo man, and "Navajo Jack," also known as "John Bitzclay," Carlisle Indian School, Carlisle, Pennsylvania, 1882. Photograph by John N. Choate. Smithsonian Institution, National Museum of Natural History, National Anthropological Archives, Photo Lot 81-12 06906900.

Chiquito, who was twenty years old when he arrived at the school, left the school at the end of August 1883 and died the next month.[58]

The ten landscapes at the end of the album having to do with Fort Sumner and Bosque Redondo (plates 41–46, 49, and 58–60) put the Navajo portraits in greater context. Most of the plates show the poor conditions under which the Indians lived; it is obvious that there are very few trees for fuel and for housing, seen very clearly in the mean housing pictured in plate 41. Plate 42 depicts one of the many ways that the Navajos and Mescaleros were put to constant work, whether it was helping the soldiers build, farming, or corn husking, likely depicted in plates 58 and 59.[59] An indication of the mixing of soldiers and interned Navajos can also be seen, particularly in plate 44. Likewise, all of the landscape plates in this section illustrate the manner in which the Navajos were anonymized groups of people to be counted (e.g., plate 49) or labeled, as the headmen seen in plate 60, for example, were accused of counterfeiting ration tickets.[60]

This last group of portraits and landscapes, plain and straightforward in their presentation (as most of the images in the *Souvenir* album are), are the earliest known photographs of Navajos. With very little exception, and not unlike most of the other portraits in this album, the *Souvenir* album is the only place these original prints are to be found. On first view, it is hard to see how these images of the Navajo internment at Bosque Redondo are connected to any if not most of the other photographs of the album, particularly the first set of portraits having to do with the French Intervention in Mexico. But, after having mined the historical context of all the images in the album, it is clear that they are indeed all intimately connected—through time and place, through the struggle for land and resources, through war and the pursuit of peace, through family and commerce, through boundaries and borders, and ultimately through bondage and the struggle to be free and autonomous. The people and places portrayed in this album are all inextricably linked in what may appear to us as surprising ways. However, in coming to some clearer understanding of the context of this album of photographs, territorial life in New Mexico 1866 is made more comprehensible, which in turn sheds light on New Mexico as we know it today.

PLATES

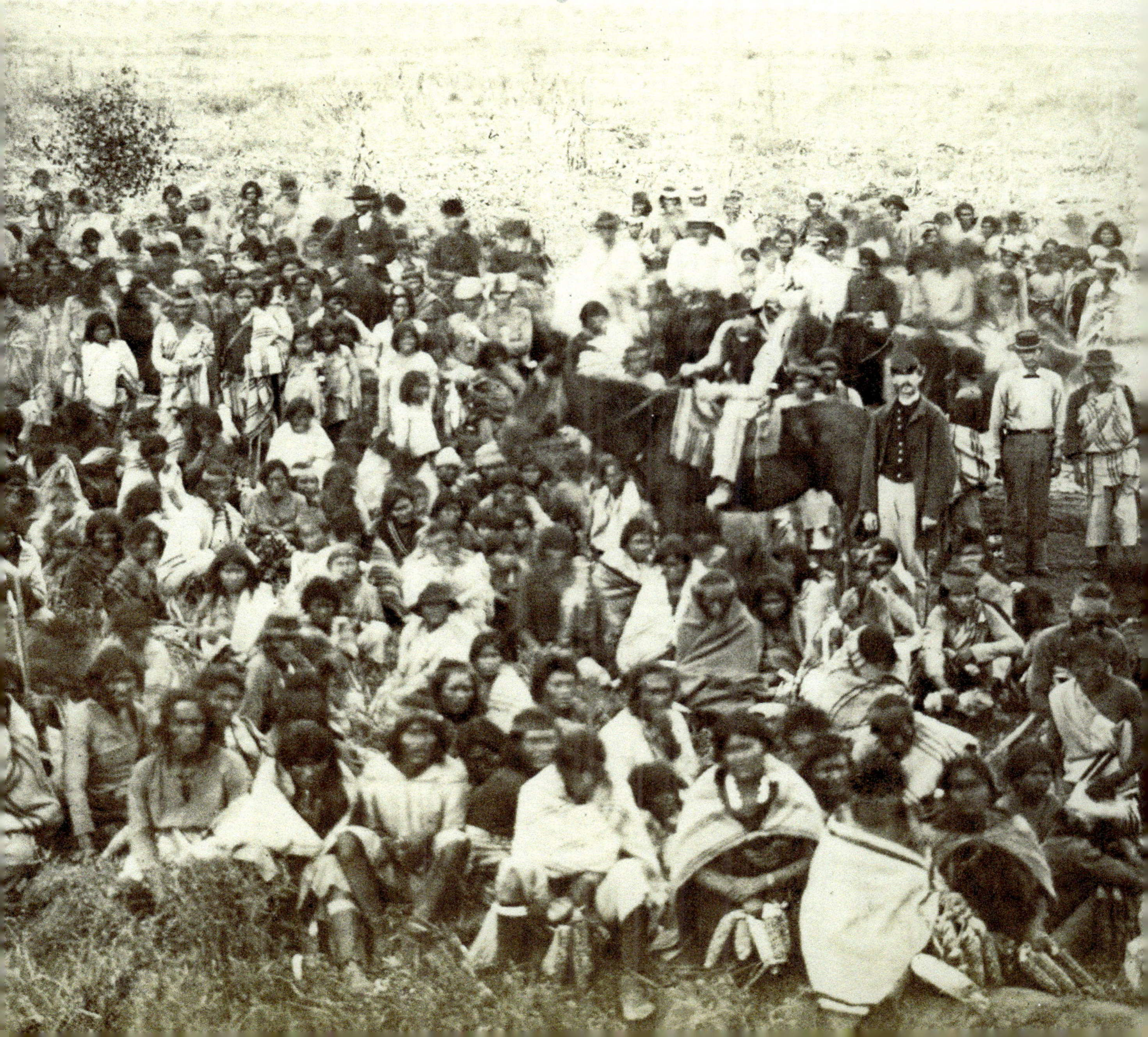

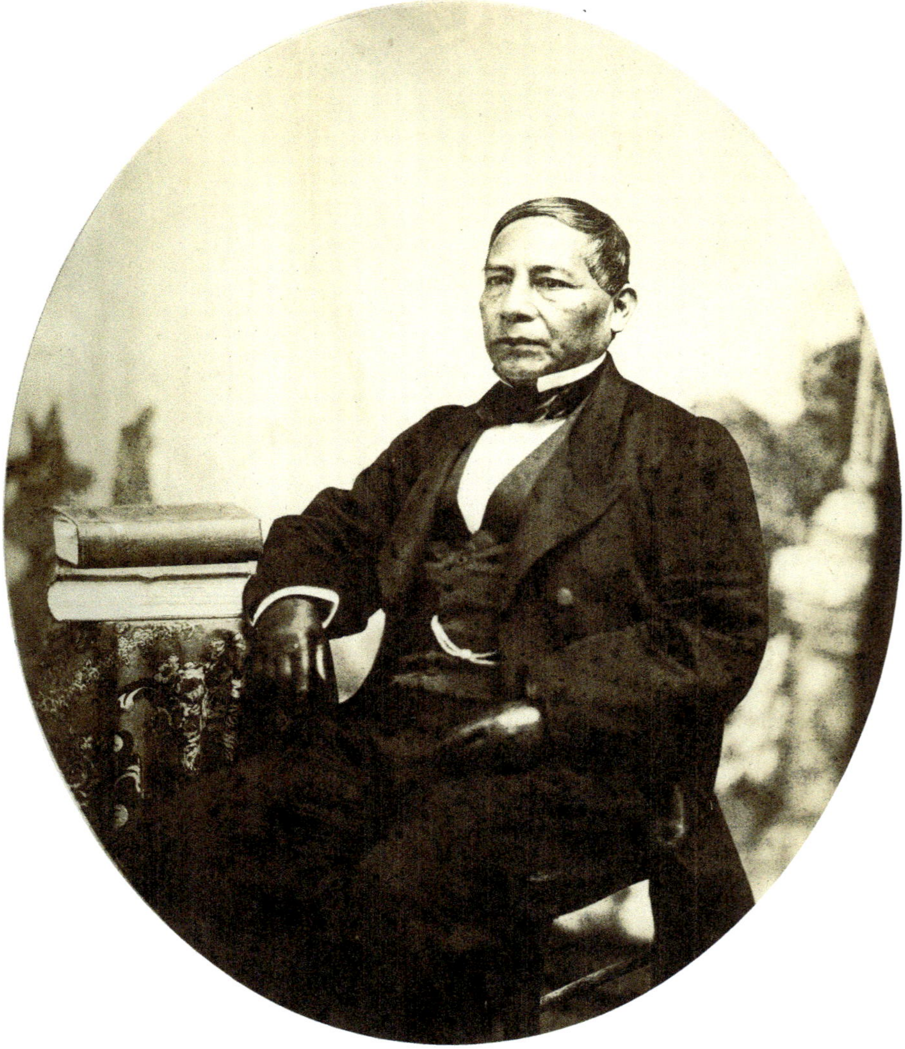

PLATE 1
President of Mexico
Benito Juárez, El Paso
del Norte (Ciudad Juárez),
Mexico, ca. February 1866.
PoG 038164

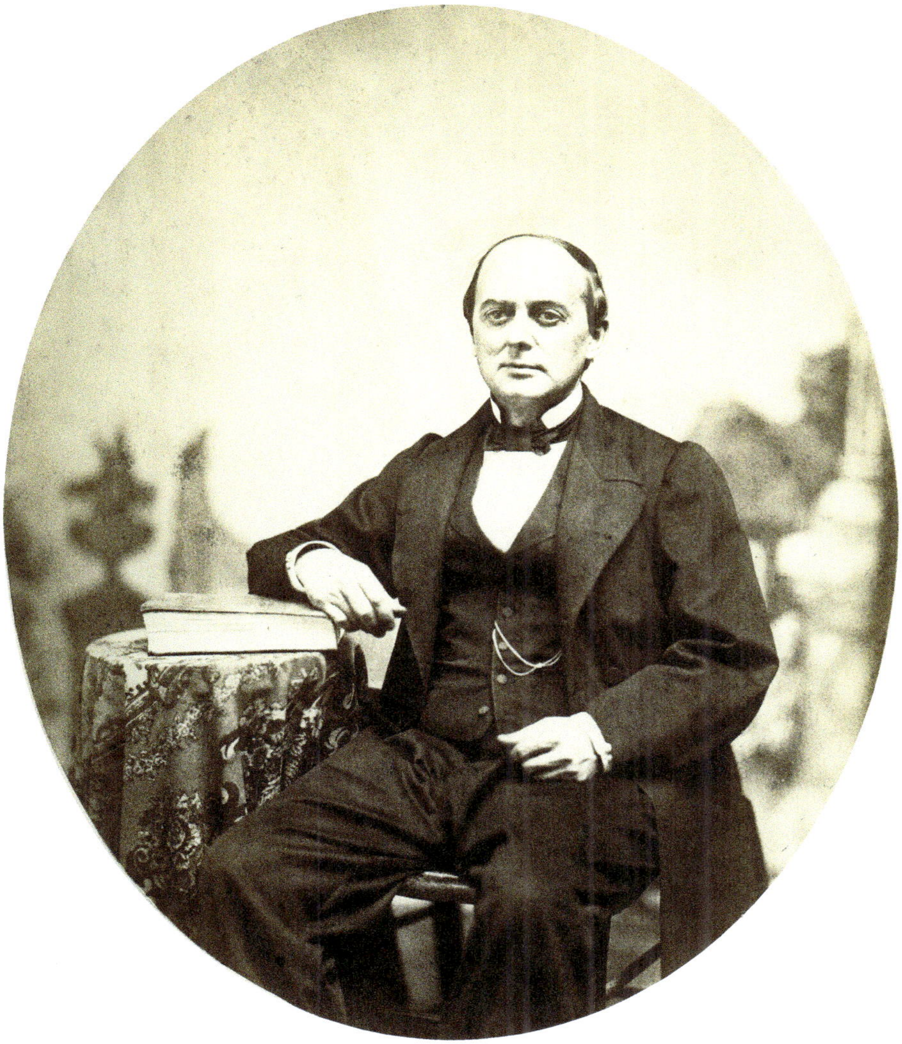

PLATE 2
Sebastián Lerdo de Tejada, minister of foreign affairs, Mexico. El Paso del Norte (Ciudad Juárez), Mexico, ca. February 1866.
PoG 038165

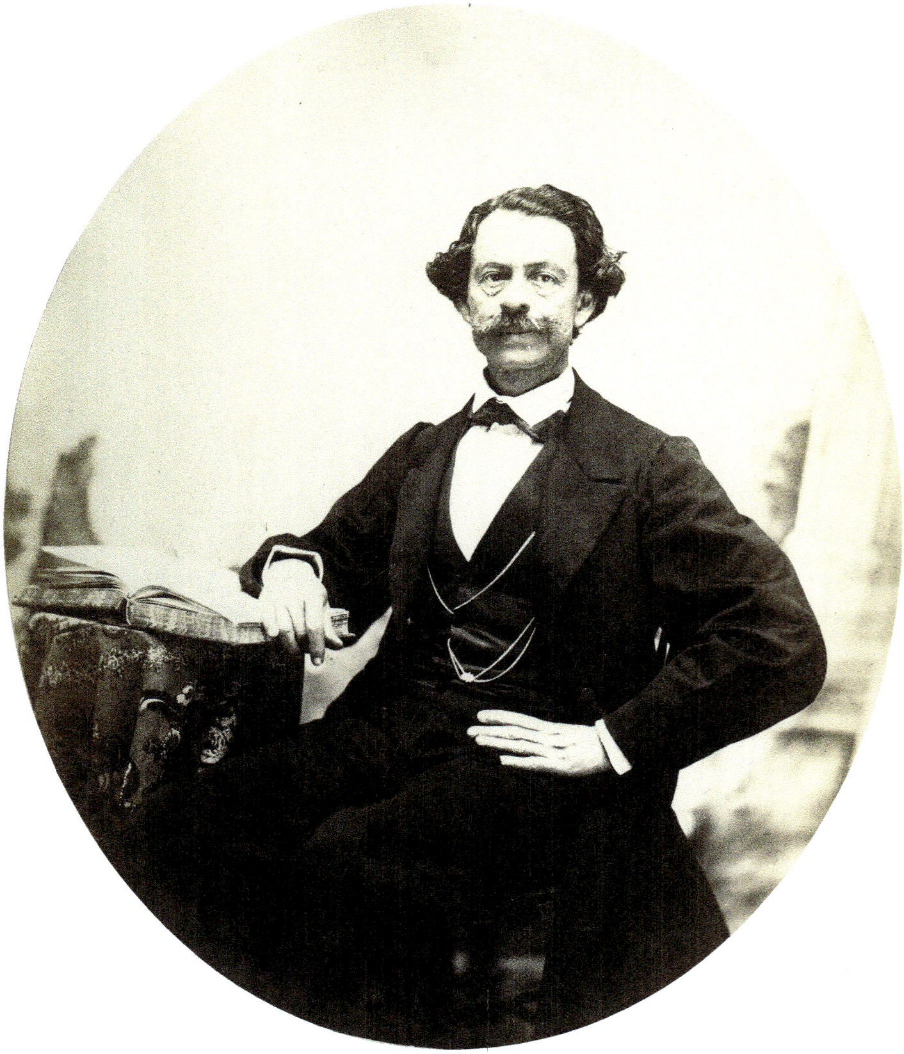

PLATE 3
General Ignacio Mejía, minister of war, El Paso del Norte (Ciudad Juárez), Mexico, ca. February 1866.
PoG 038166

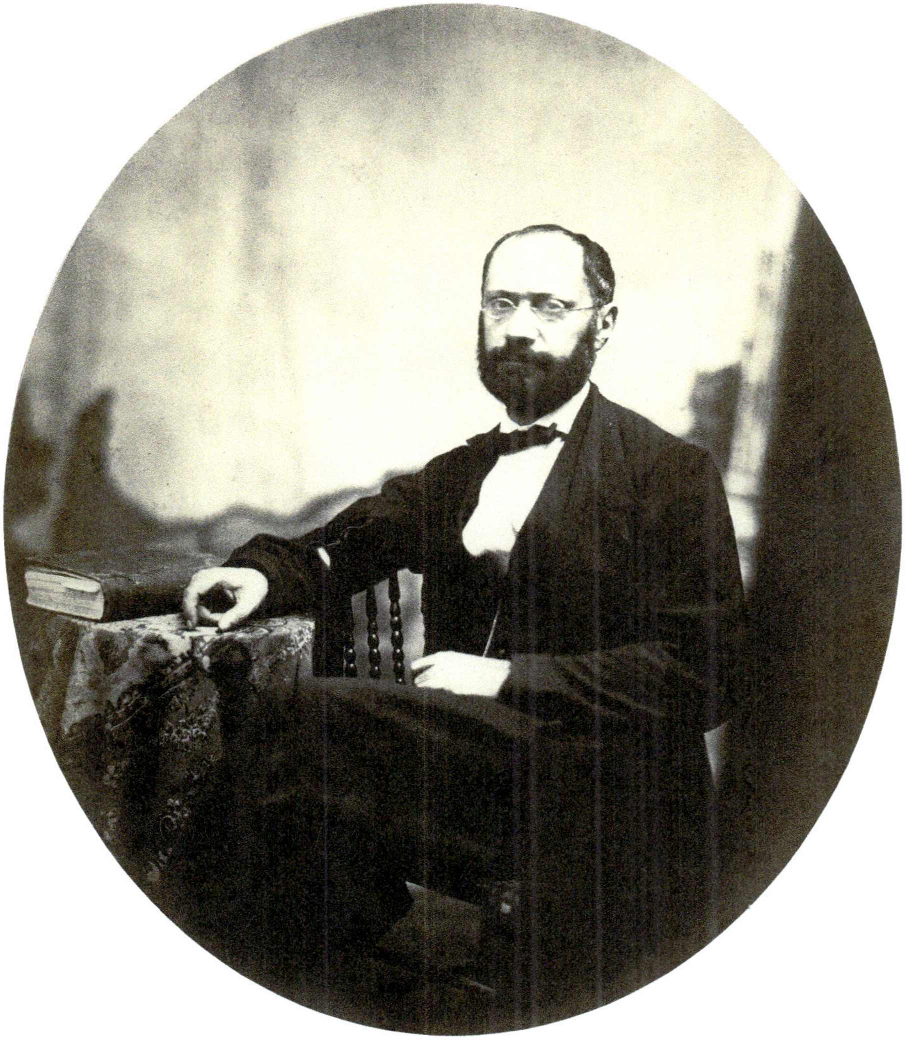

PLATE 4
José María Iglesias, minister of public instruction, El Paso del Norte (Ciudad Juárez), Mexico, ca. February 1866.
PoG 038167

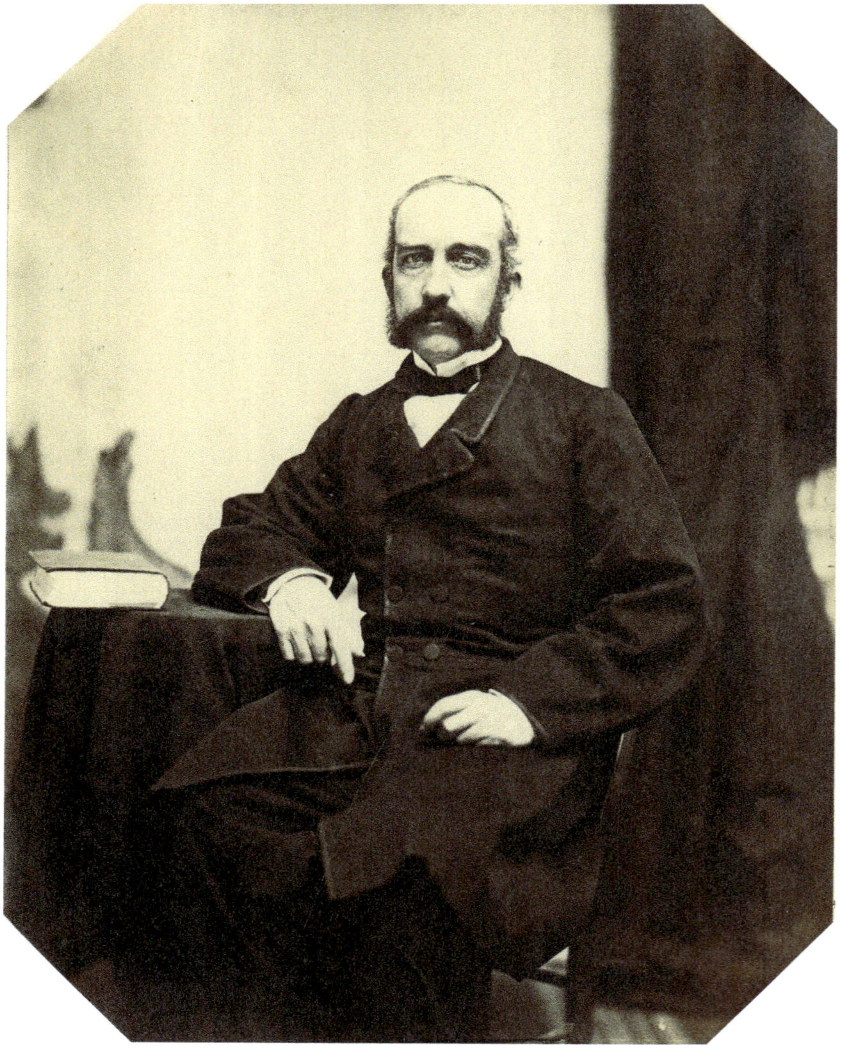

PLATE 5
Señor Gotien, steward of the household, El Paso del Norte (Ciudad Juárez), Mexico, ca. February 1866.
PoG 038168

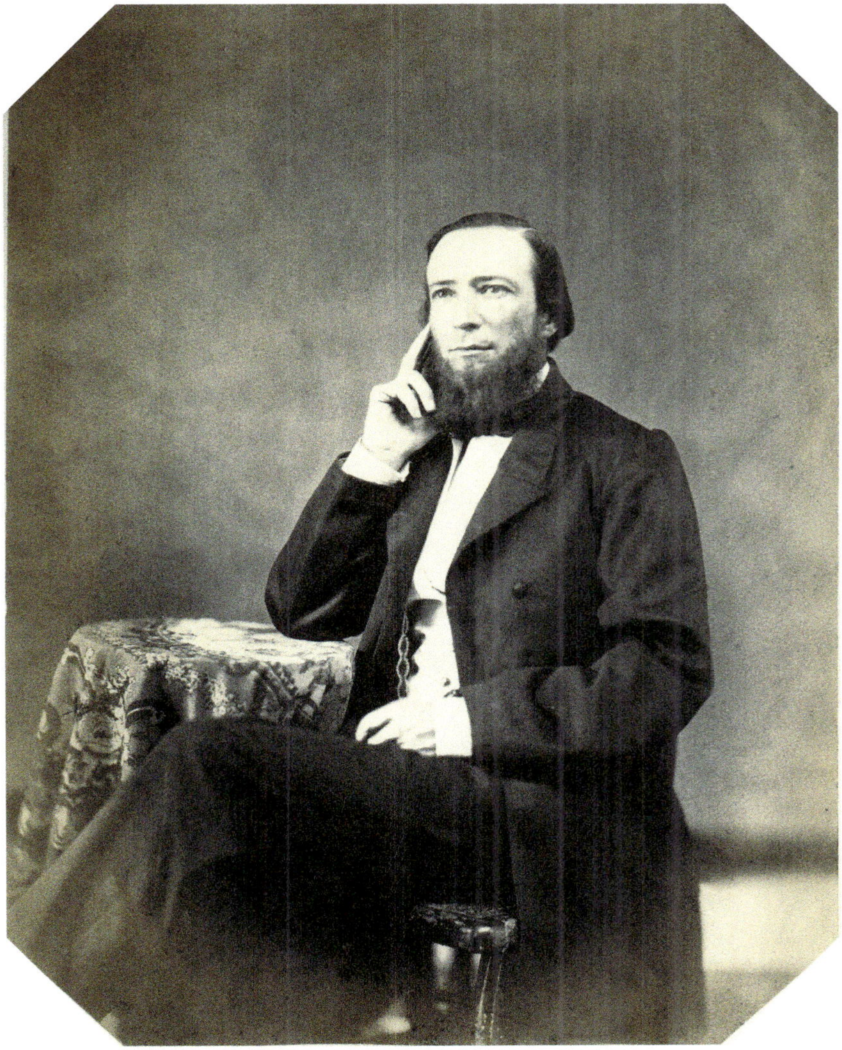

PLATE 6
Henry Cuniffe, American consul, Franklin (El Paso), Texas, 1866.
PoG 038169

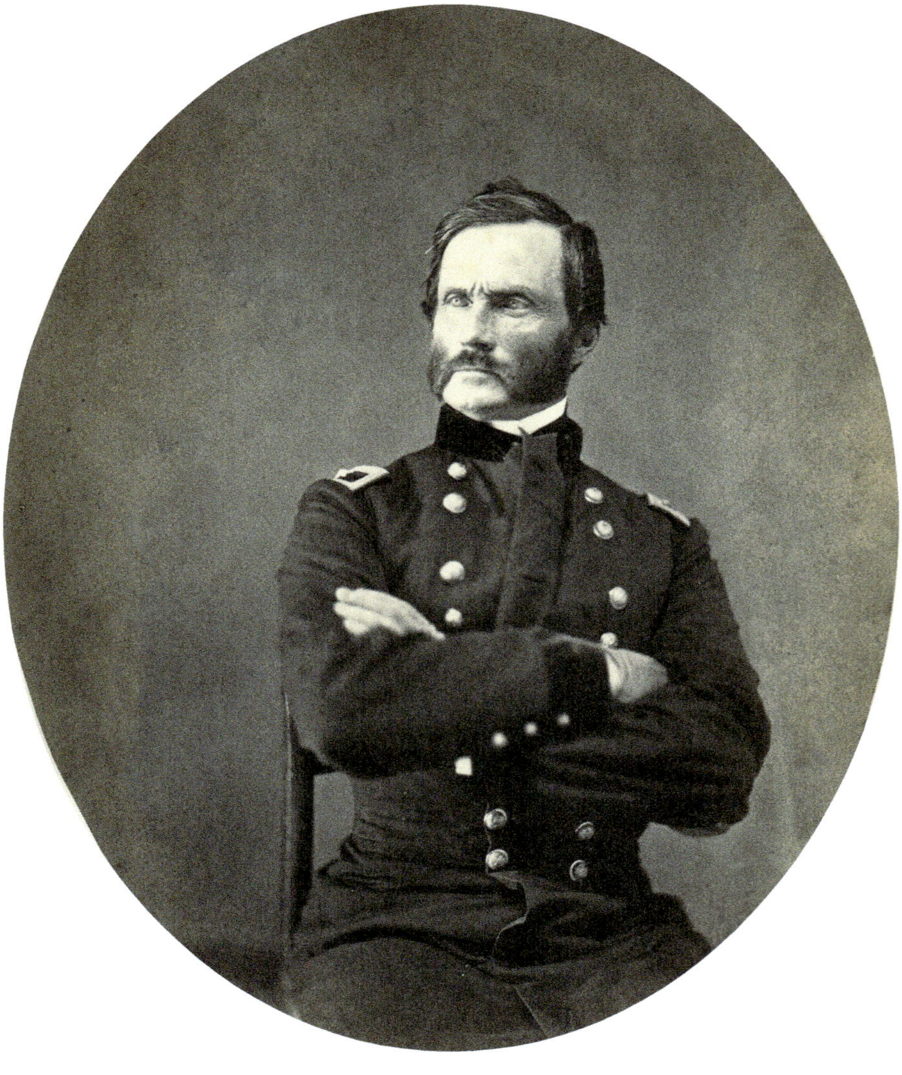

PLATE 7
Brevet Brigadier General James Henry Carleton, in command of the Department of New Mexico, U.S. Army, Franklin (El Paso), Texas, ca. 1866.
PoG 022938

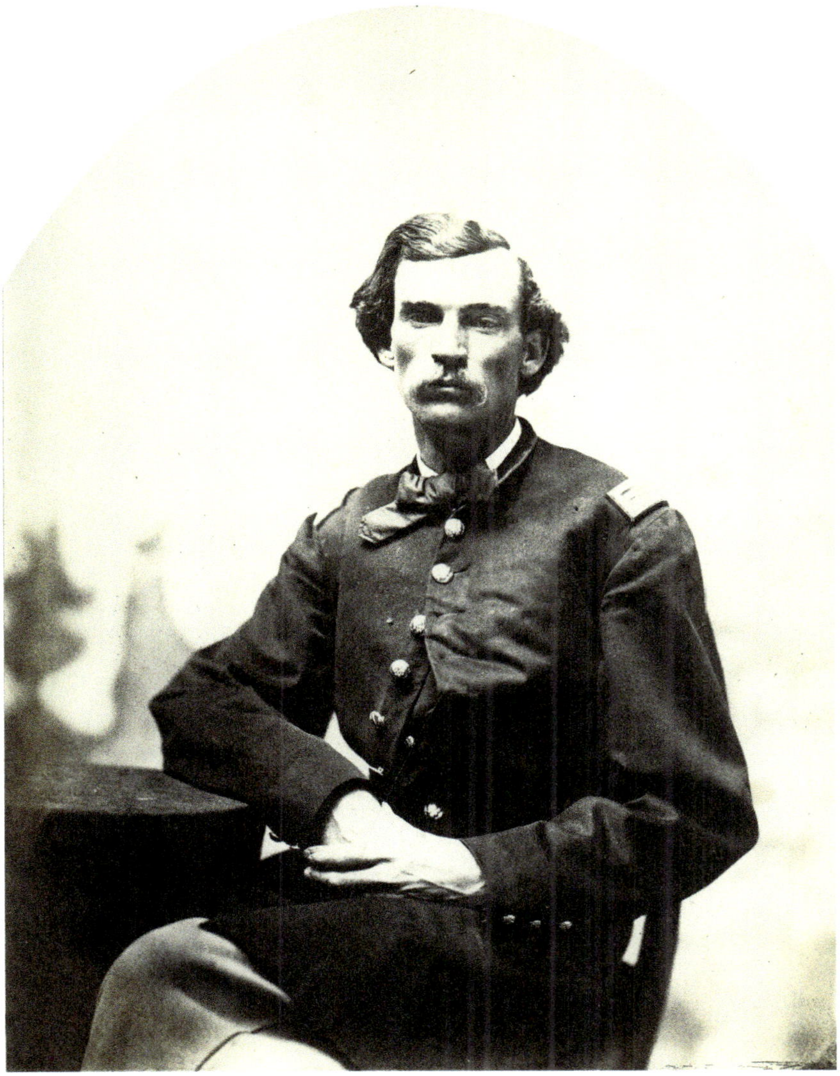

PLATE 8
Captain David Hammett Brotherton, Fifth U.S. Infantry, El Paso del Norte (Ciudad Juárez), ca. February 1866.
PoG 023138

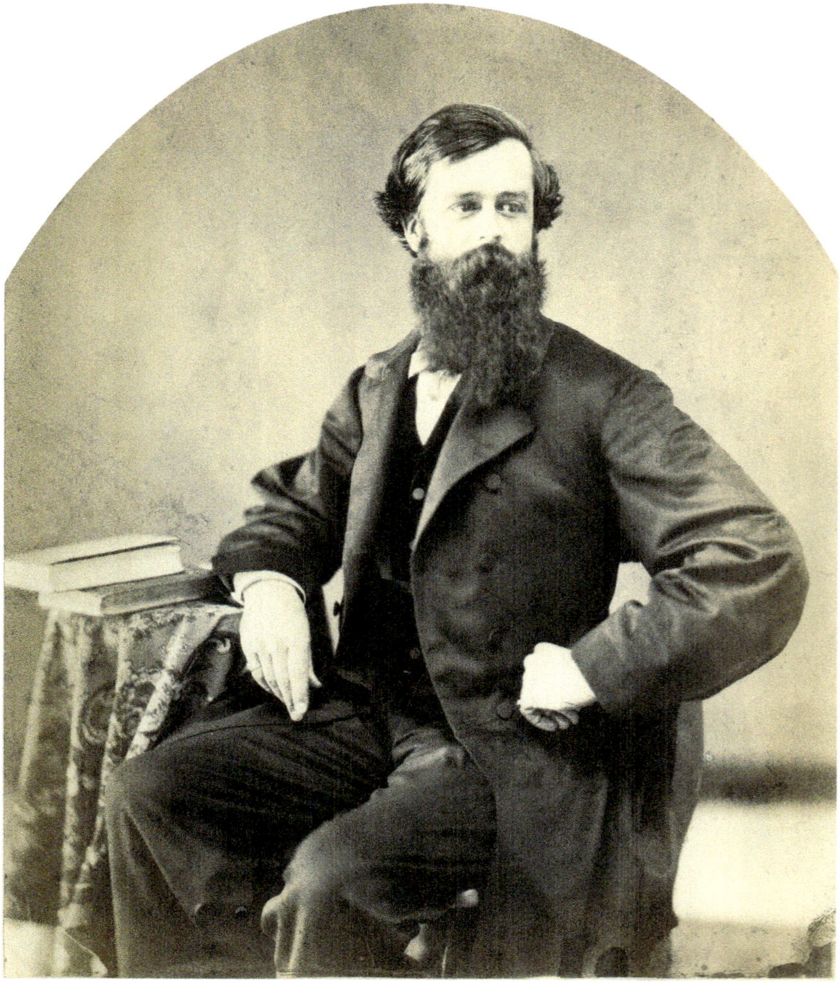

PLATE 9
Major Cyrus Curtis Clark, U.S. Army paymaster, Franklin (El Paso), Texas, ca. 1866.
PoG 038170

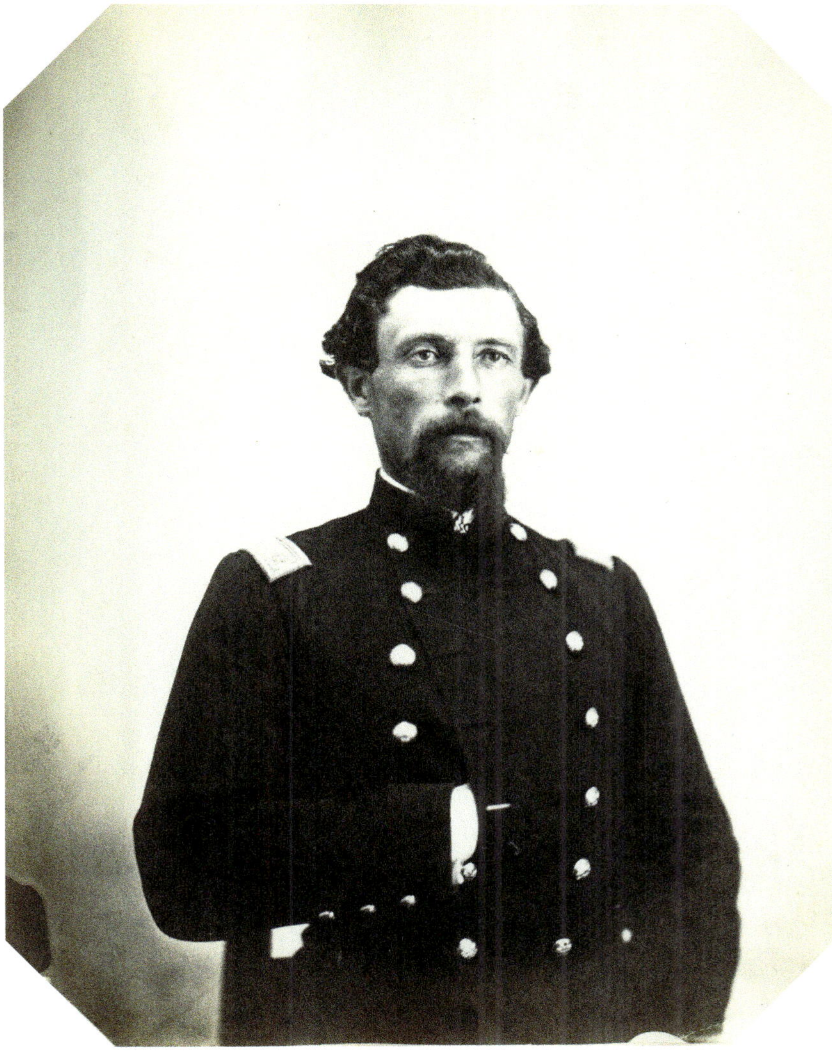

PLATE 10
Captain Emil Fritz, Franklin (El Paso), Texas, ca. 1866.
PoG 023137

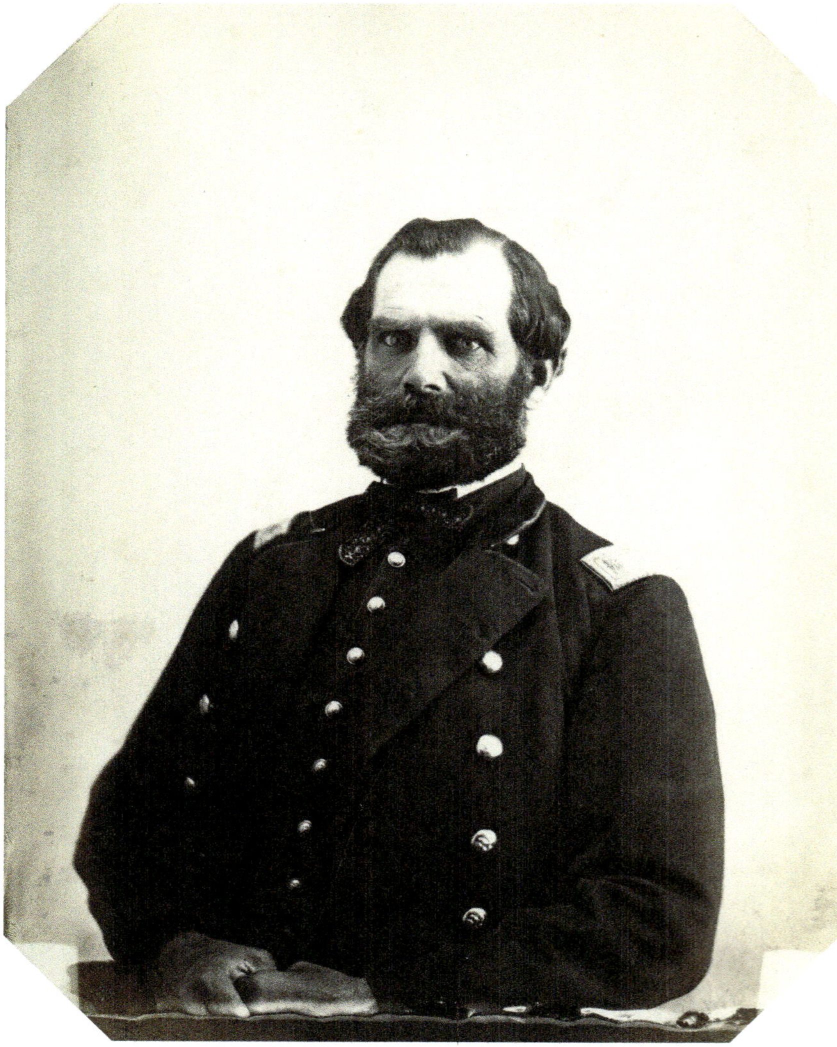

PLATE 11
Major William McCleave,
Franklin (El Paso), Texas,
ca. 1866.
PoG 009152

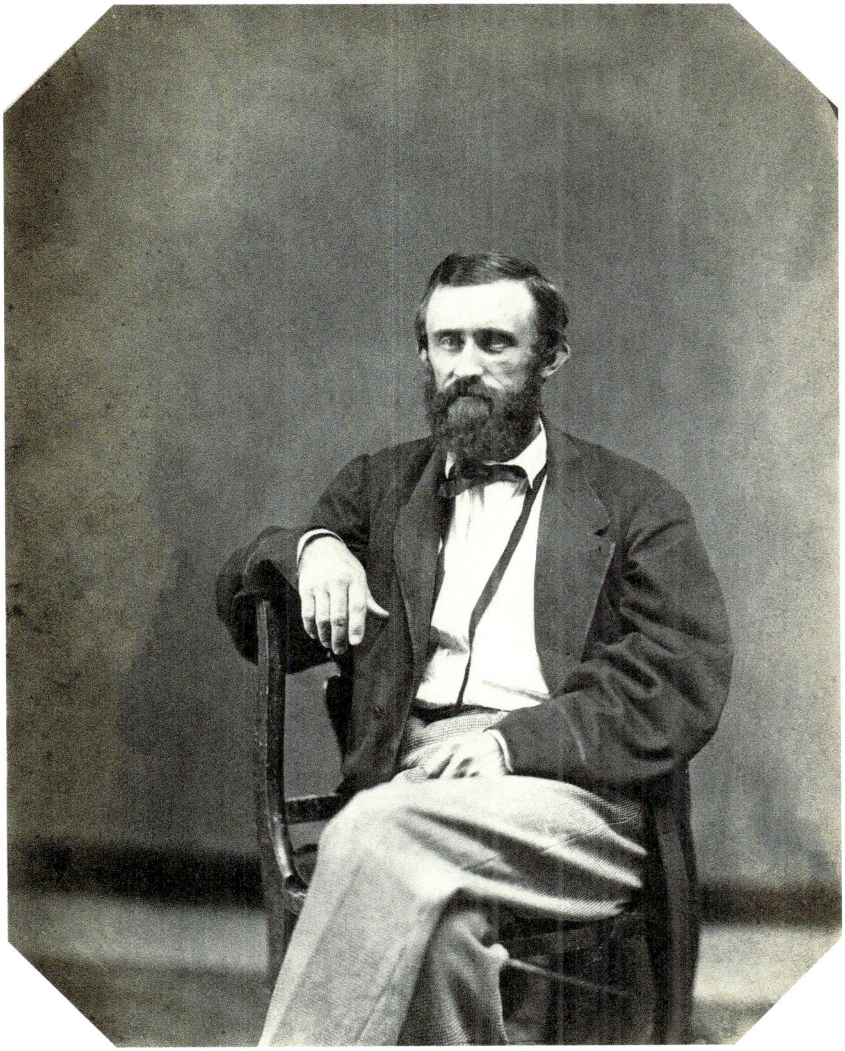

PLATE 12
Nathan Webb, Franklin
(El Paso), Texas, ca. 1866.
PoG 038173

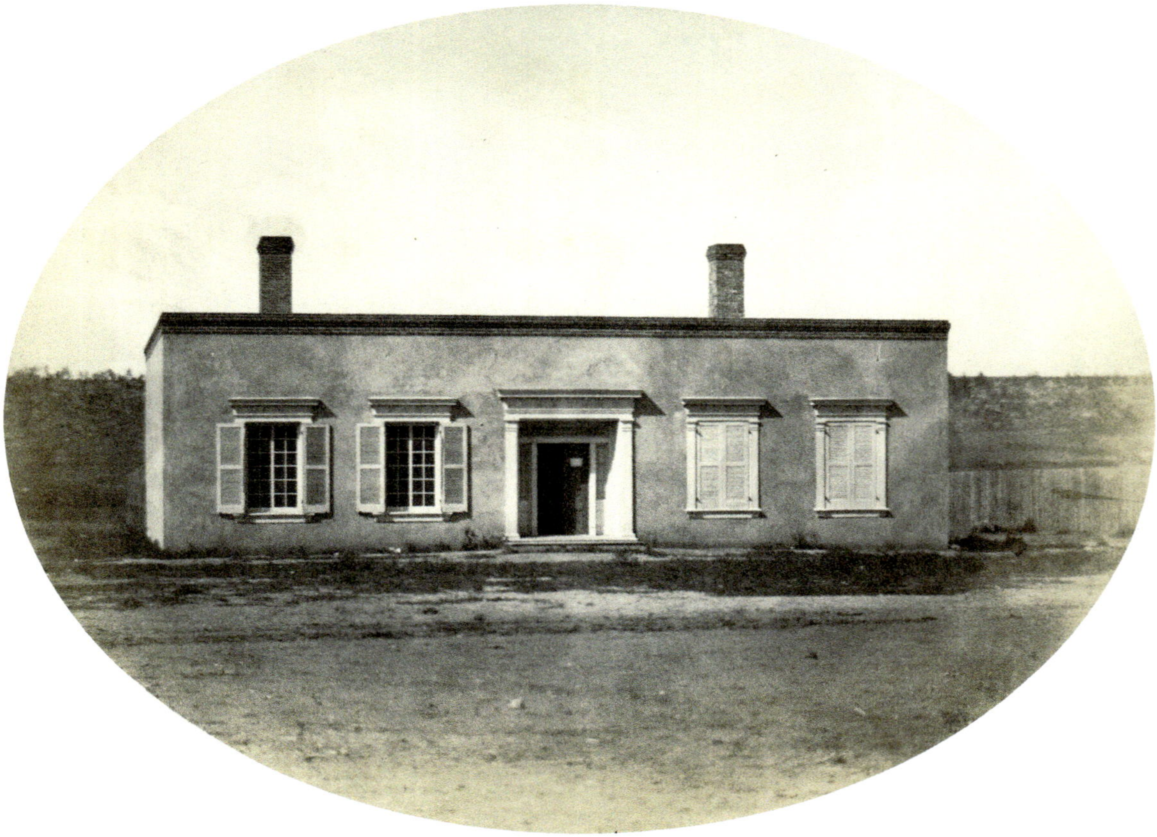

PLATE 13
Officers' quarters,
Fort Union, New Mexico
Territory, ca. 1865.
P0G 038172

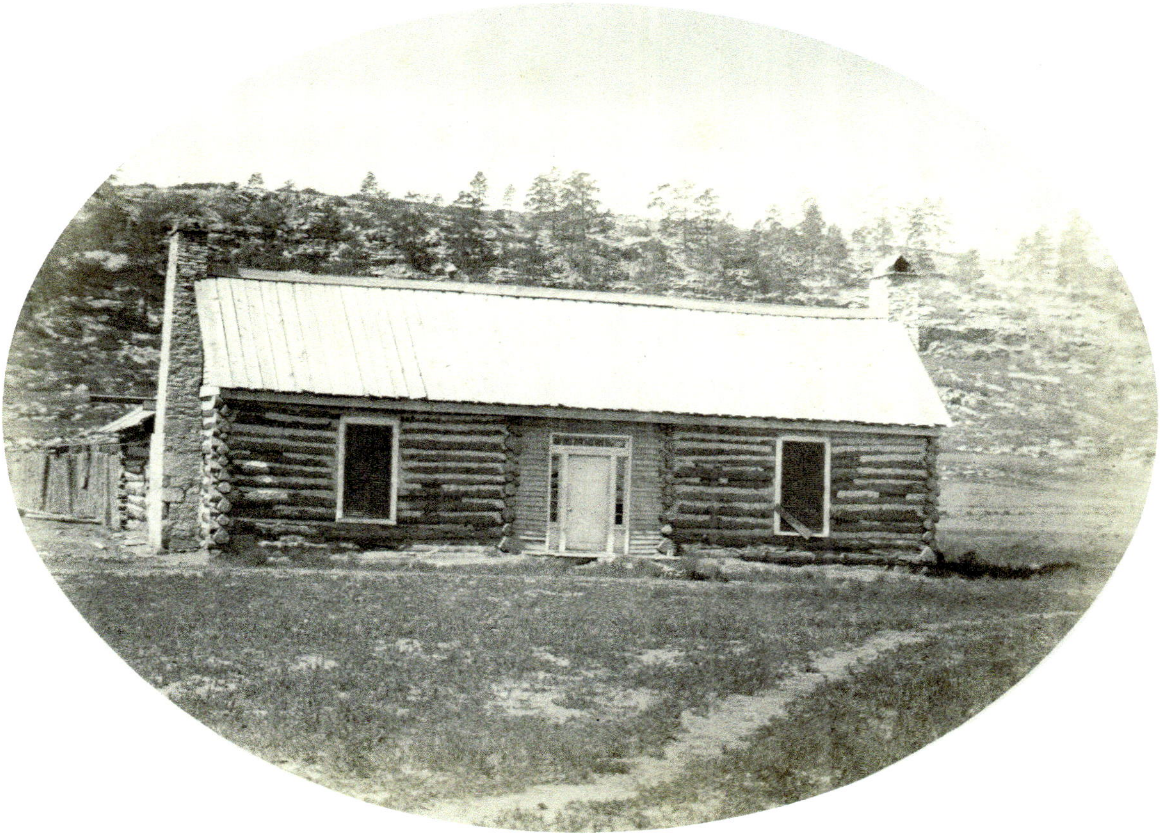

PLATE 14
Officers' quarters,
Fort Union, New Mexico
Territory, ca. 1865.
PoG 038174

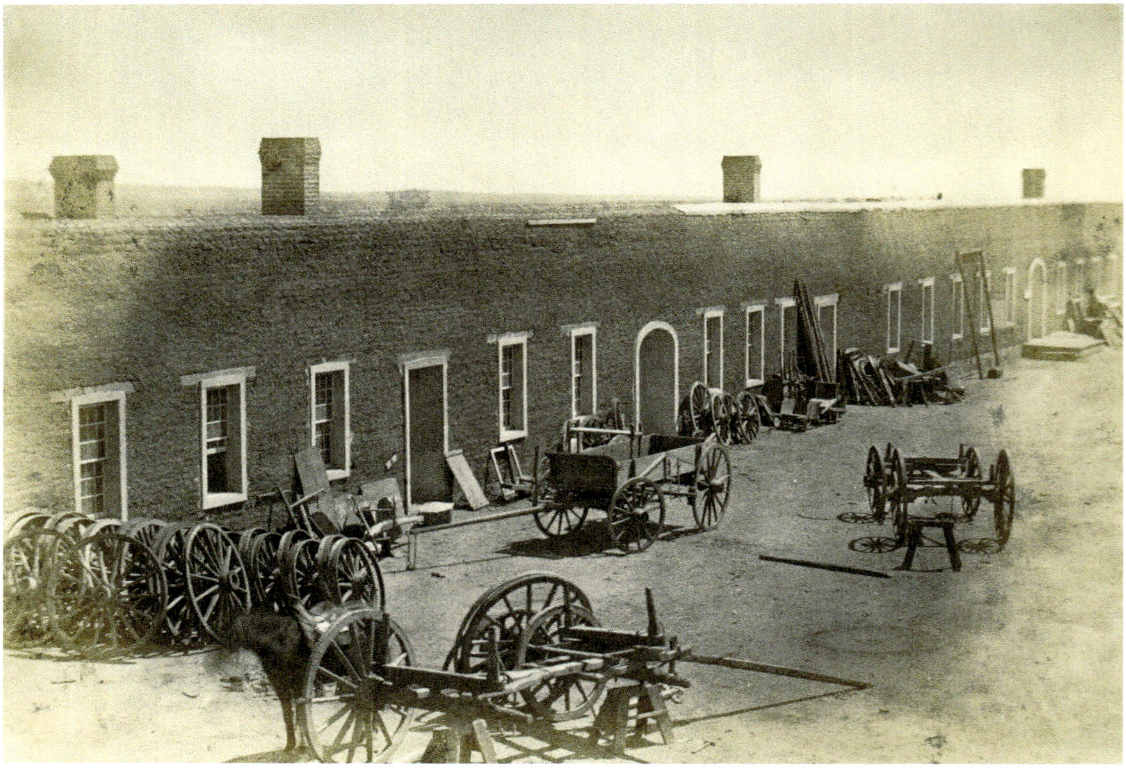

PLATE 15
Government repair workshops, Fort Union, New Mexico Territory, ca. 1865.
PoG 001839

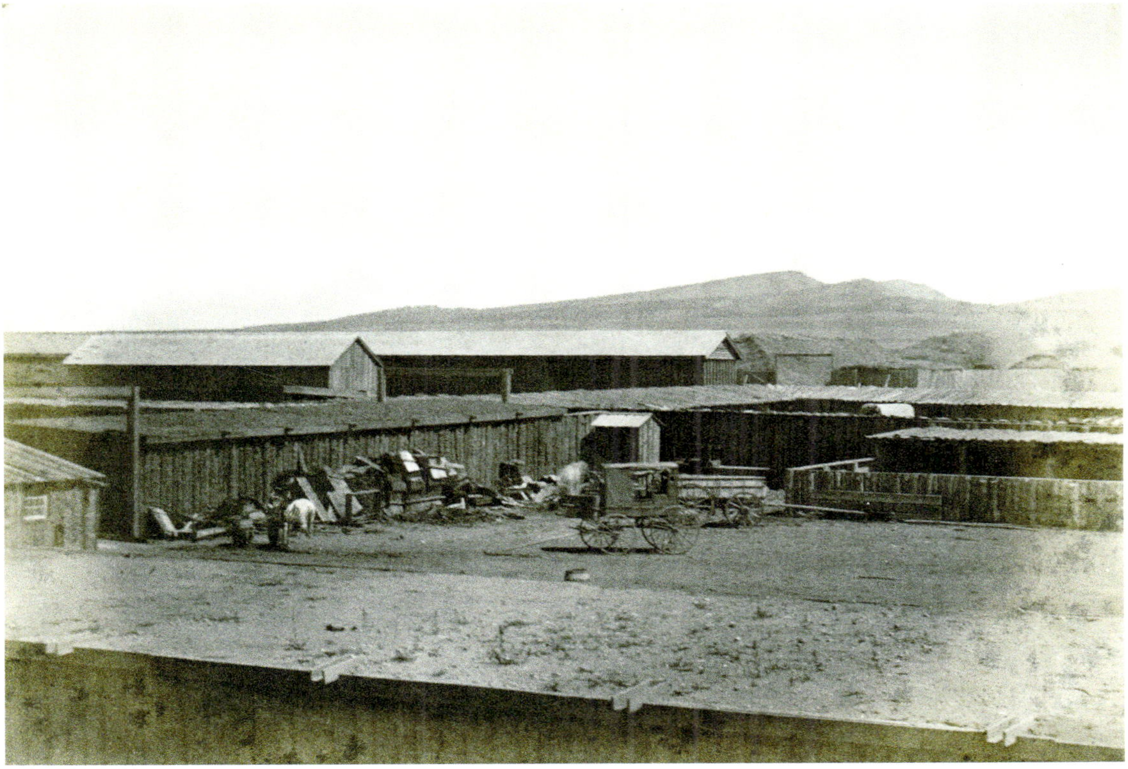

PLATE 16
Government corn cribs, Fort Union, New Mexico Territory, ca. 1865.
PoG 014533

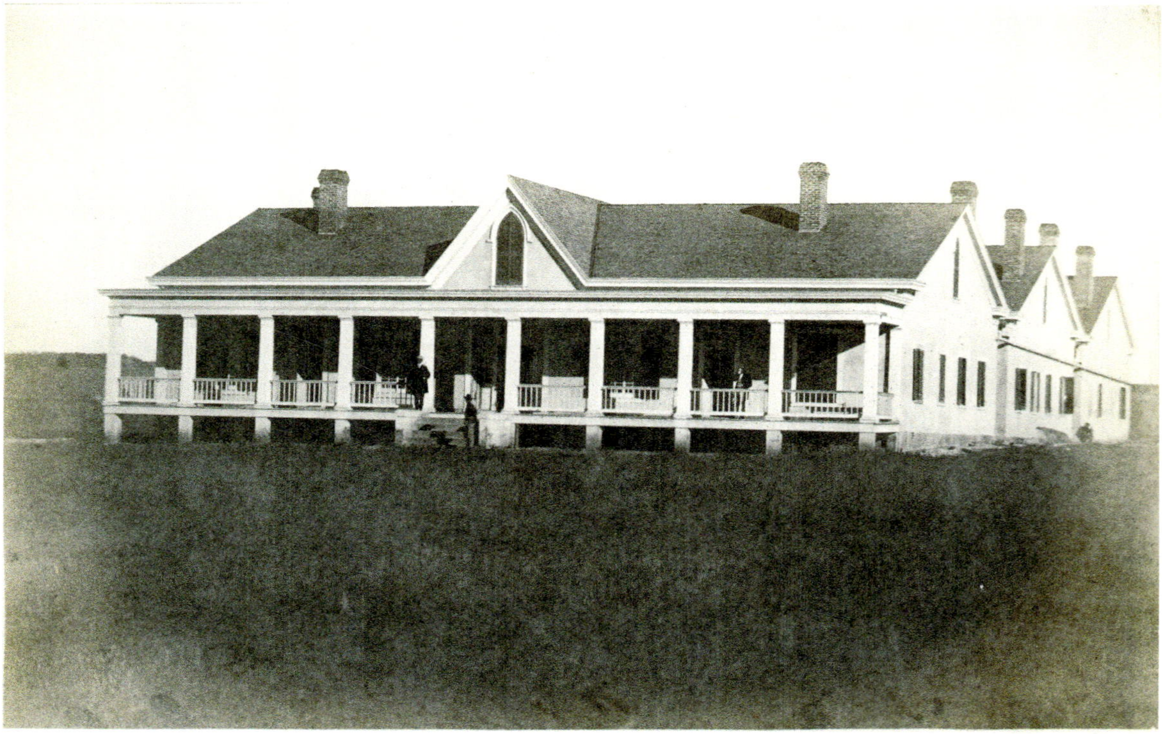

PLATE 17
United States Army General Hospital, Fort Union, New Mexico Territory, ca. 1865.
PoG 014543

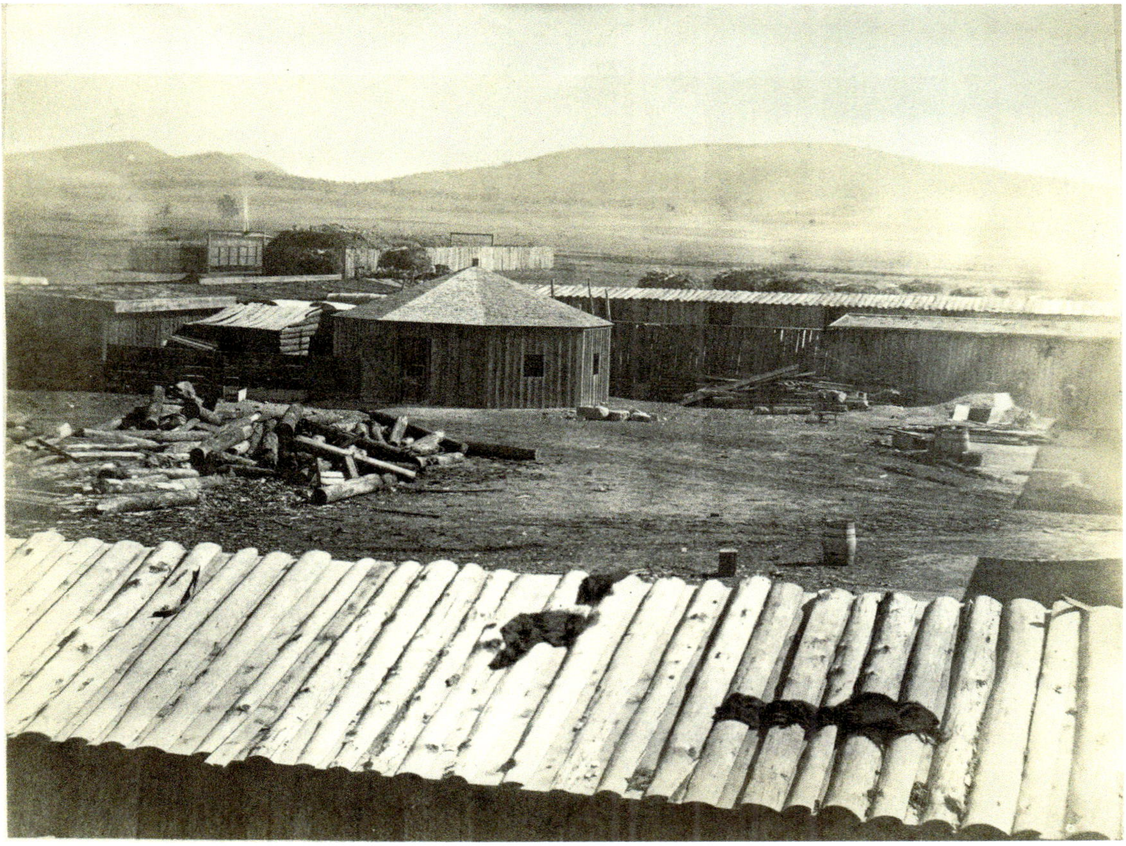

PLATE 18
Government buildings and corrals at Fort Union, New Mexico Territory, ca. 1865.
PoG 014545

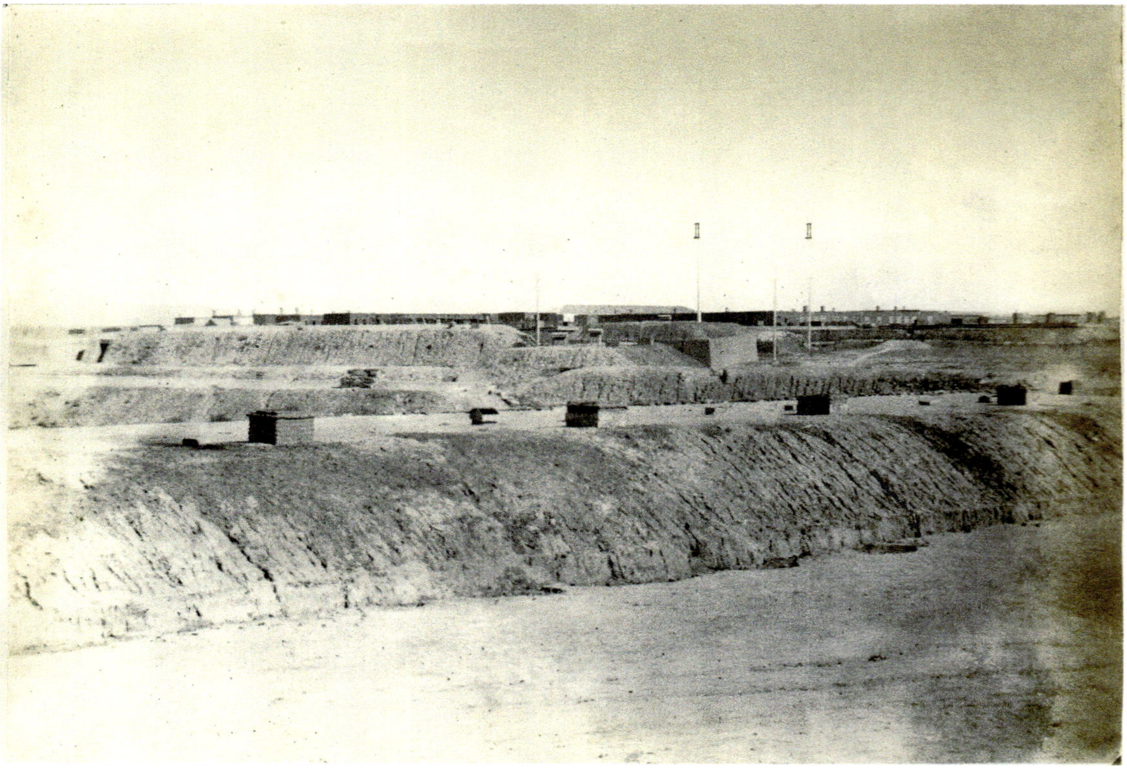

PLATE 19
Fort Union, New Mexico Territory, ca. 1865.
PoG 014548

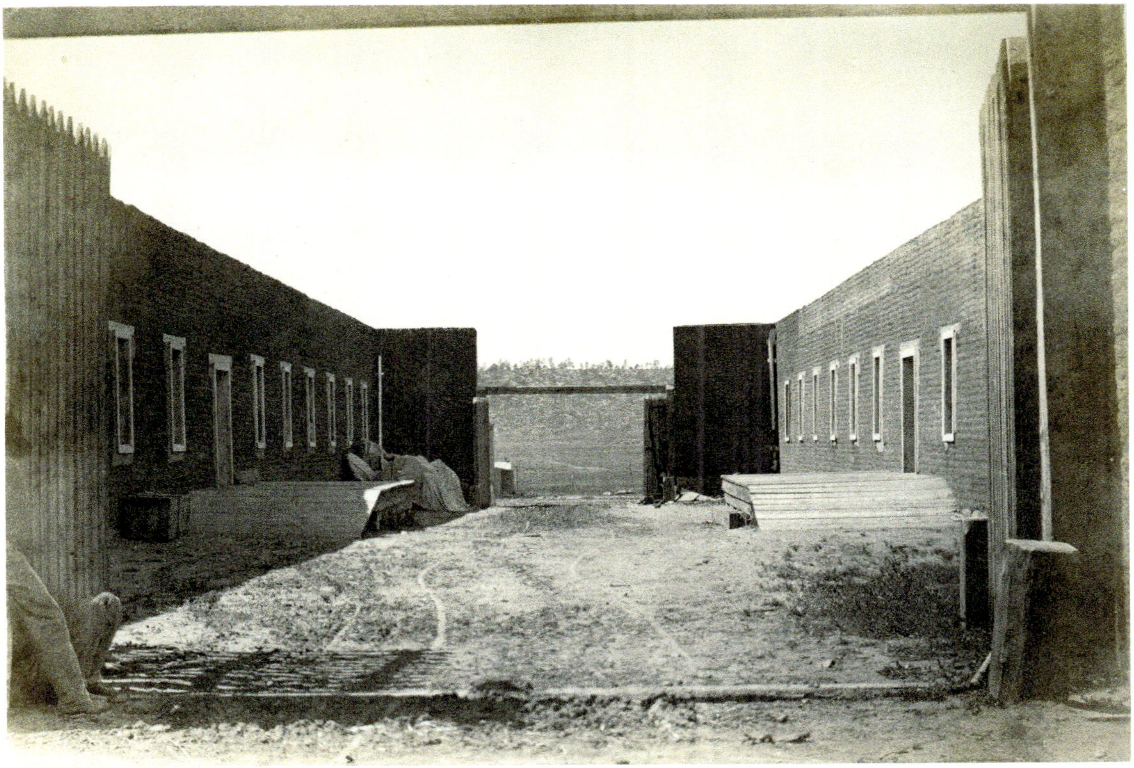

PLATE 20
Government storehouses, Fort Union, New Mexico Territory, ca. 1865.
PoG 03817

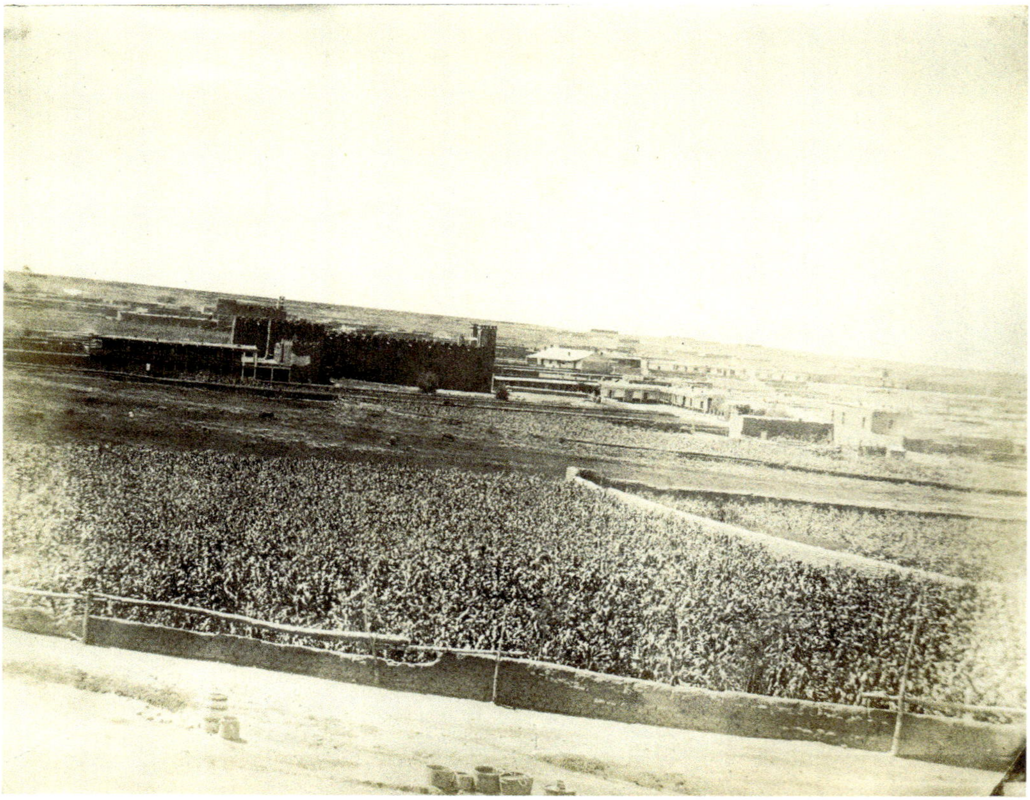

PLATE 21
View looking south, showing La Parroquia Church, Santa Fe, New Mexico Territory, ca. 1865.
PoG 038176

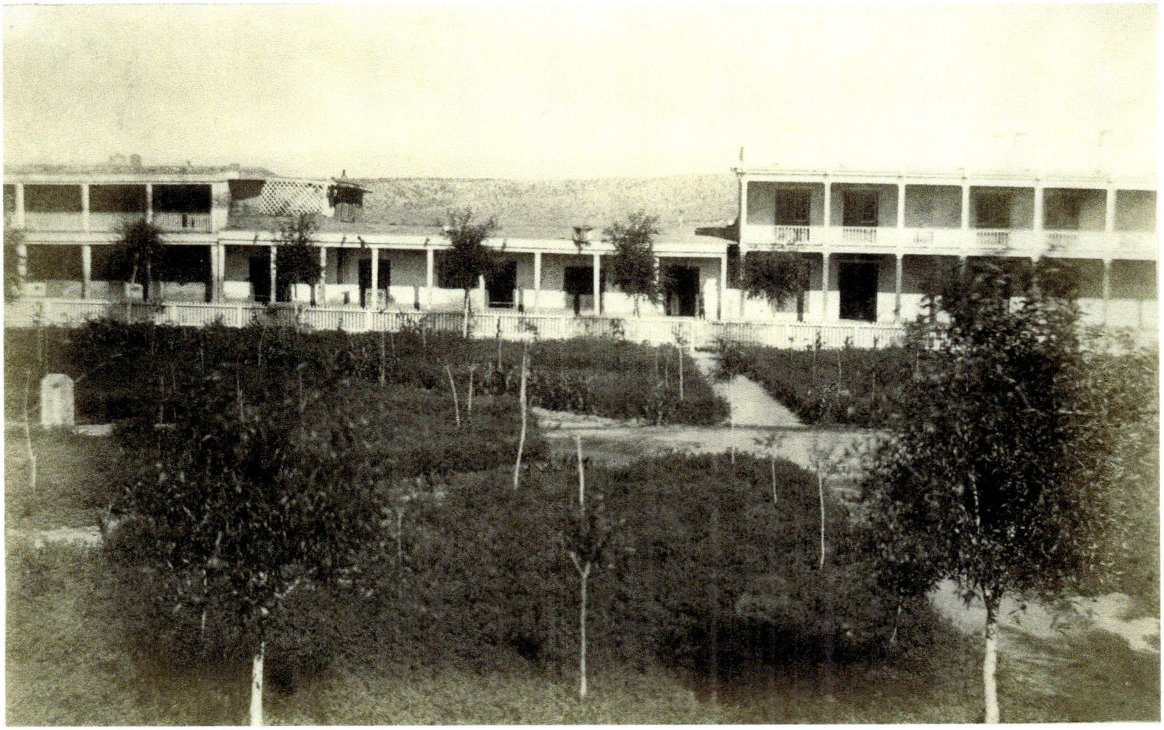

PLATE 22
View of the west side of the Plaza, Santa Fe, New Mexico Territory, ca. 1865.
PoG 023136

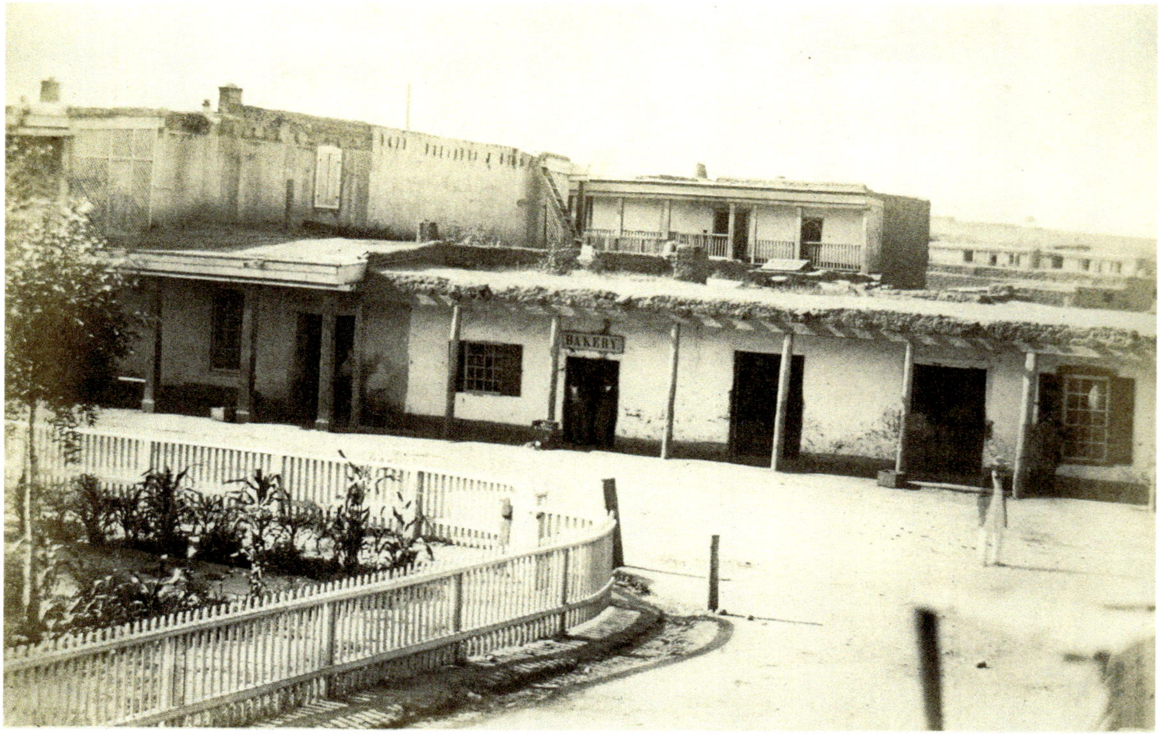

PLATE 23
View of the southwest corner of the Plaza, Santa Fe, New Mexico Territory, ca. 1865.
PoG 038178

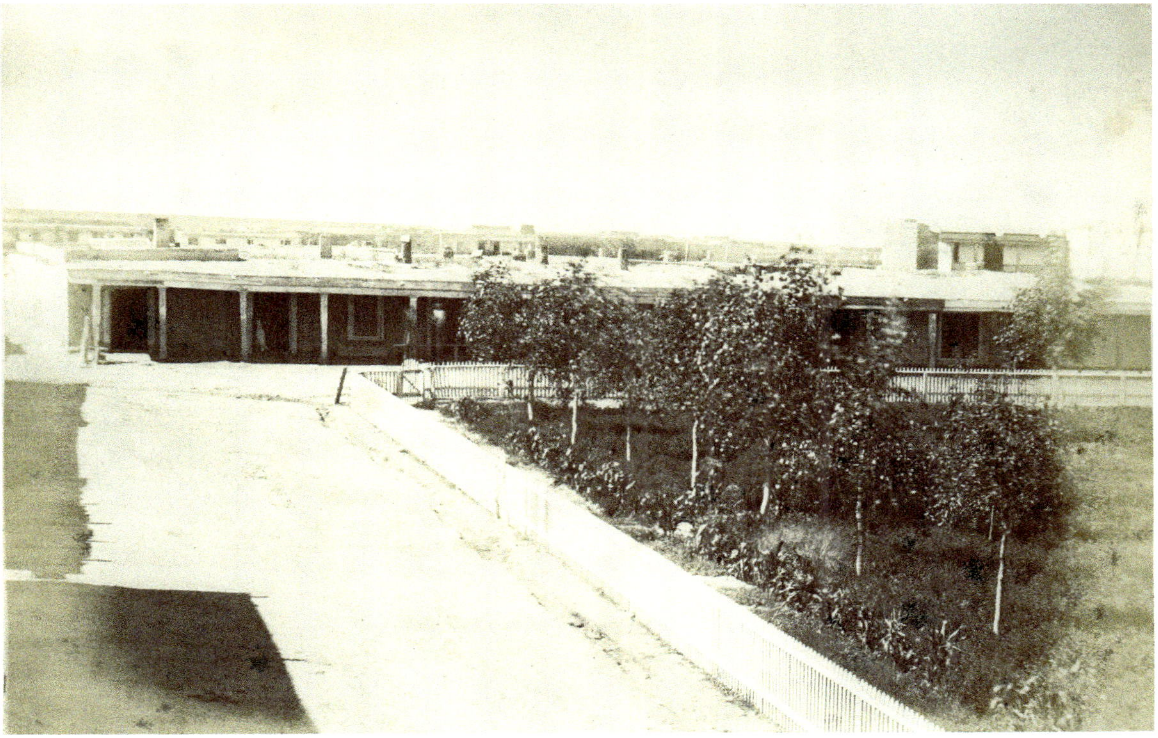

PLATE 24
View of the southeast corner of the Plaza, Santa Fe, New Mexico Territory, ca. 1865.
PoG 038179

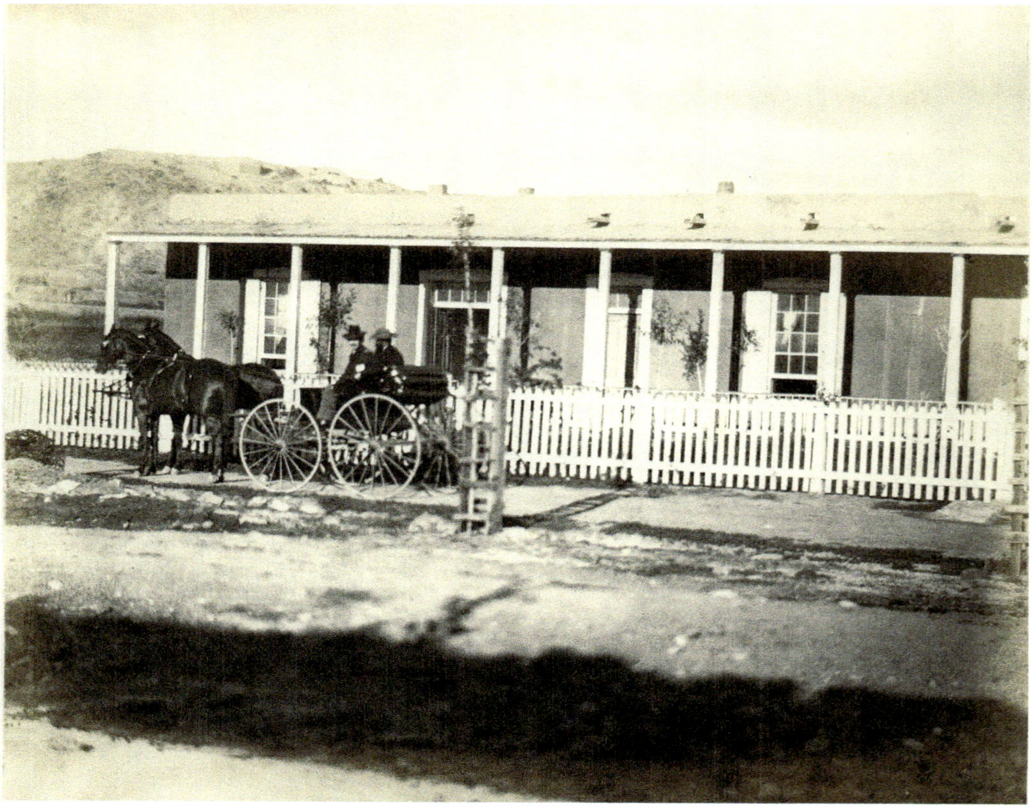

PLATE 25
View of General
J. H. Carleton's quarters,
Santa Fe, New Mexico
Territory, ca. 1865.
PoG 038180

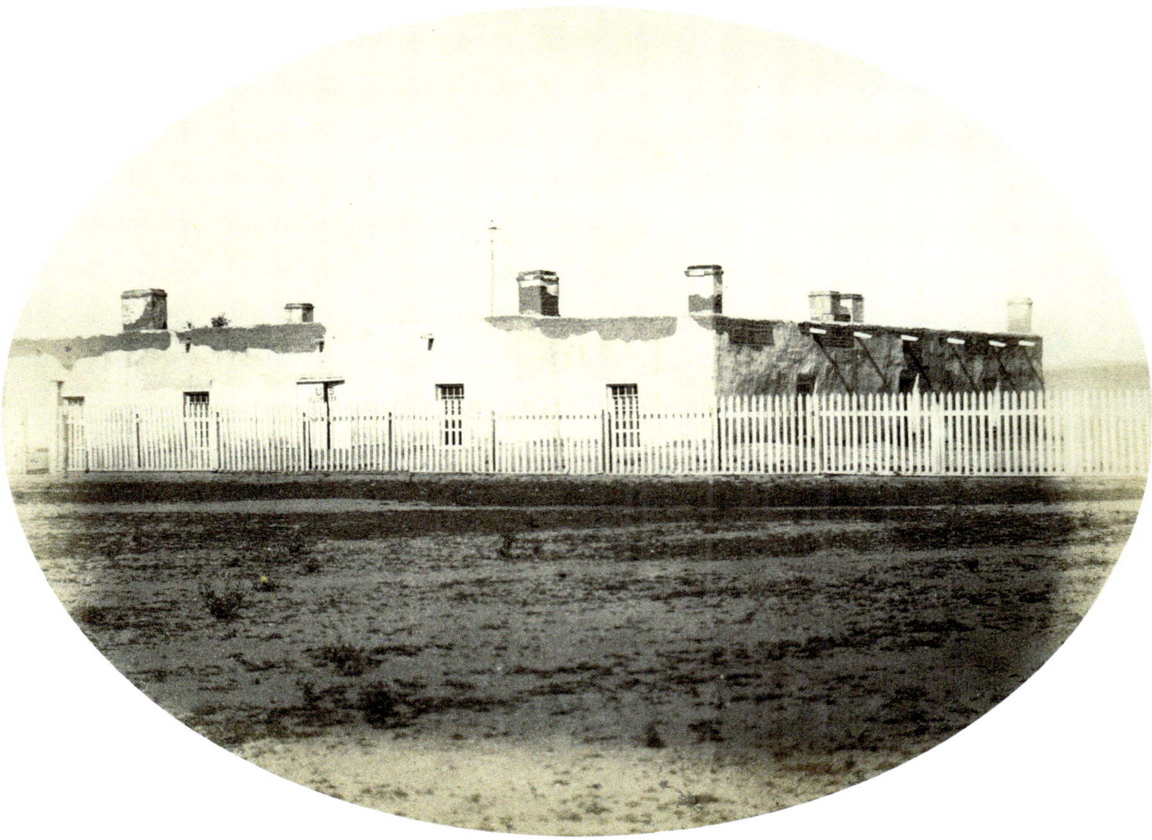

PLATE 26
U.S. Hospital at Fort Marcy,
Santa Fe, New Mexico
Territory, ca. 1865.
PoG 001700

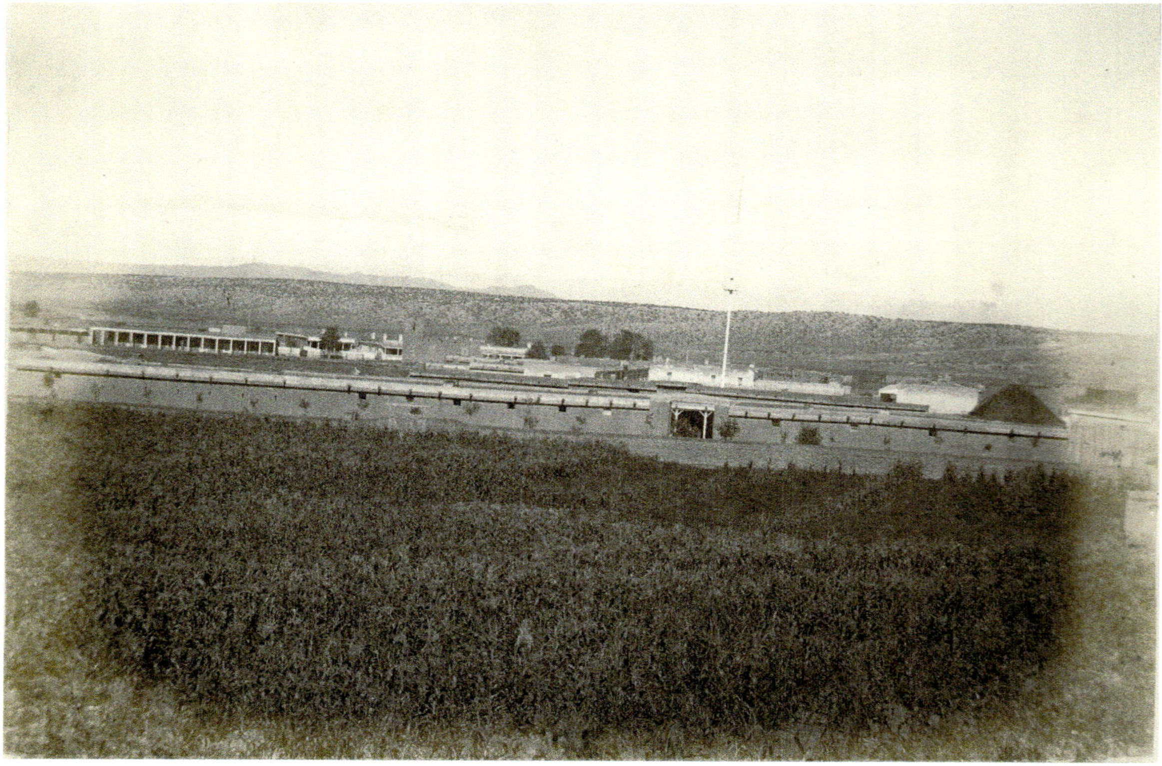

PLATE 27
View of Fort Marcy looking west, Santa Fe, New Mexico Territory, ca. 1865.
PoG 038181

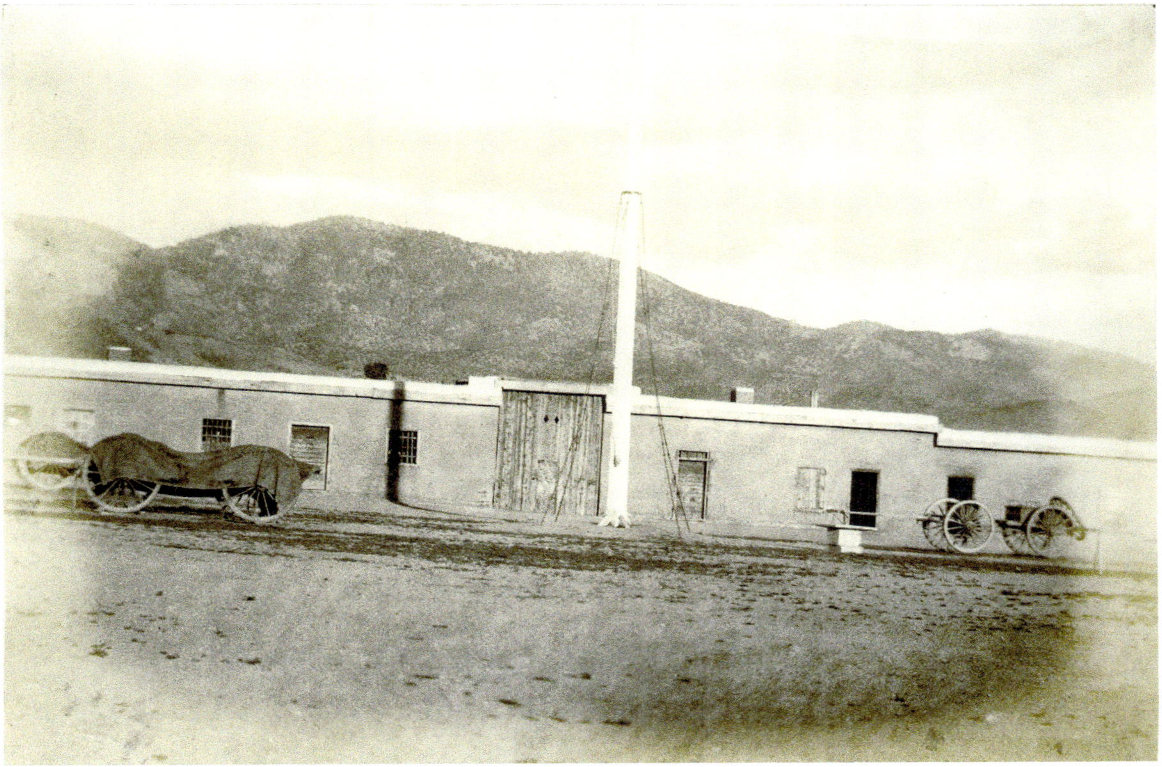

PLATE 28
View inside Fort Marcy looking east, Santa Fe, New Mexico Territory, ca. 1865.
PoG 038182

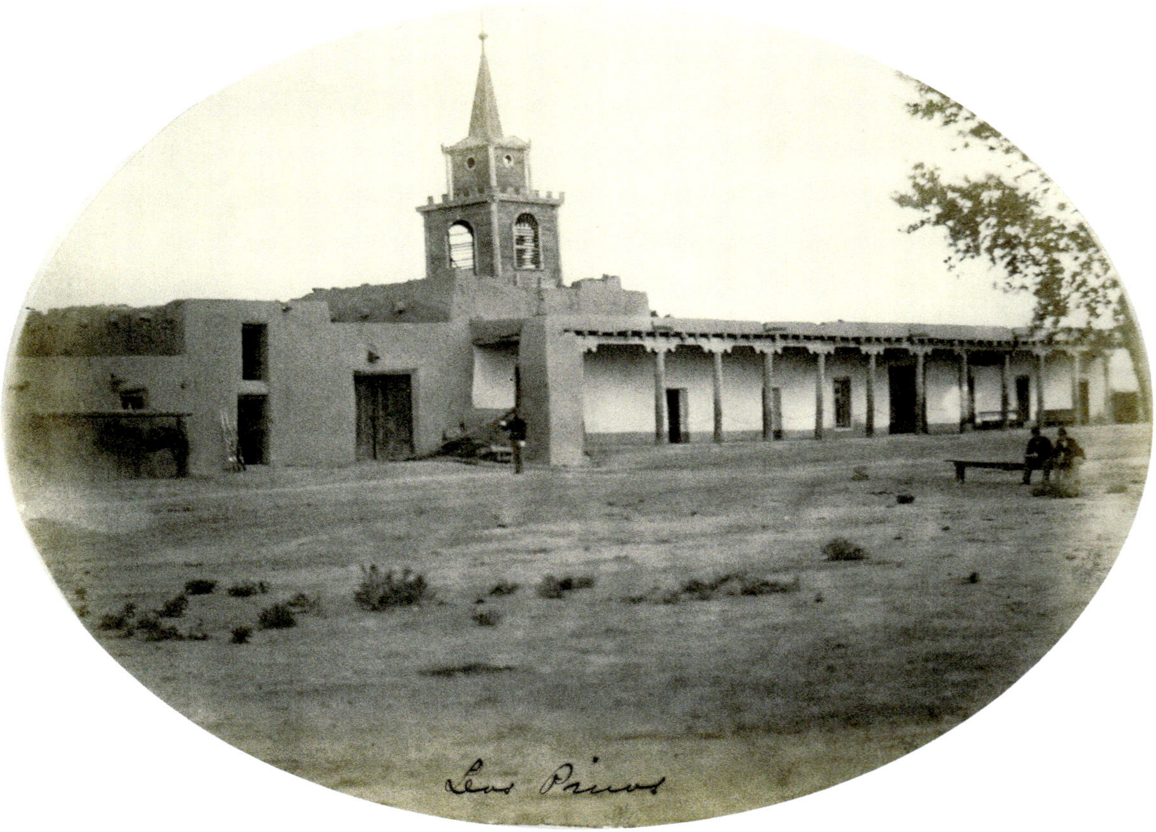

PLATE 29
Los Pinos Church at Los Pinos encampment, Pecos, New Mexico Territory, ca. 1865.
PoG 101938

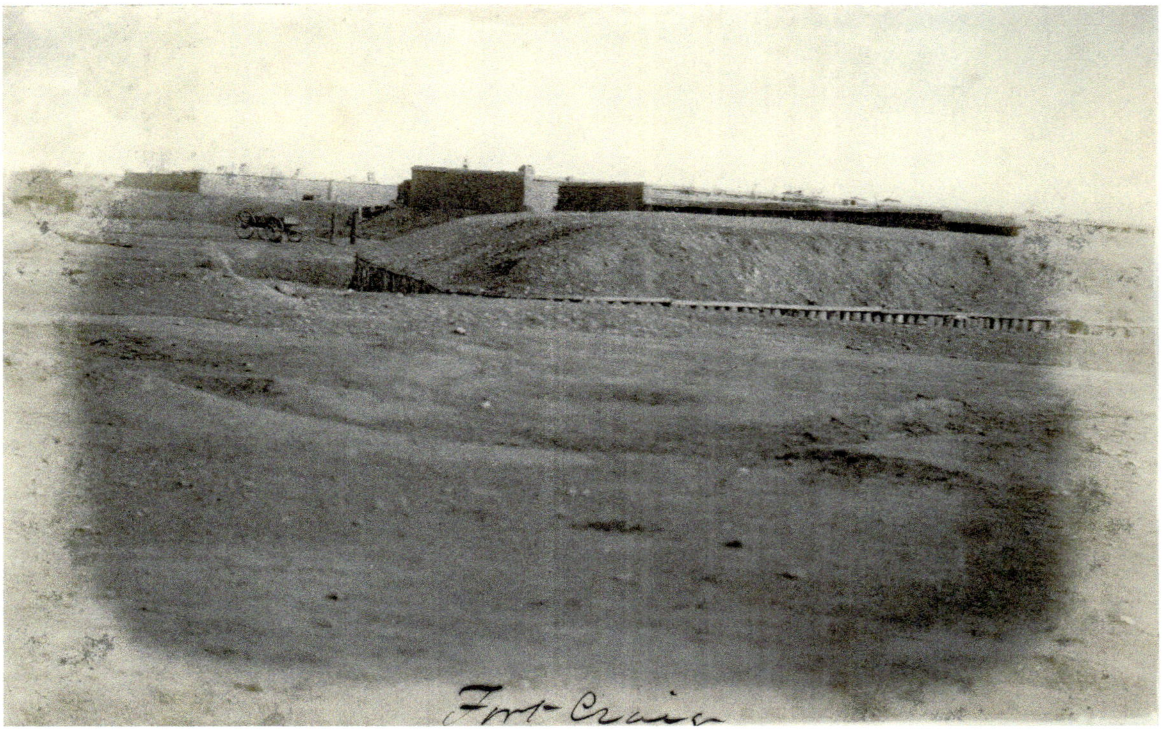

PLATE 30
Earthworks at Fort Craig, San Antonio, New Mexico Territory, ca. 1865.
PoG 014510

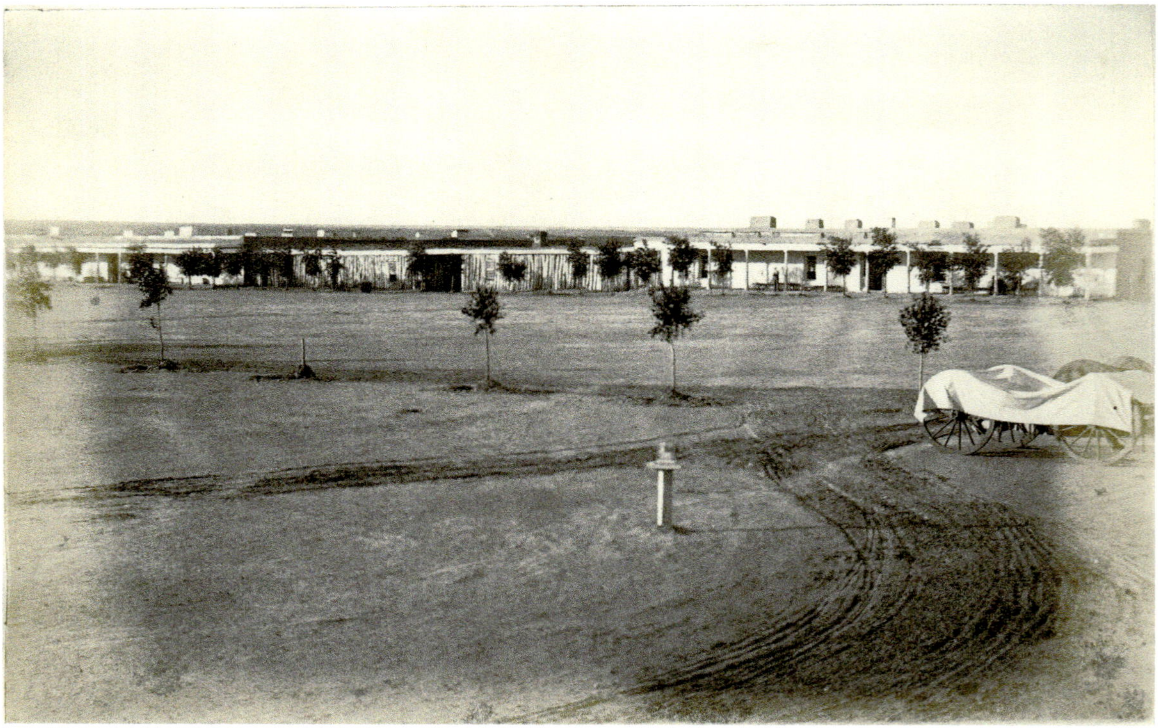

PLATE 31
Soldiers' quarters, Fort Craig, San Antonio, New Mexico Territory, ca. 1865.
PoG 014514

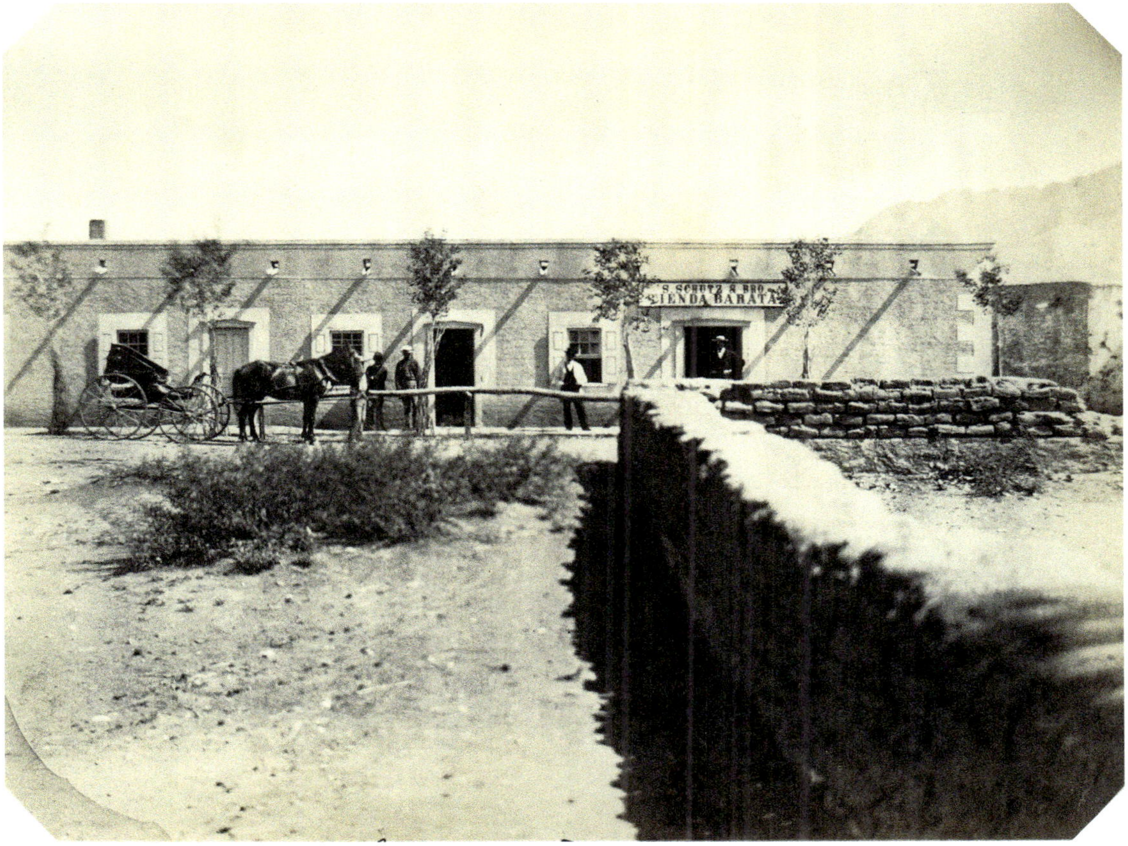

PLATE 32
Street scene showing
"S. Schutz & Bro., Tienda
Barata," Franklin (El Paso),
Texas, ca. 1865.
PoG 038183

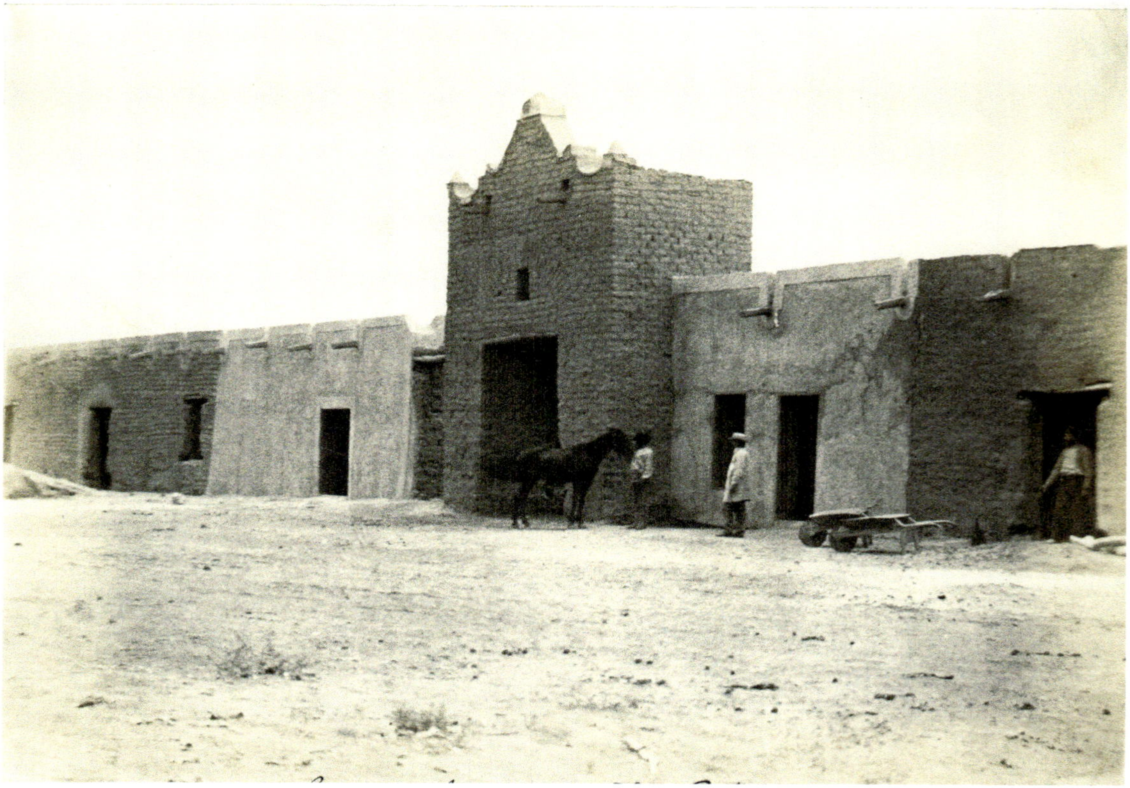

PLATE 33
Sally port, Fort Bliss, Franklin (El Paso), Texas, ca. 1865.
PoG 038184

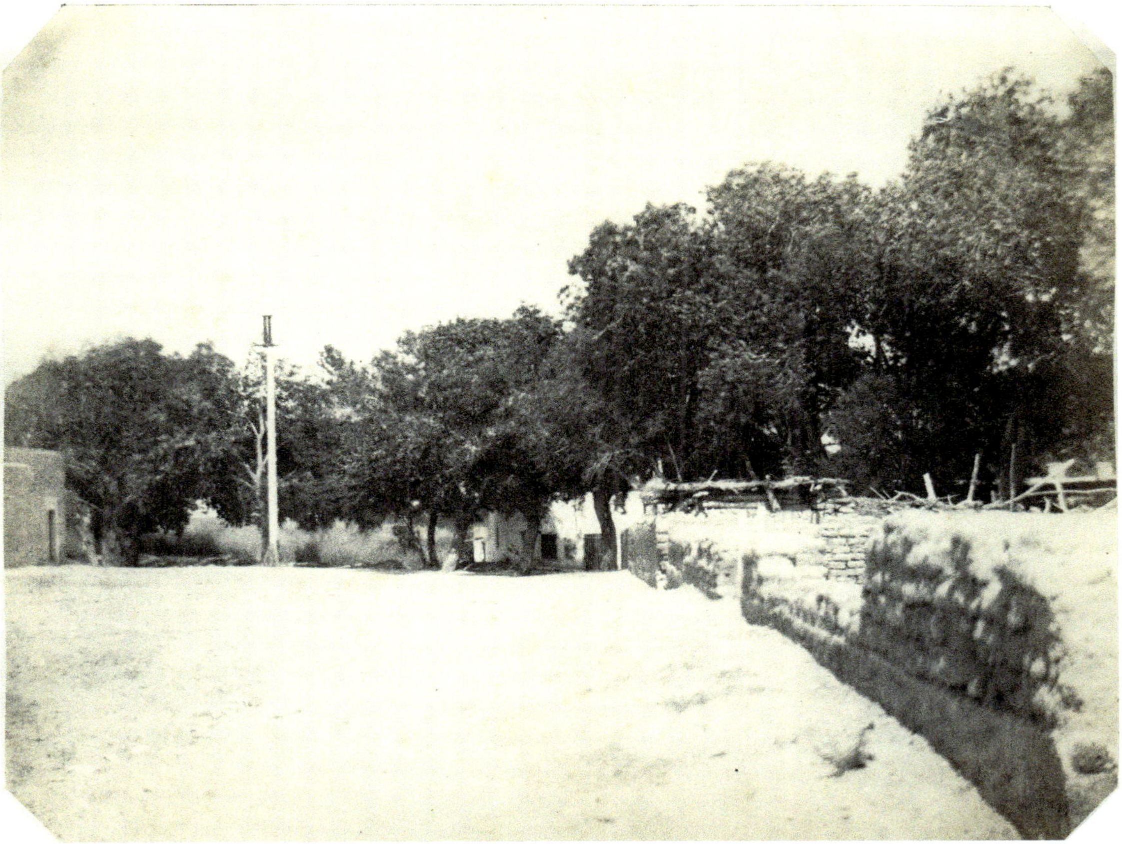

PLATE 34
Grounds of Fort Bliss,
Franklin (El Paso), Texas,
ca. 1865.
PoG 038185

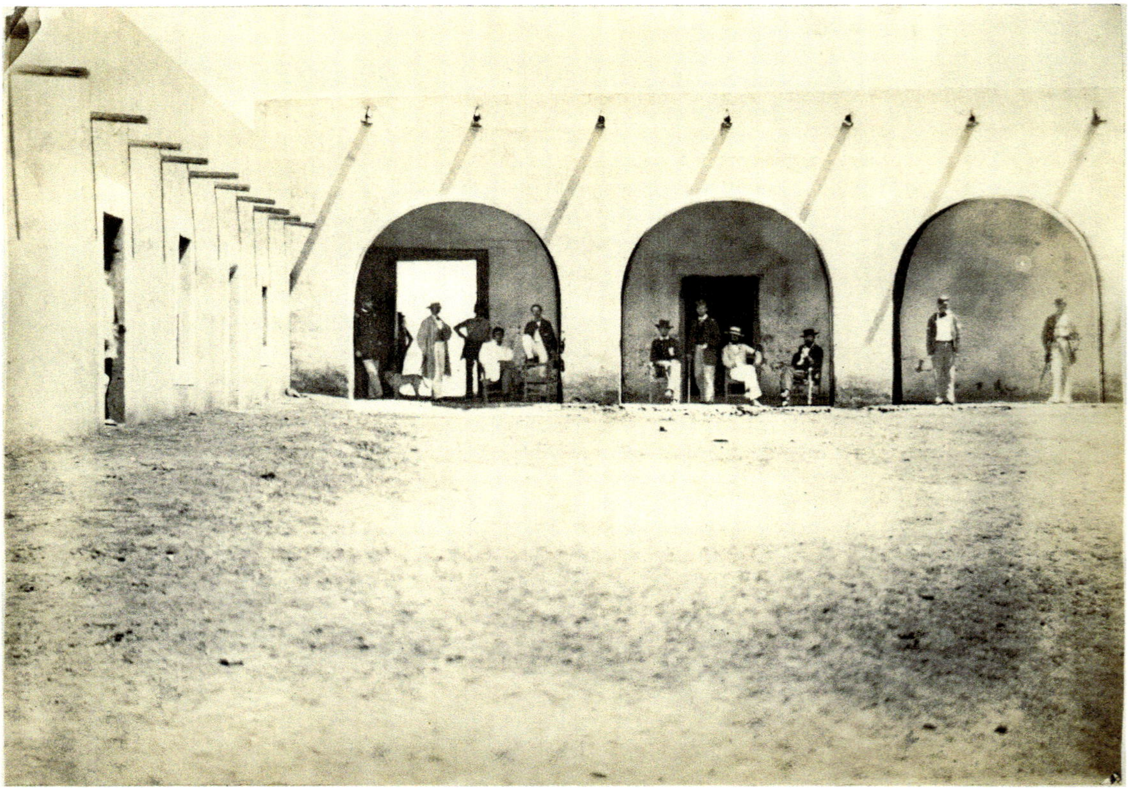

PLATE 35
Arches at Fort Bliss, Franklin (El Paso), Texas, ca. 1865.
PoG 038186

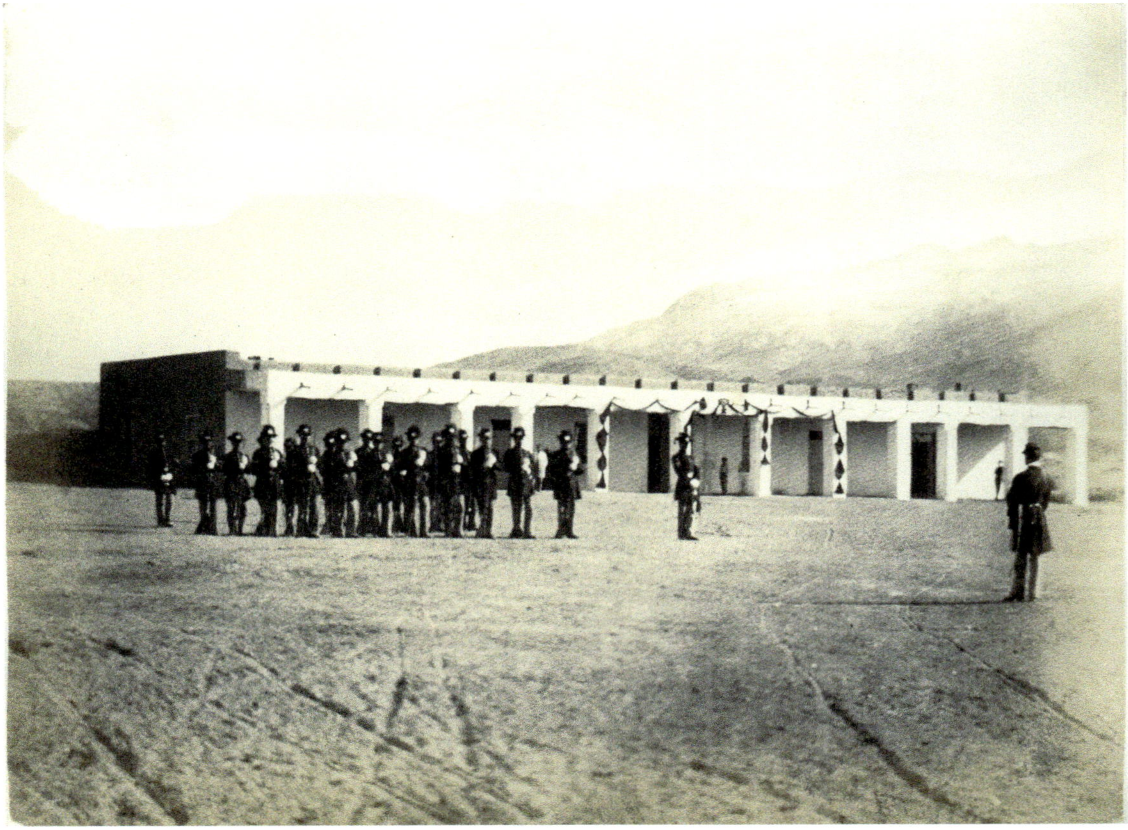

PLATE 36
Soldiers on review at Fort Bliss, Franklin (El Paso), Texas, ca. 1865.
PoG 038187

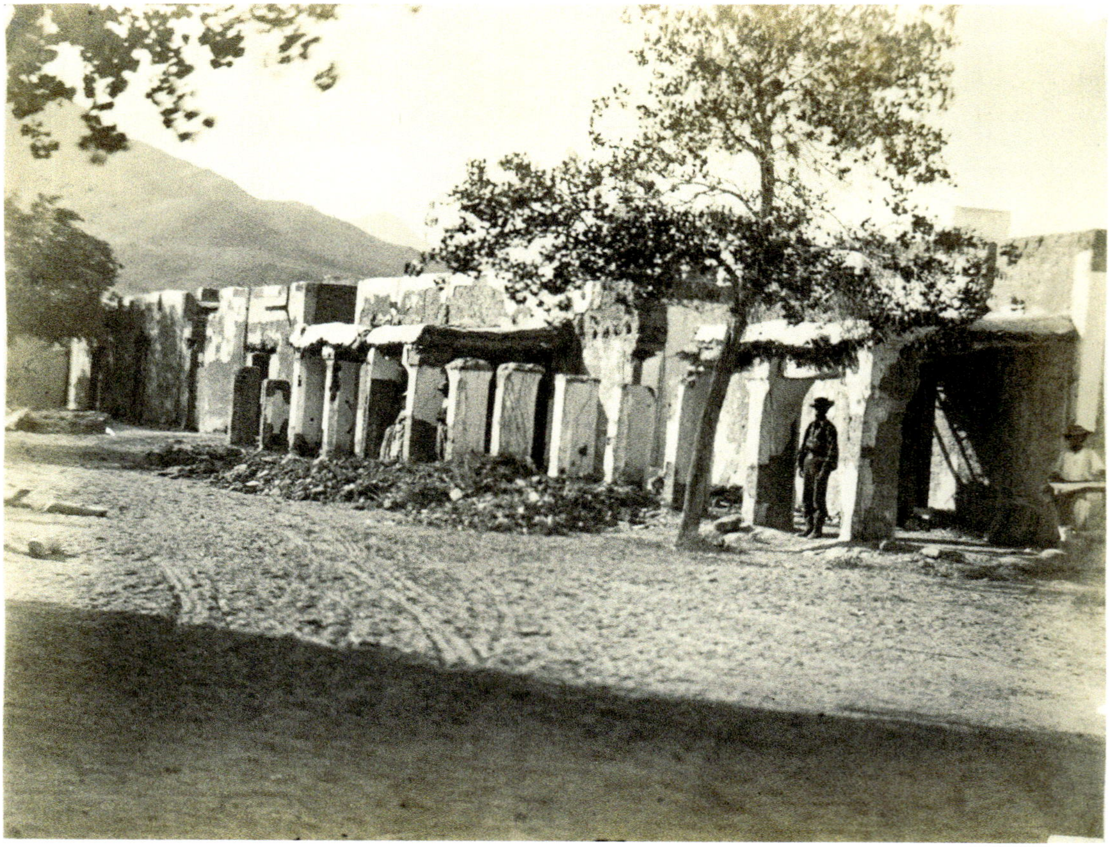

PLATE 37
Officers' quarters, Fort Bliss, Franklin (El Paso), Texas, ca. 1865.
PoG 014504

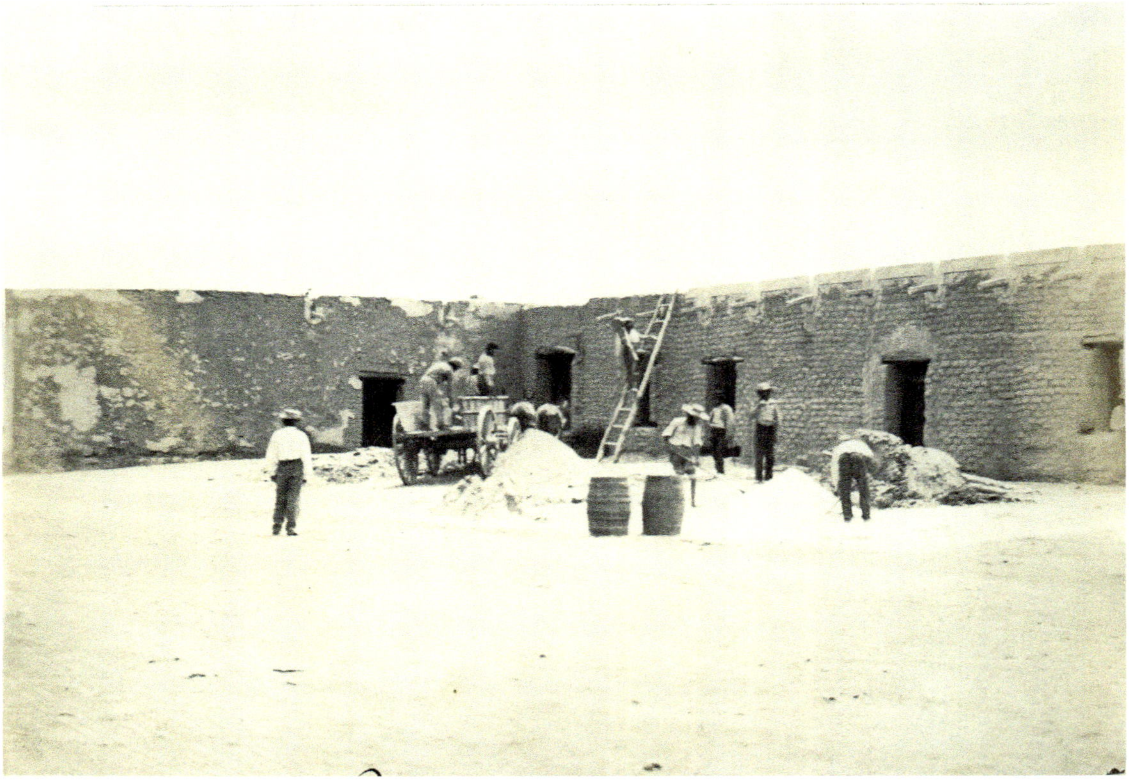

PLATE 38
Repairing adobe buildings, Fort Bliss, Franklin (El Paso), Texas, ca. 1865.
PoG 038188

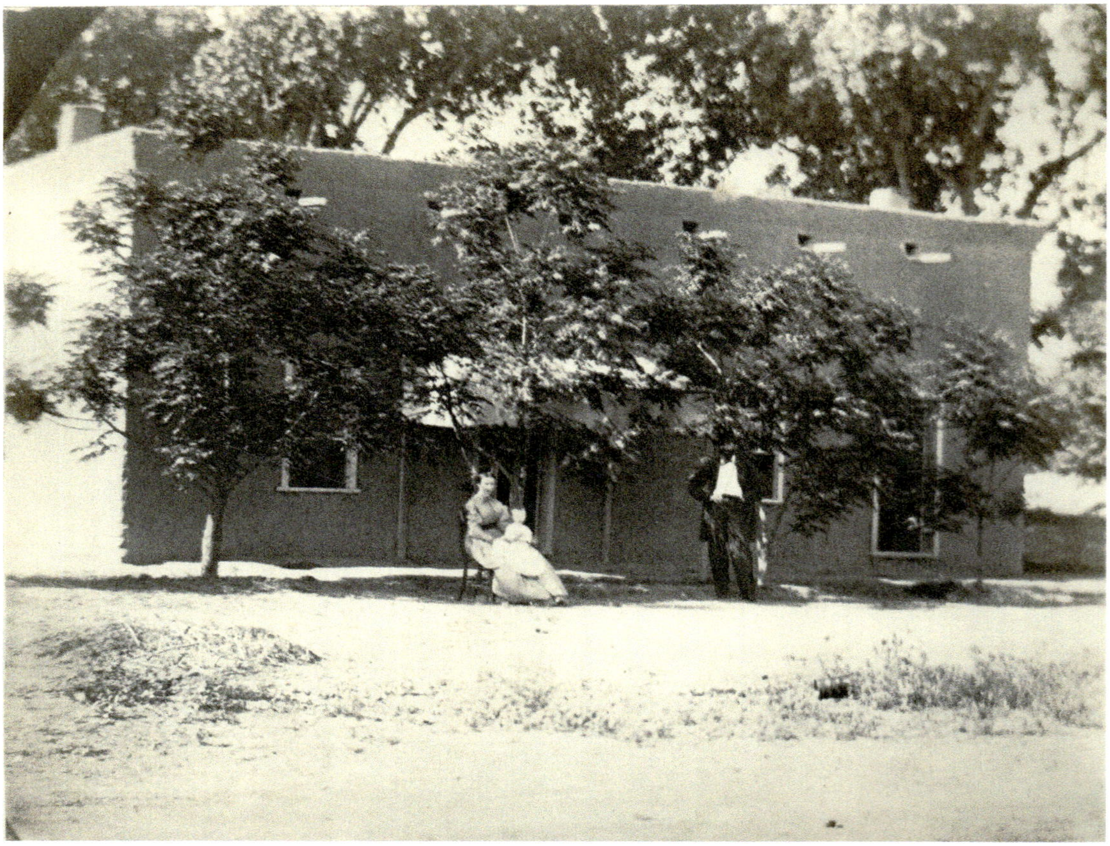

PLATE 39
Family scene at Fort Bliss, Franklin (El Paso), Texas, ca. 1865.
PoG 038189

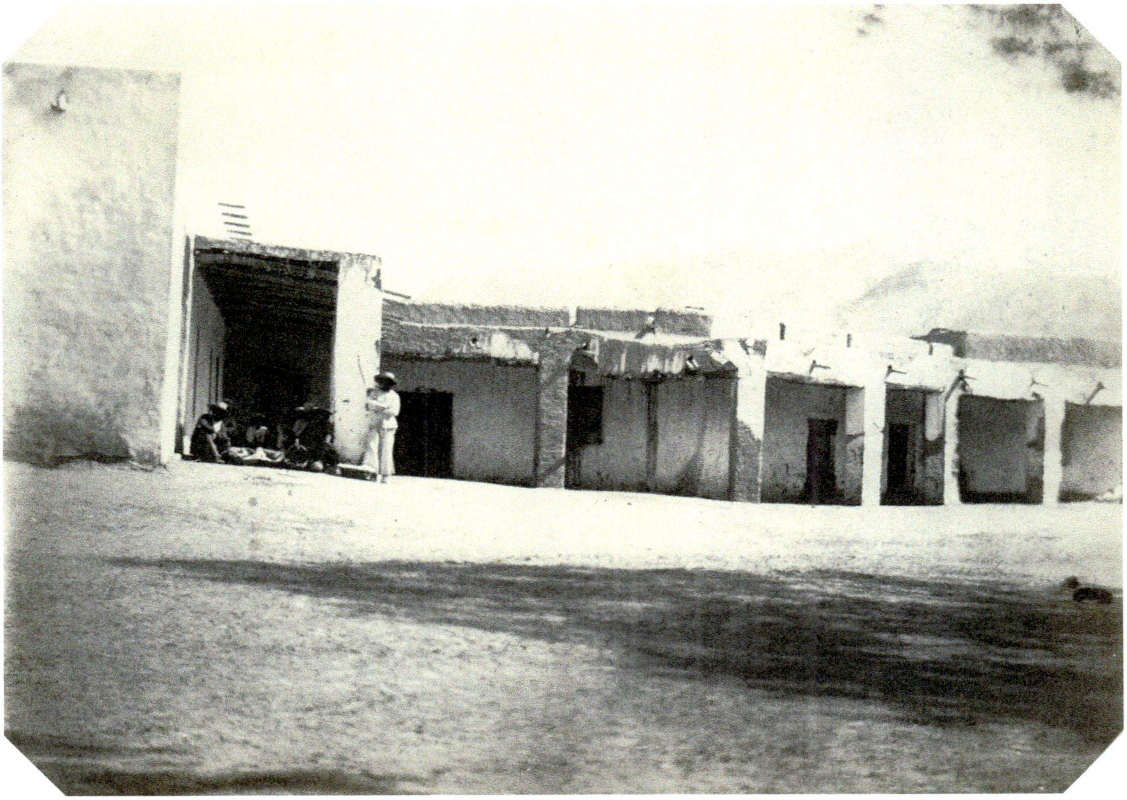

PLATE 40
View at Fort Bliss, Franklin (El Paso), Texas, ca. 1865.
PoG 038190

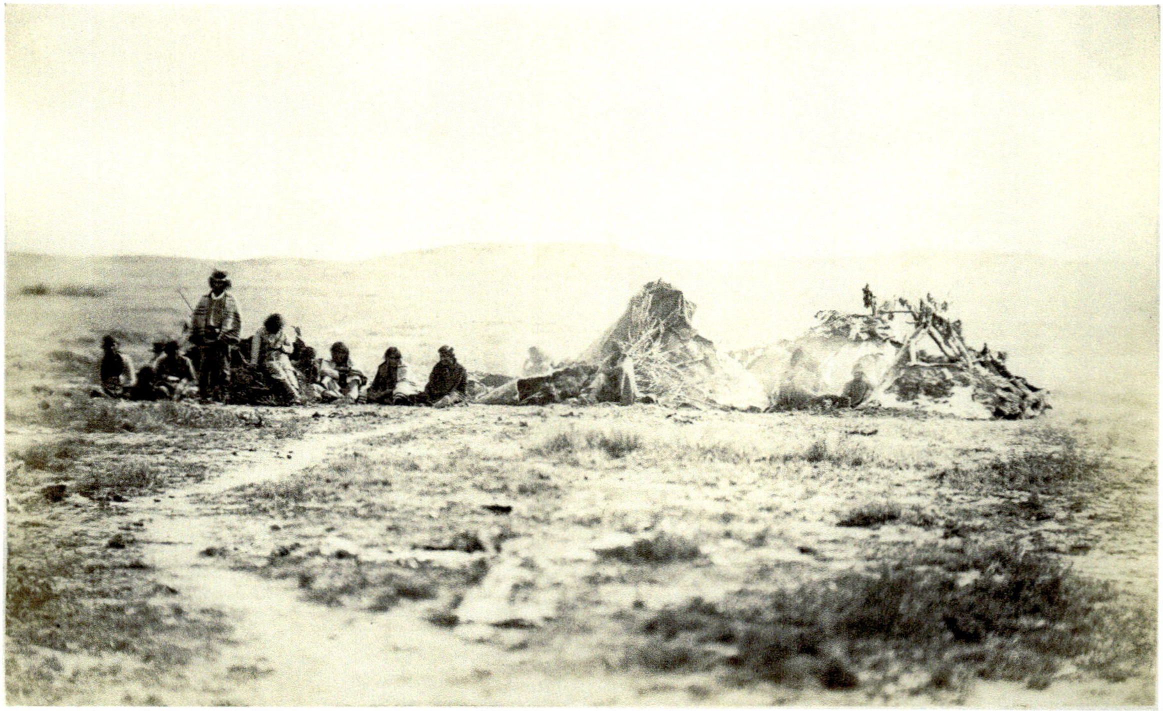

PLATE 41
Group of Navajo captives, Bosque Redondo era, Fort Sumner, New Mexico Territory, ca. 1865.
PoG 038191

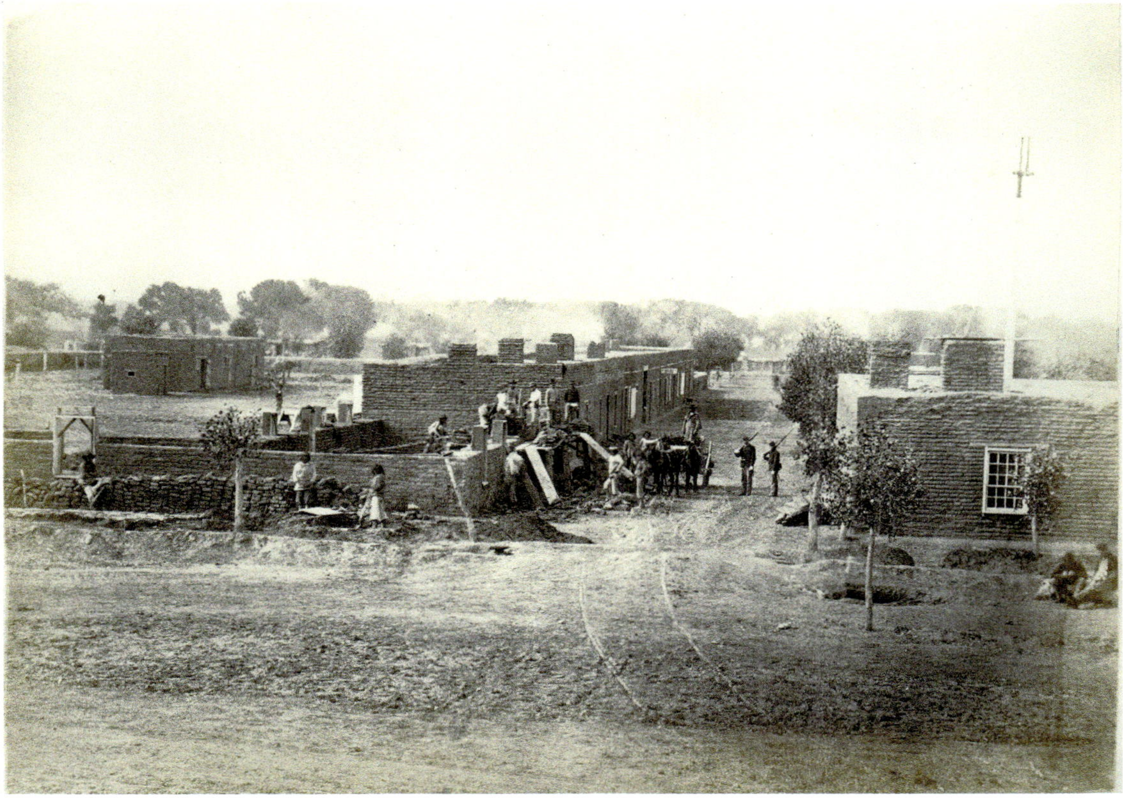

PLATE 42
Indian captives building the fort, Fort Sumner, New Mexico Territory, ca. 1865.
PoG 001816

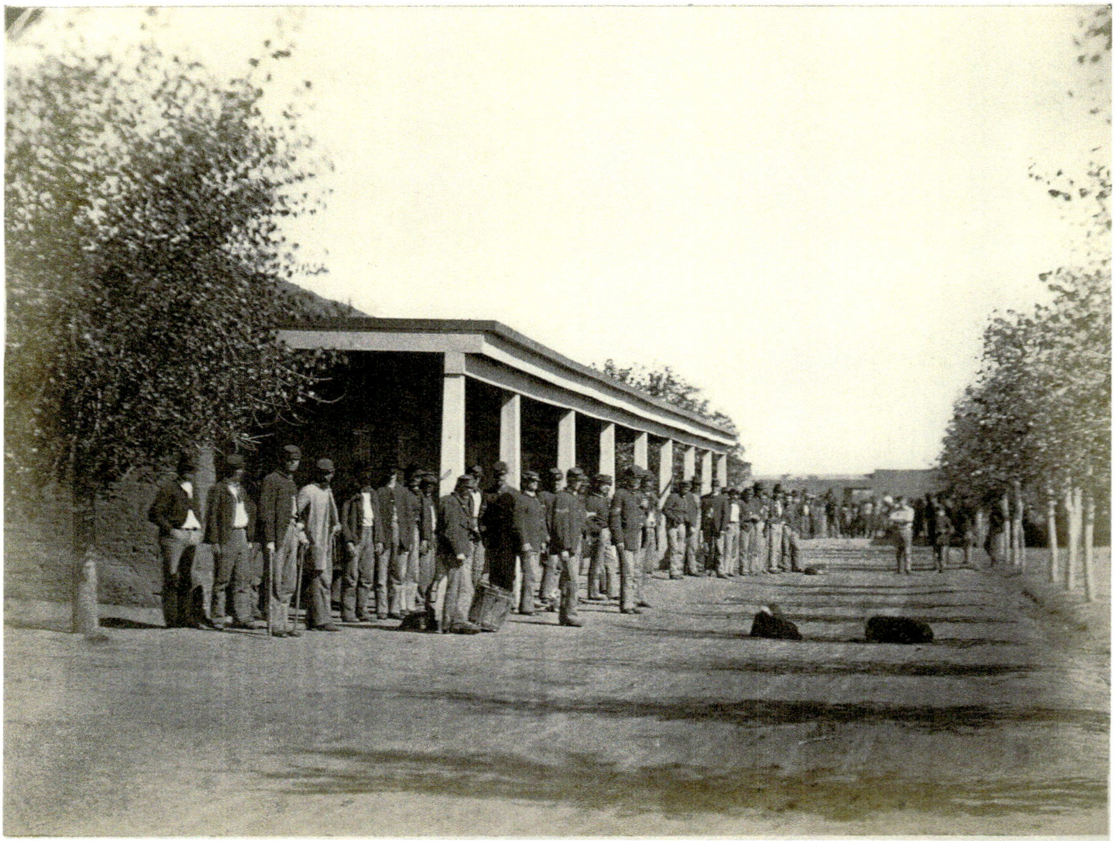

PLATE 43
Soldiers at Fort Sumner, New Mexico Territory, ca. 1865.
PoG 028537

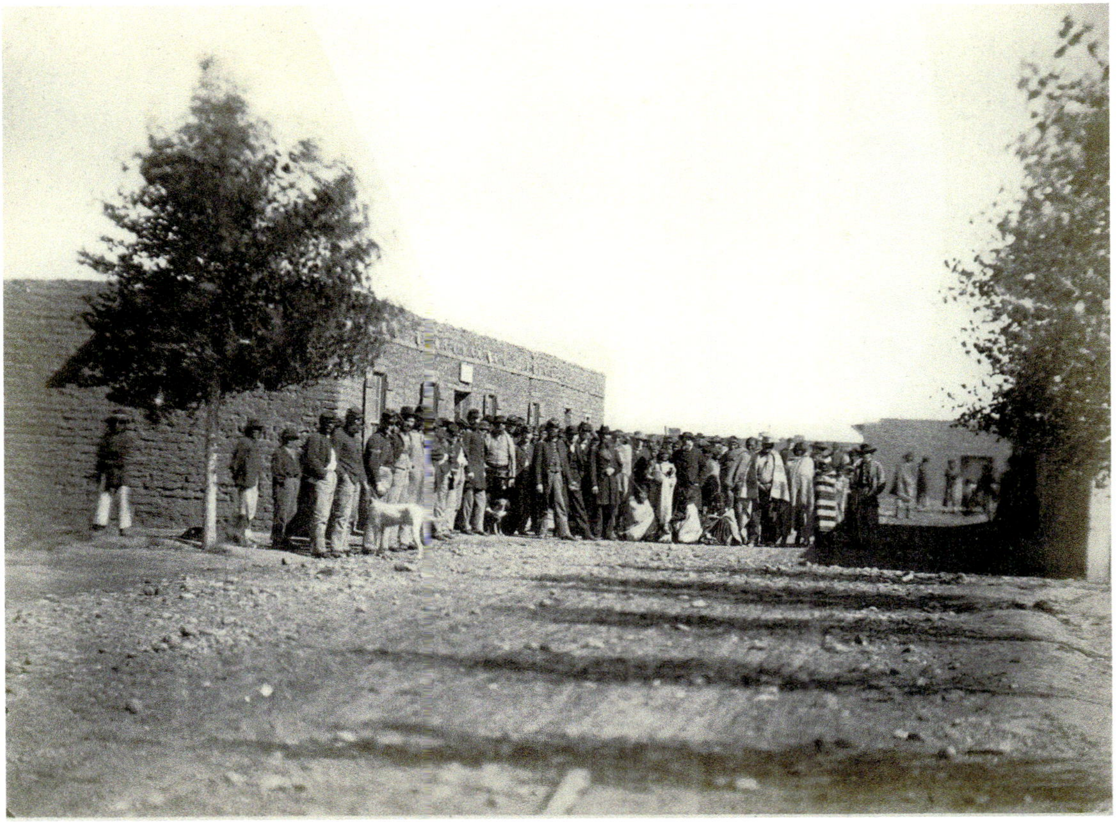

PLATE 44
Group of soldiers and Navajos gathered in street, Fort Sumner, New Mexico Territory, ca. 1865.
PoG 001817

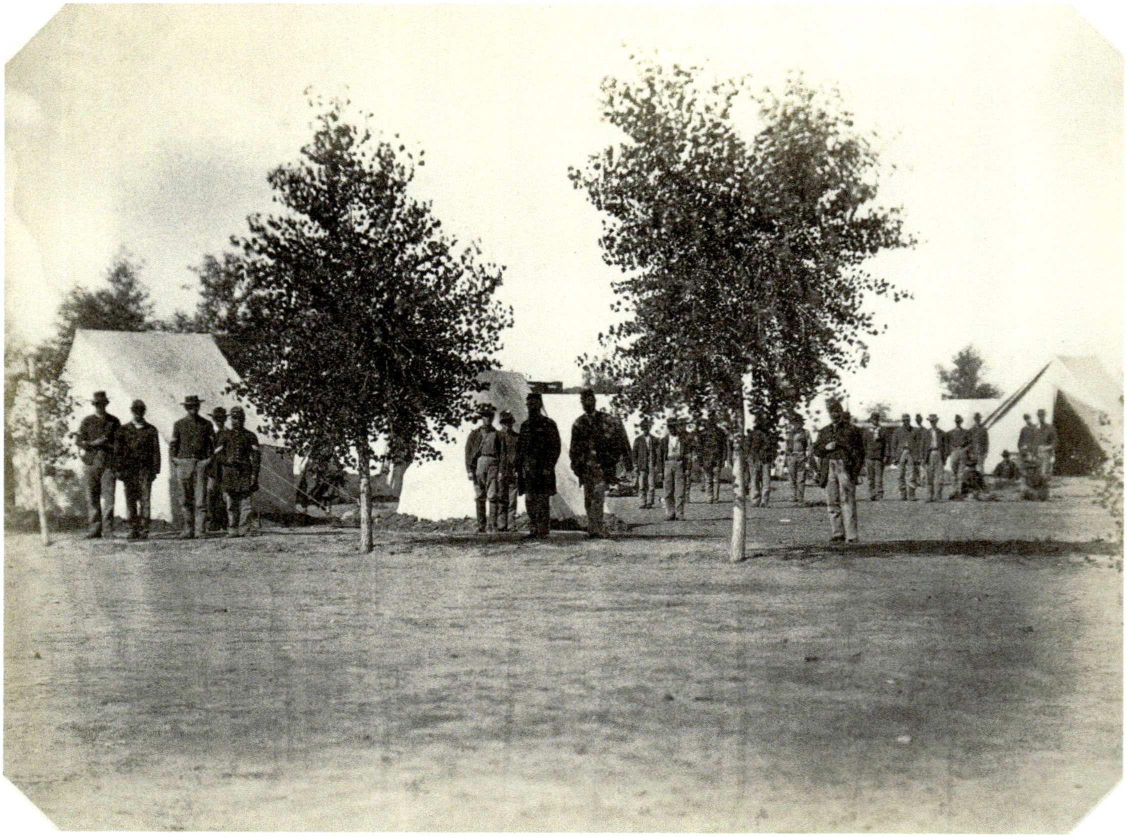

PLATE 45
Soldiers and tents, likely Company B, First New Mexican Infantry, Fort Sumner, New Mexico, ca. 1865.
PoG 023128

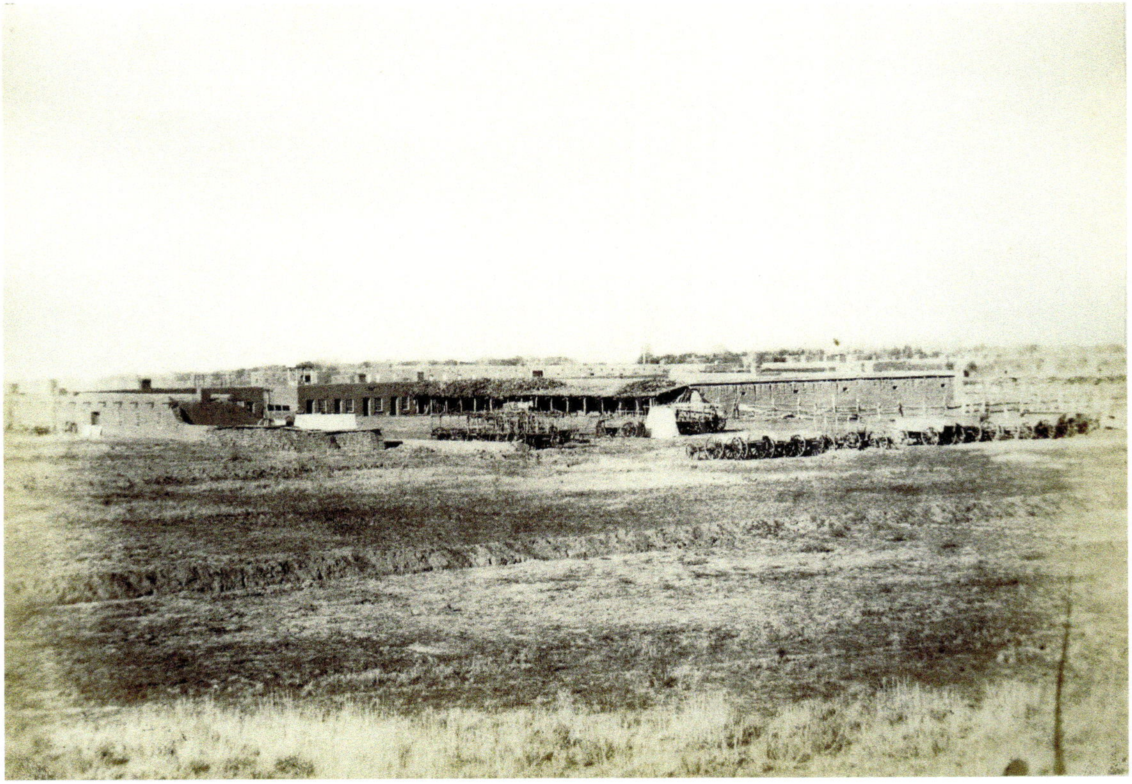

PLATE 46
Fort Sumner, New Mexico Territory, ca. 1865.
PoG 023129

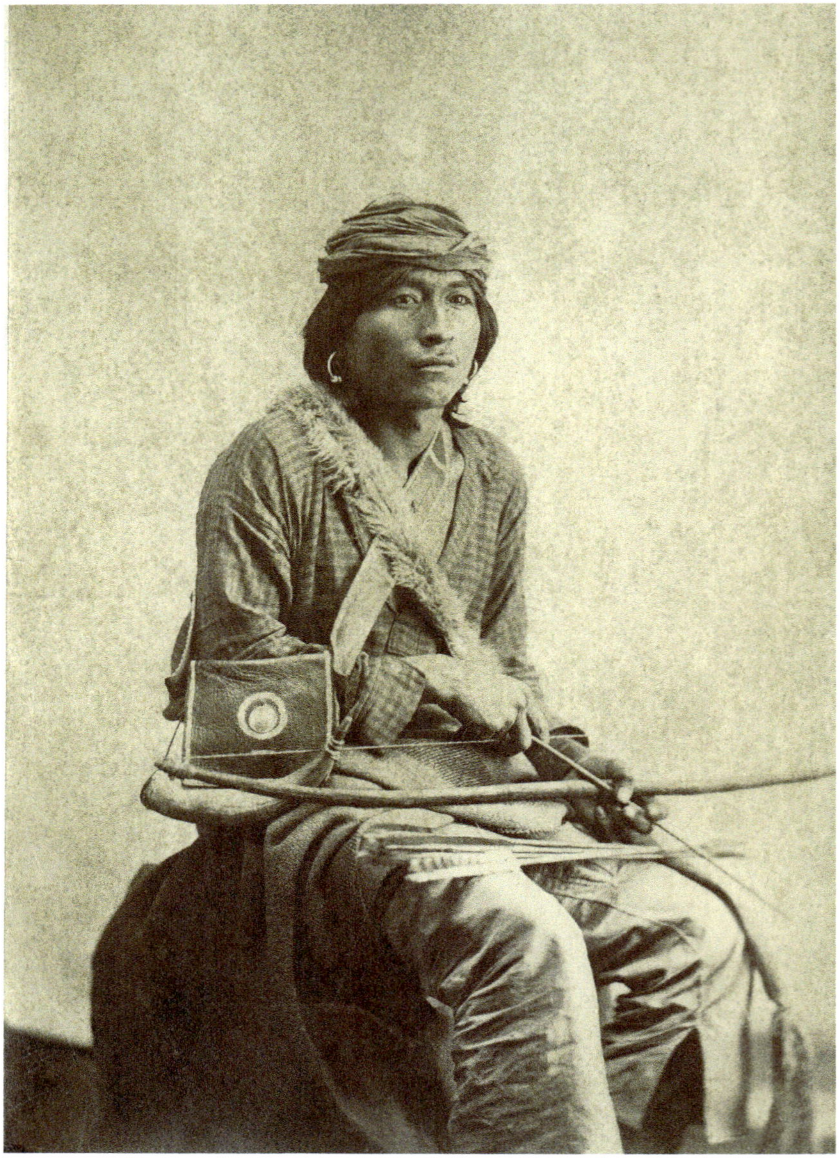

PLATE 47
Navajo man en route to or at Fort Sumner, New Mexico Territory, ca. September 1866.
PoG 038192
See also figure 19a, page 36.

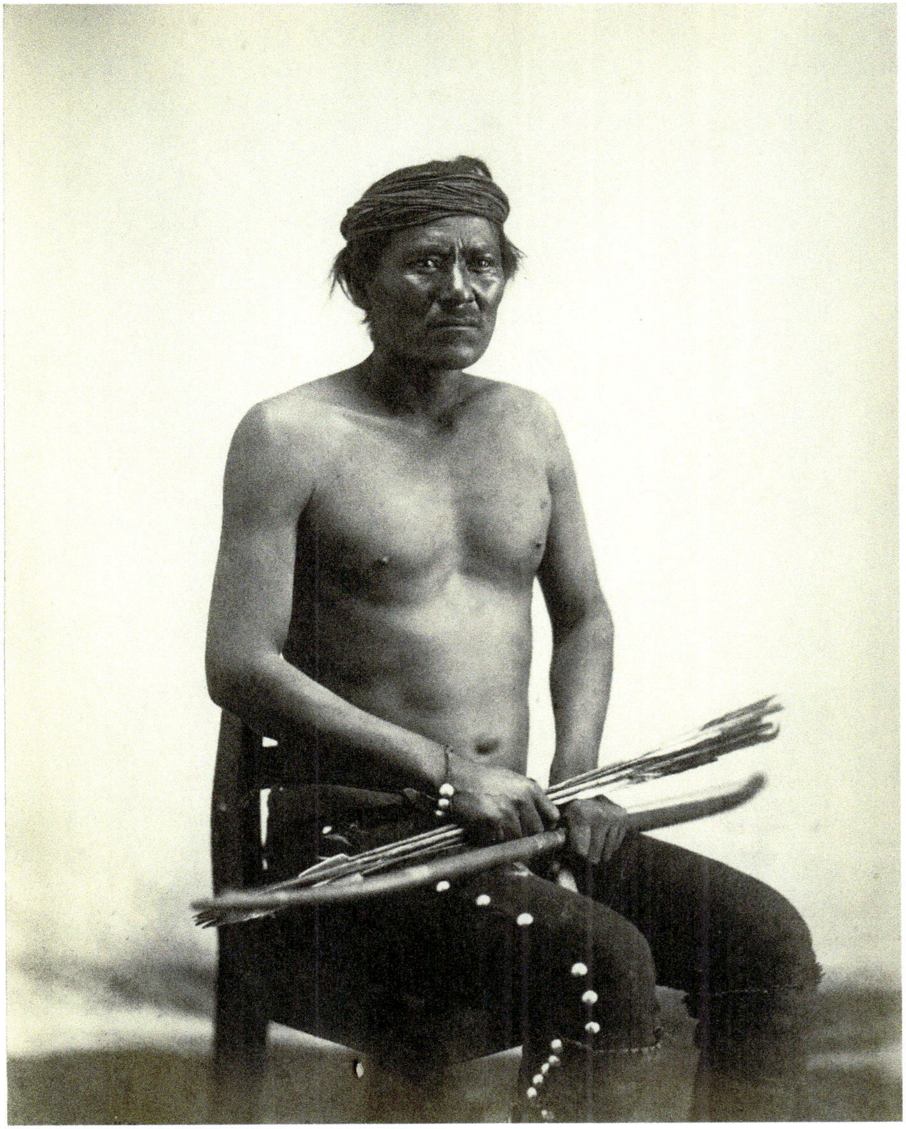

PLATE 48
"Pistol Bullet," Navajo chief Manuelito en route to or at Fort Sumner, New Mexico Territory, ca. September 1866.
PoG 023130

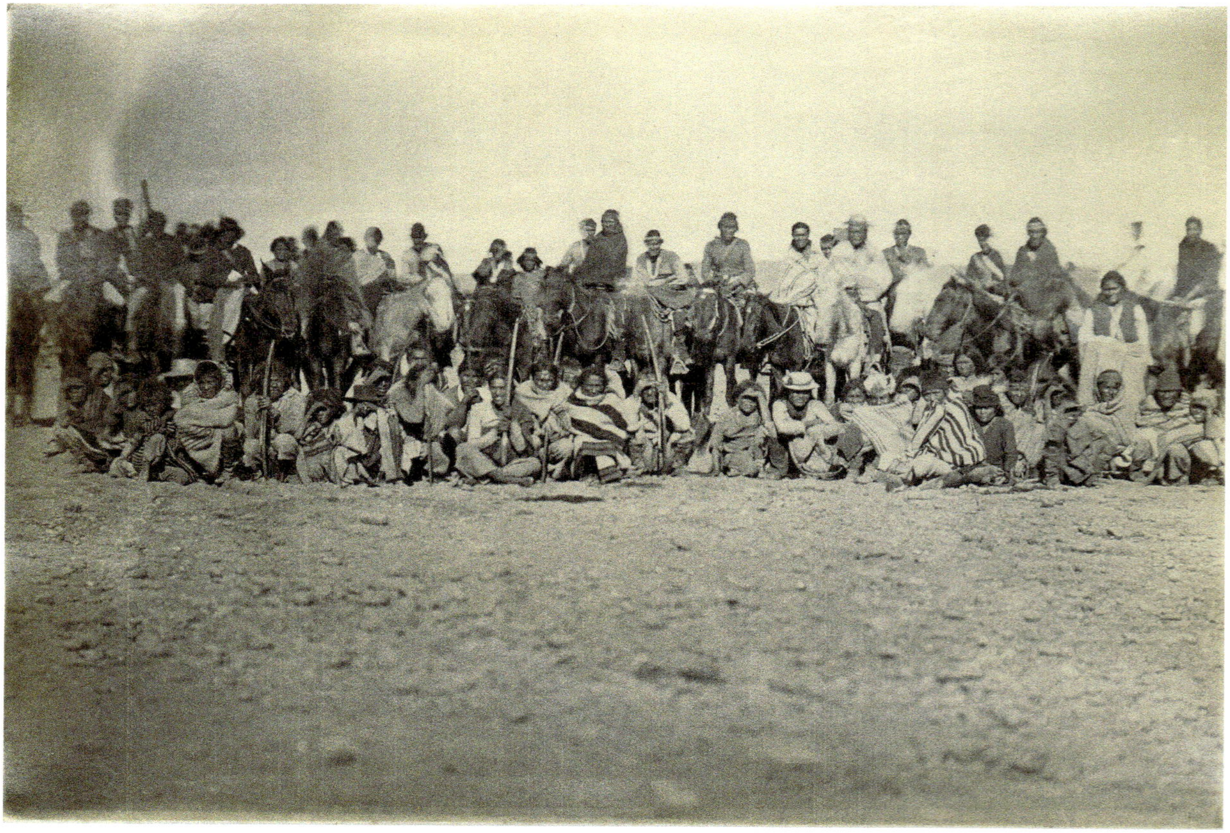

PLATE 49
Large group of Navajo captives at Fort Sumner, New Mexico Territory, ca. 1865.
PoG 038194

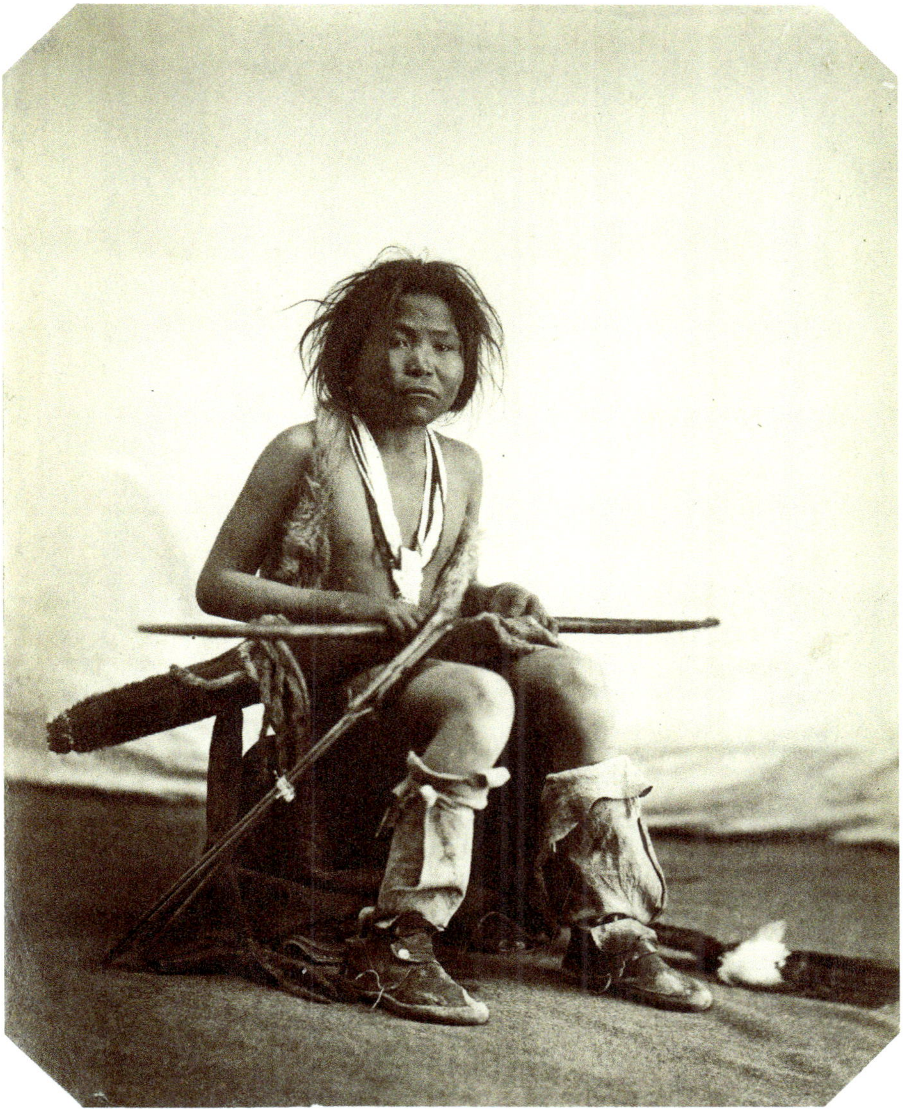

PLATE 50
Apache boy en route to or at Fort Sumner, New Mexico Territory, ca. September 1866.
PoG 038195

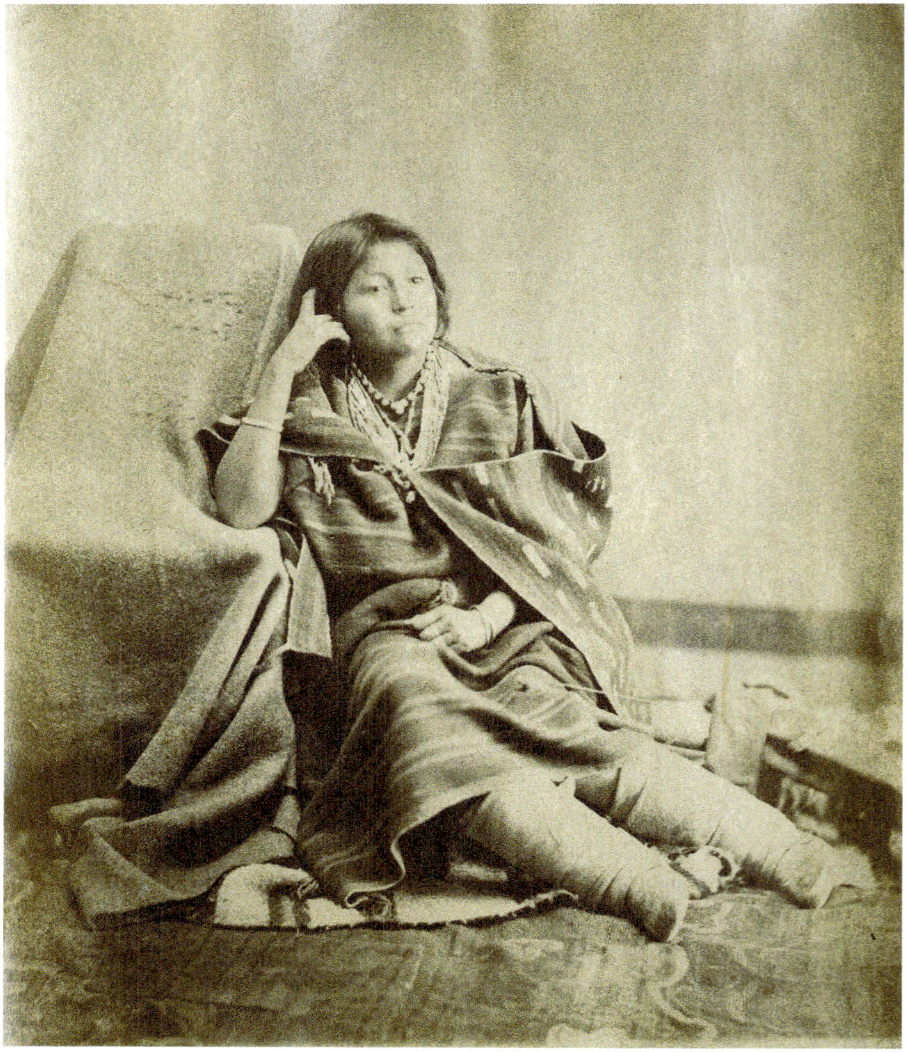

PLATE 51
Navajo girl en route to or at Fort Sumner, New Mexico Territory, ca. September 1866.
PoG 038196

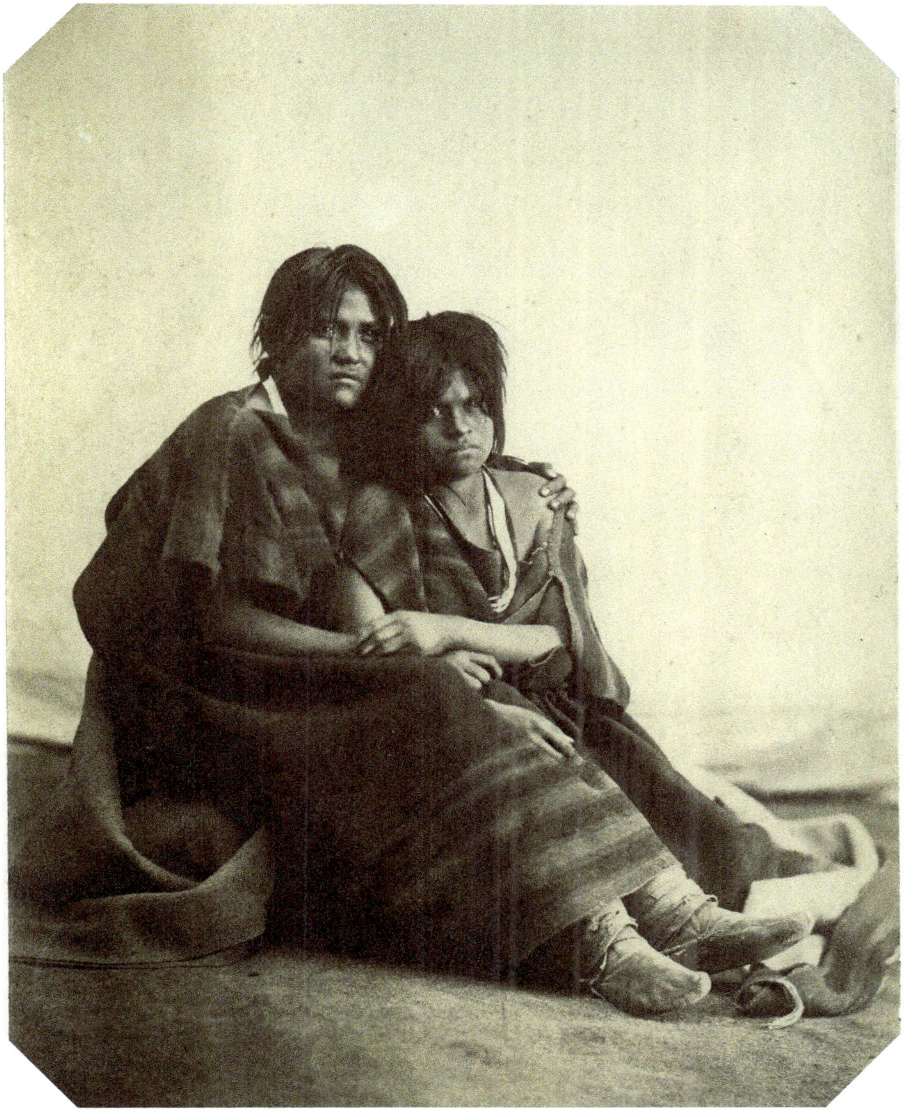

PLATE 52
Two Navajo girls en route to or at Fort Sumner, New Mexico Territory, ca. September 1866.
PoG 03819

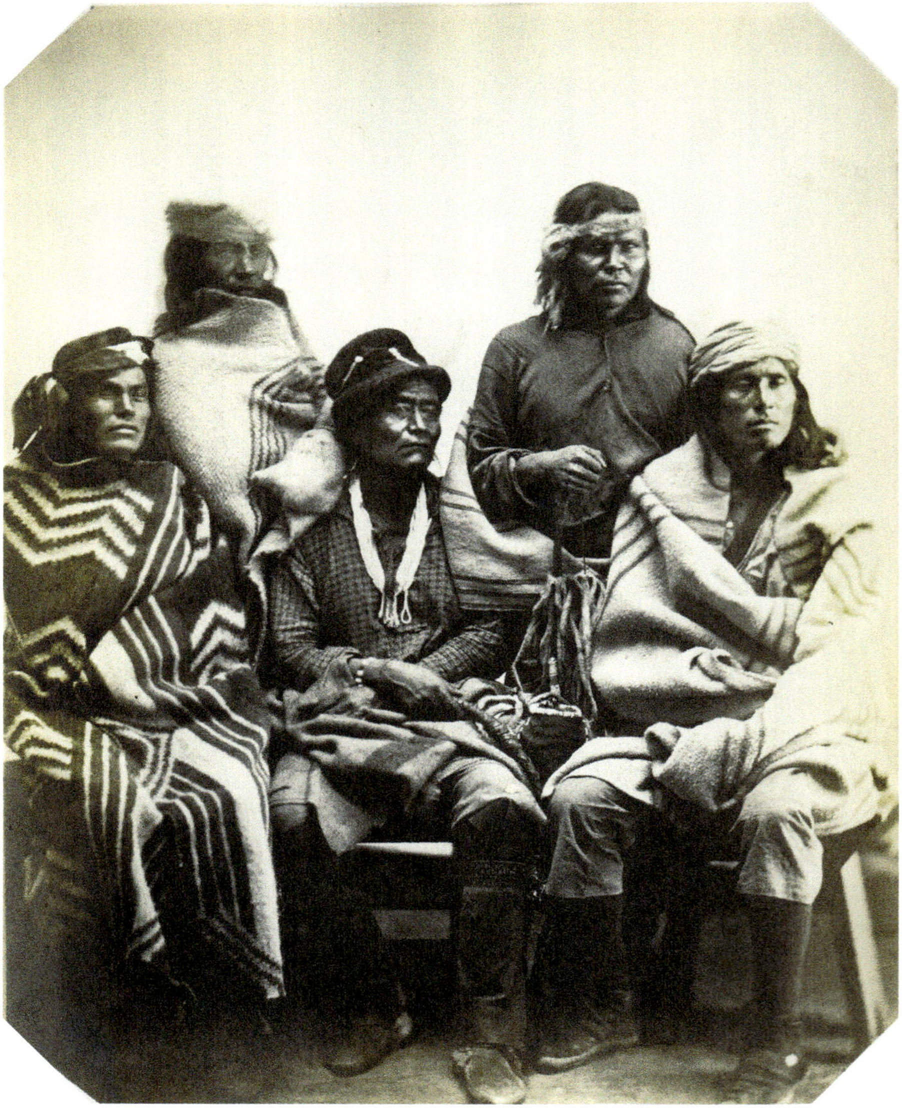

PLATE 53
Navajo men en route to or at Fort Sumner, New Mexico Territory, ca. September 1866. (*Seated, lower left*) Possibly El Ciego, Manuelito's older brother, and (*seated, right*) possibly Mariano.
PoG 030332

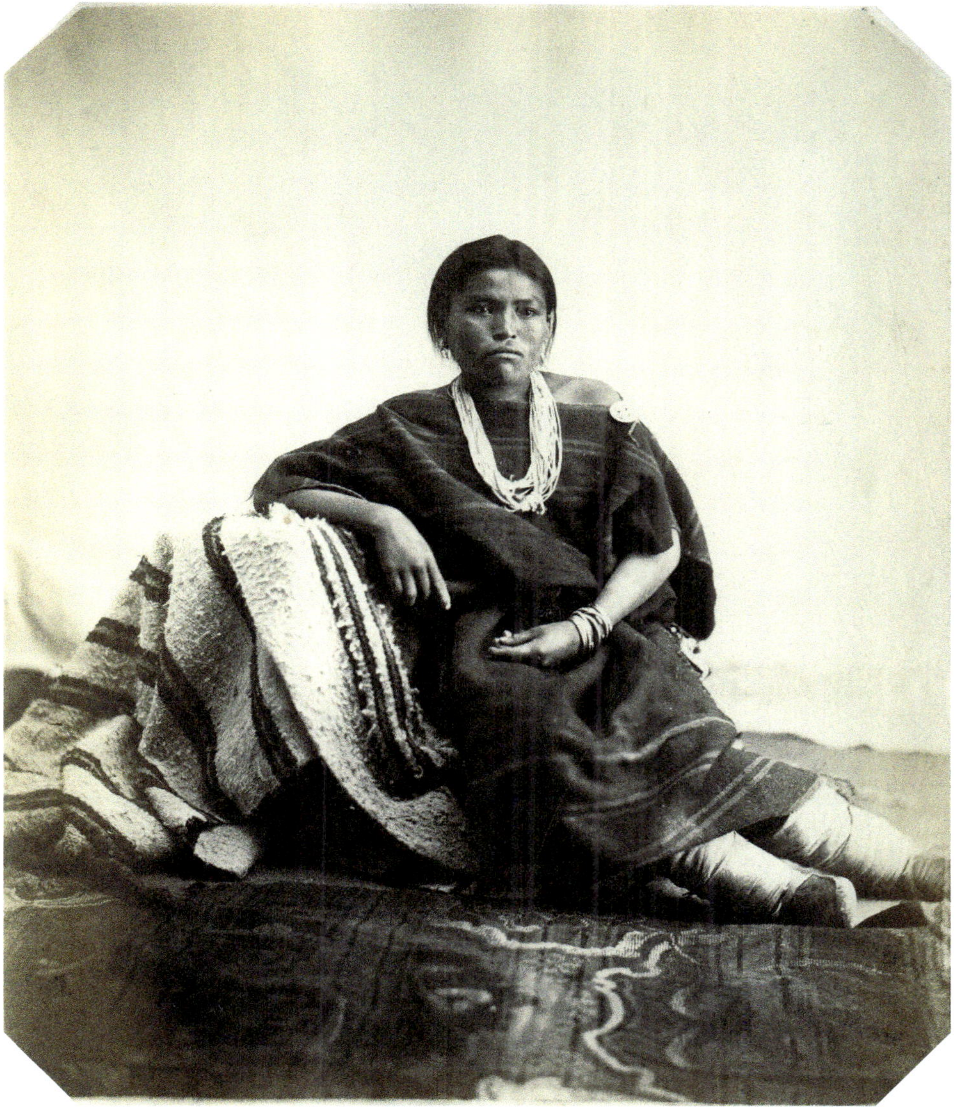

PLATE 54
"The Belle of the Navajos,"
Navajo girl en route to or at
Fort Sumner, New Mexico
Territory, ca. September 1866.
PoG 038199

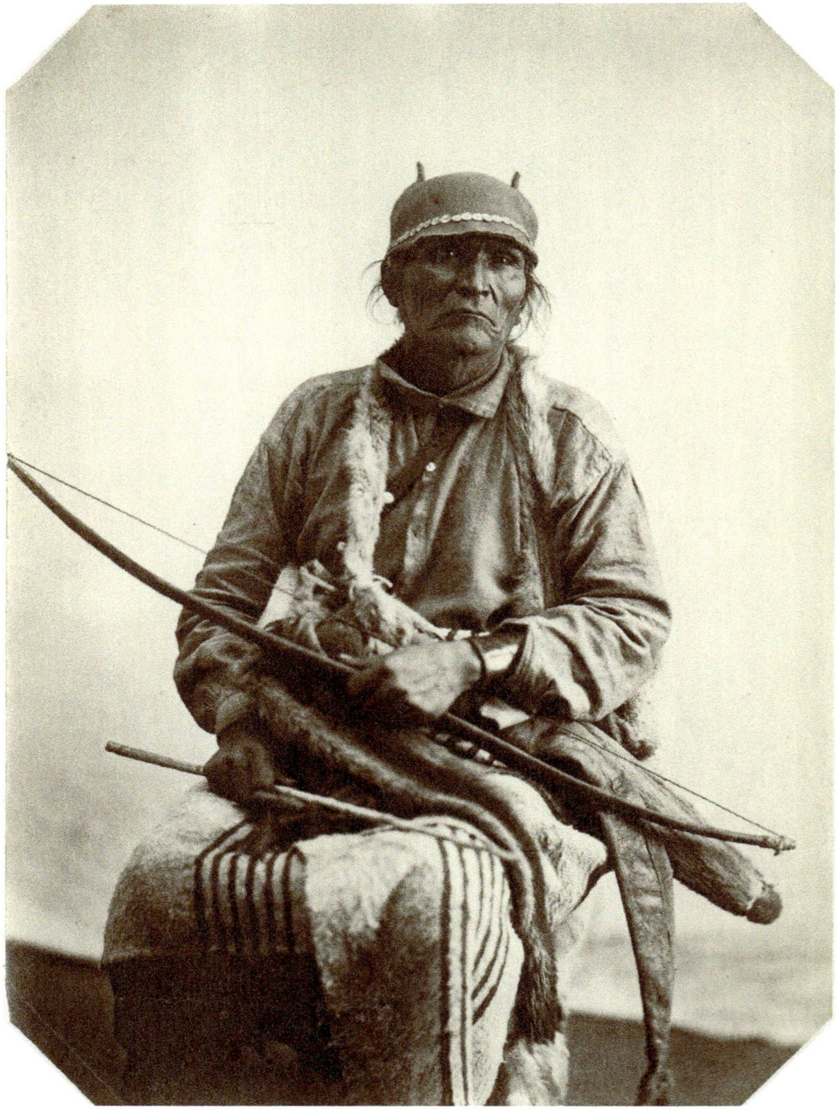

PLATE 55
Navajo man en route to or at Fort Sumner, New Mexico Territory, ca. September 1866.
PoG 038200

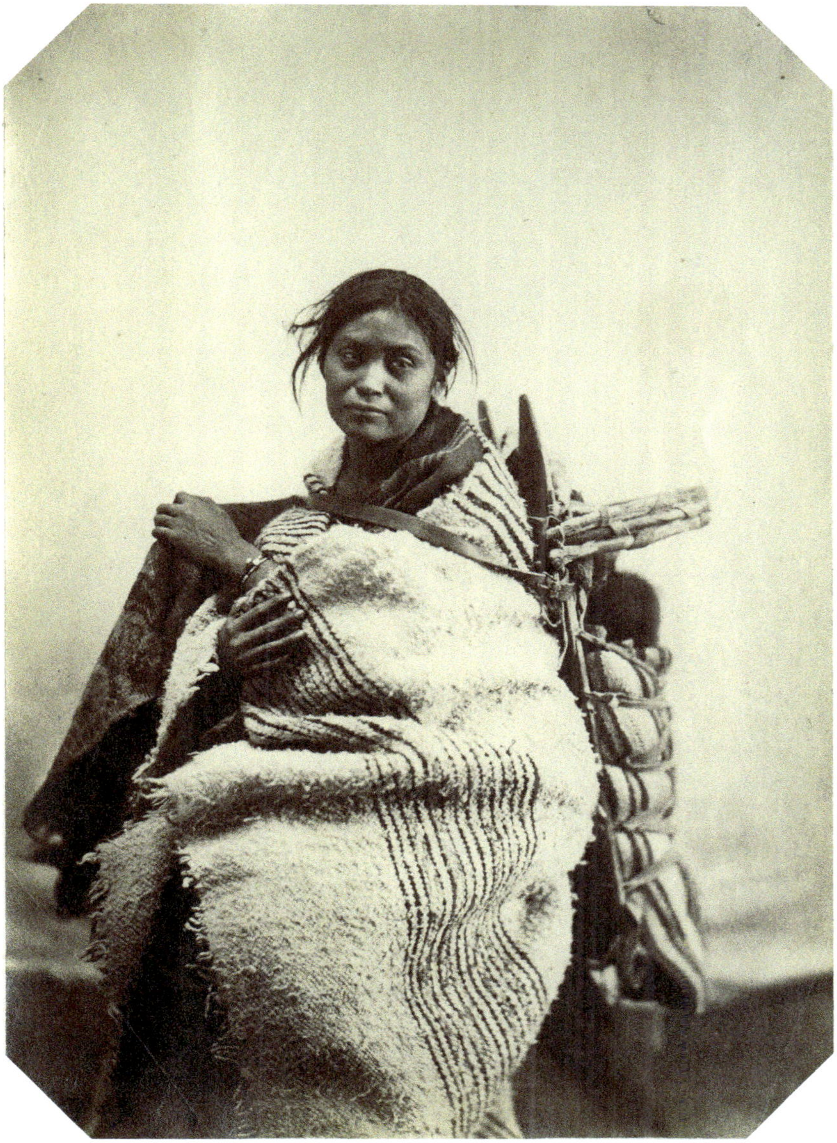

PLATE 56
Navajo woman and baby en route to or at Fort Sumner, New Mexico Territory, ca. September 1866.
PoG 003242

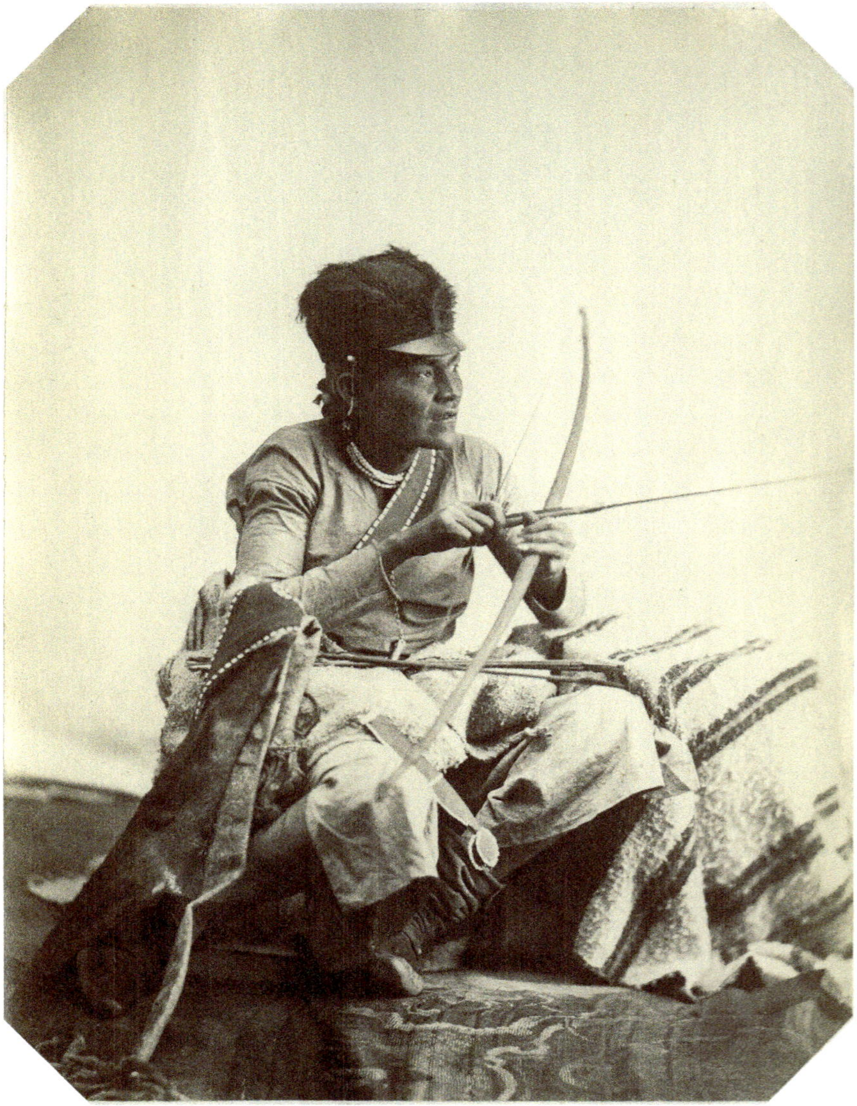

PLATE 57A
Navajo man en route to or at Fort Sumner, New Mexico Territory, ca. September 1866.
PoG 038202

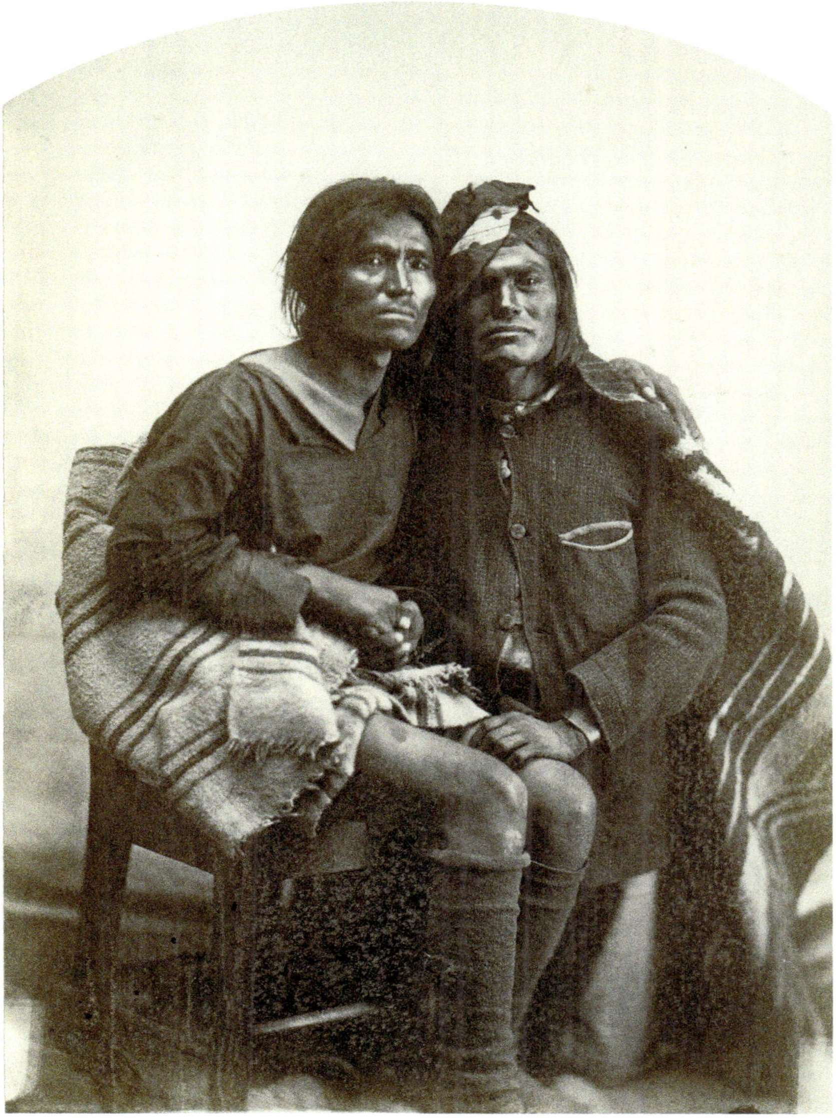

PLATE 57B
"Navajo Thieves," Navajo men en route to or at Fort Sumner, New Mexico Territory, ca. September 1866. (*Seated, right*) Possibly El Ciego, Manuelito's older brother.
PoG 038203

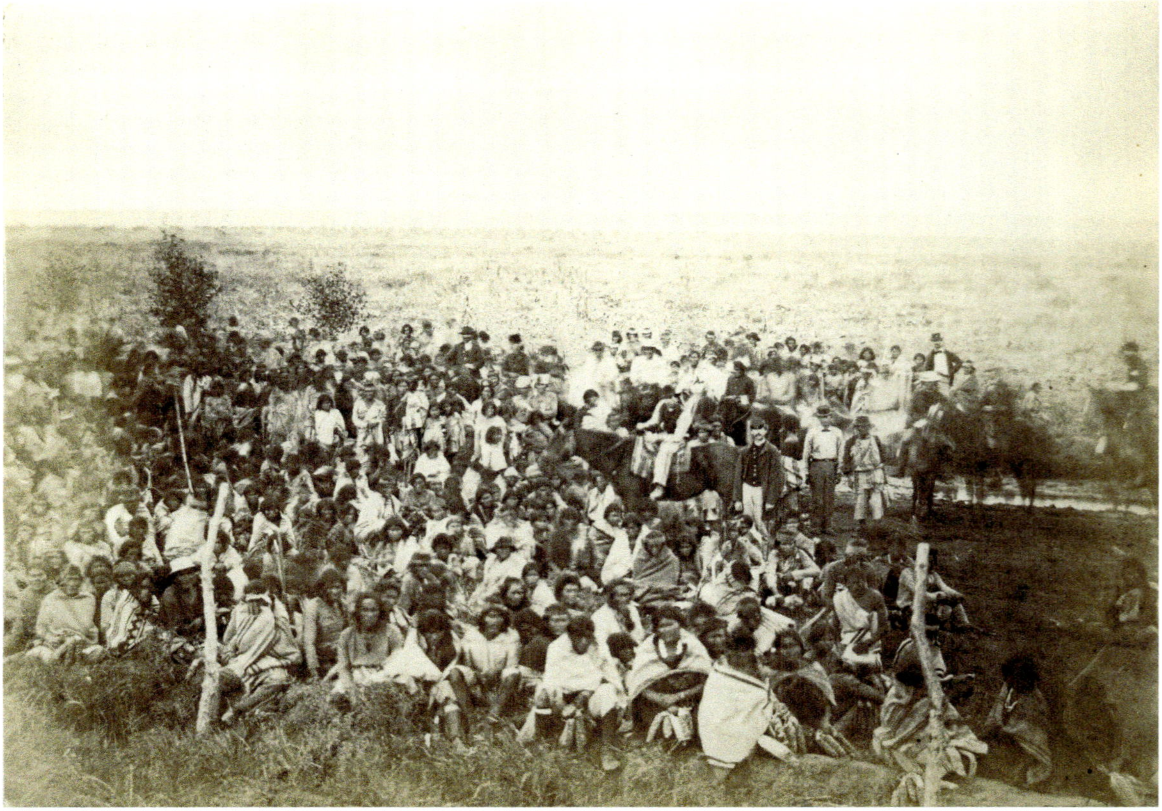

PLATE 58
Navajo Indians, possibly gathered to husk corn, at Fort Sumner, New Mexico Territory, ca. 1865.
PoG 038204

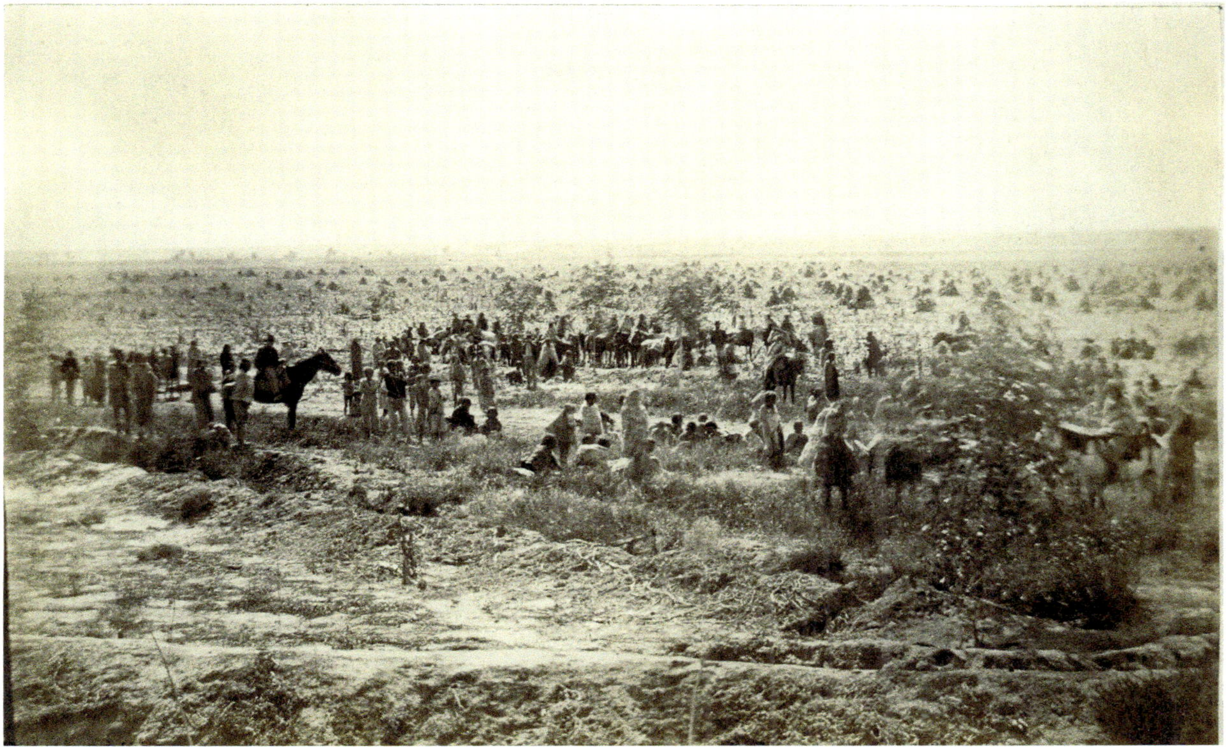

PLATE 59
Navajo Indians, possibly gathered to husk corn, at Fort Sumner, New Mexico, ca. 1865.
PoG 038205

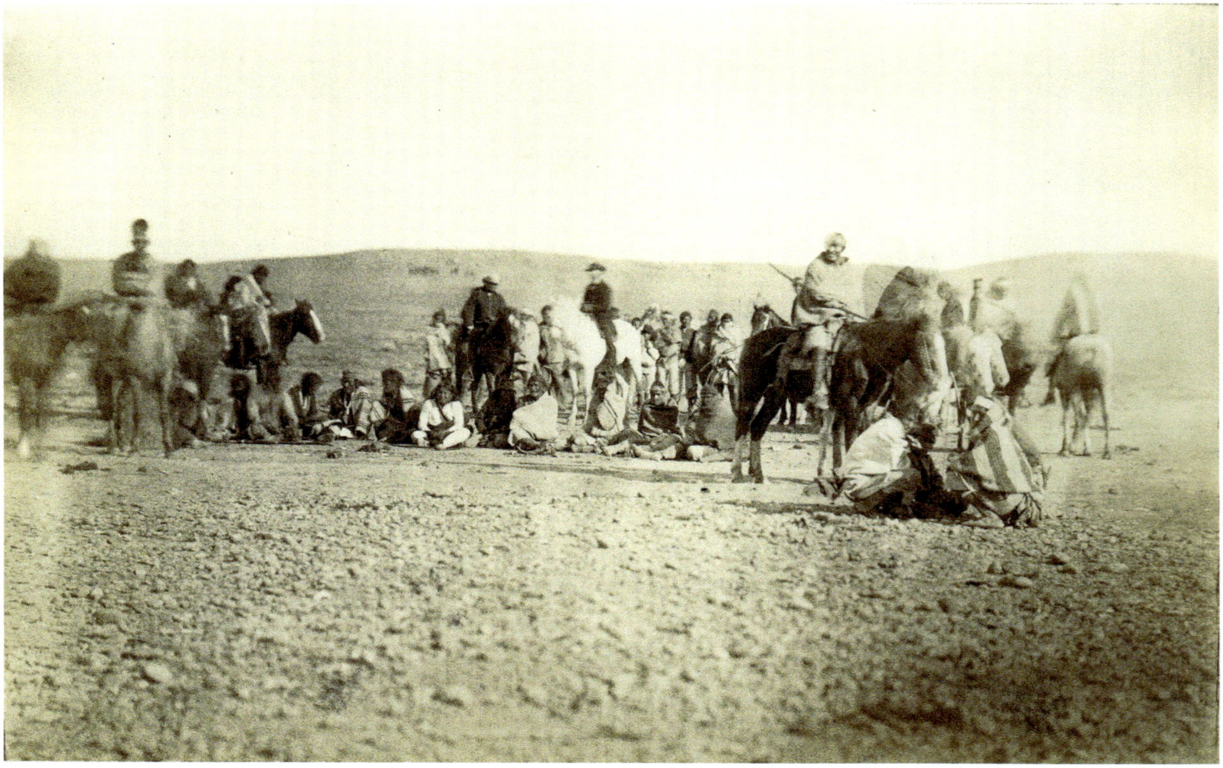

PLATE 60
A group of Navajo headmen accused of counterfeiting ration tickets, New Mexico Territory, ca. 1865.
PoG 038206

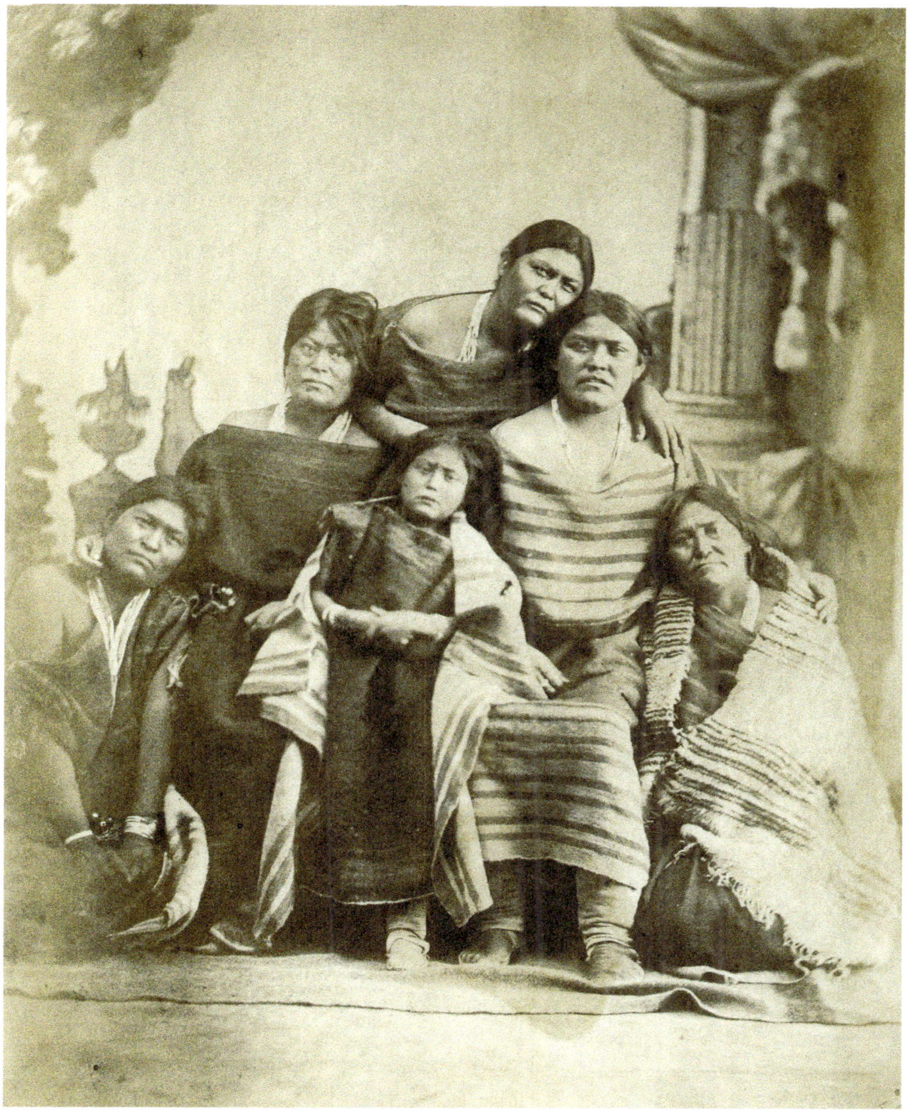

PLATE 61
Navajo women and children en route to or at Fort Sumner, New Mexico Territory, ca. September 1866.
PoG 038207

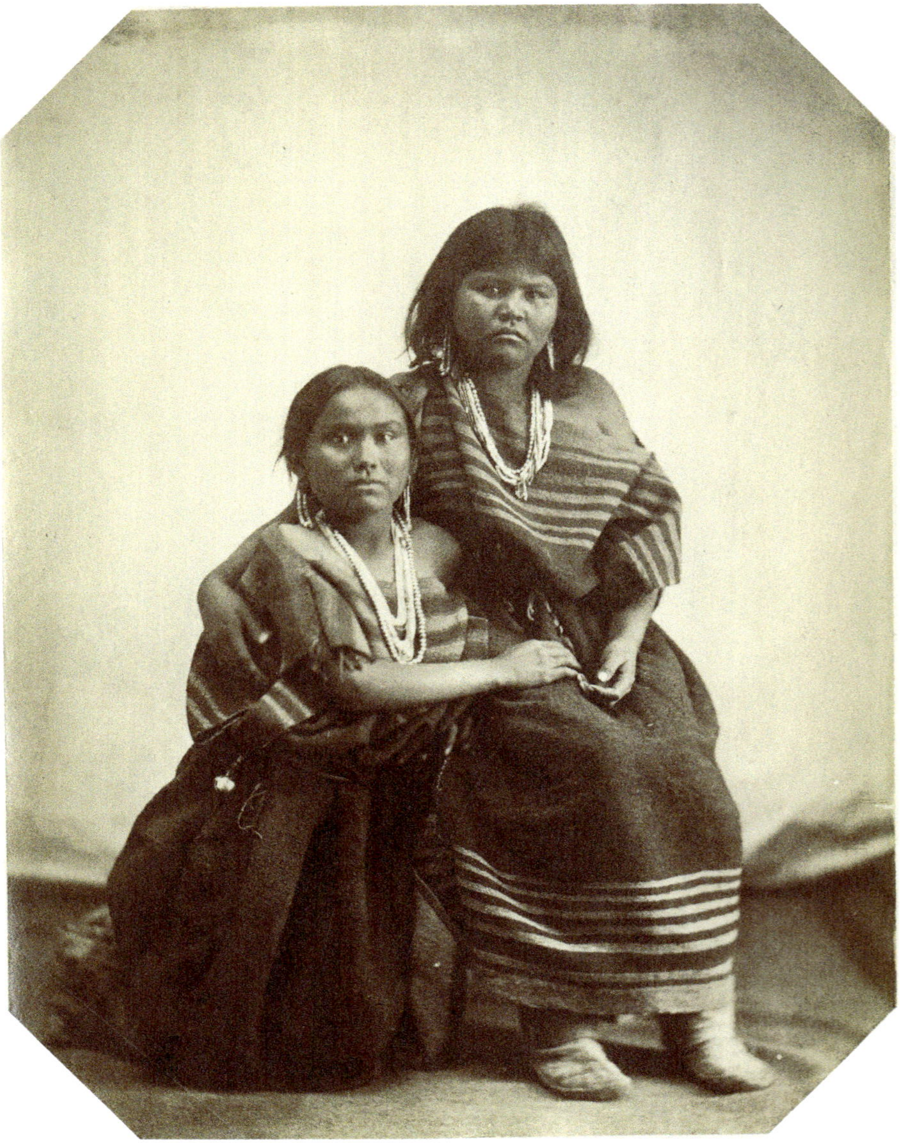

PLATE 62
Navajo girls en route to or at Fort Sumner, New Mexico Territory, ca. September 1866.
PoG 038208

NOTES

INTRODUCTION

1. The rule of Spain in Mexico ended in 1821 with the signing of the Treaty of Córdoba at the end of the Mexican War of Independence. The United States acquired lands, including the Territory of New Mexico, from Mexico in 1848 at the conclusion of the Mexican-American War with the signing of the Treaty of Guadalupe Hidalgo. New Mexico became a state on January 6, 1912.
2. The *Souvenir* album depicts events related to the Civil War, the French Intervention in Mexico, early days in the New Mexico Territory, slavery of indigenous people of the Southwest, and the Navajo internment at Bosque Redondo. Many excellent scholarly books have been published on these themes independently. For scholarship about the Civil War and Reconstruction, see Charles B. Dew, *Apostles of Disunion* (Charlottesville: University of Virginia Press, 2017); James McPherson, *Battle Cry of Freedom: The Civil War Era*; Drew Gilpin Faust, *This Republic of Suffering: Death and the American Civil War* (New York: Vintage, 2008); Eric Foner, *Reconstruction: America's Unfinished Revolution, 1863–1877* (New York: Harper and Row, 1988); and specific to New Mexico, see Jerry D. Thompson, *A Civil War History of the New Mexico Volunteers and Militia* (Albuquerque: University of New Mexico Press, 2015). Regarding the French Intervention in Mexico, see Jaspar Ridley, *Maximilian and Juárez* (London: Phoenix Press, 1992); and M. M. McAllen, *Maximilian and Carlota: Europe's Last Empire in Mexico* (San Antonio, Tex.: Trinity University Press, 2015). Regarding slavery and indigenous people of the Southwest, see James Brooks, *Captives and Cousins: Slavery, Kinship, and Community in the Southwest Borderlands* (Chapel Hill: Omohundro Institute of Early American History and Culture and University of North Carolina Press, 2011), and Andrés Reséndez, *The Other Slavery: The Uncovered Story of Indian Enslavement in America* (Boston: Houghton Mifflin Harcourt, 2016). For the Navajo Long Walk and internment at Bosque Redondo, see Jennifer Denetdale, *The Long Walk: The Forced Navajo Exile* (New York: Chelsea House, 2008), and Peter Iverson and Monty Roessel, *Diné: A History of the Navajos* (Albuquerque: University of New Mexico Press, 2003), especially chapter 2, by Peter Iverson.
3. Dauber and Pine, antiquarian book dealers of New York City (83 Fourth Avenue, and later, 66 Fifth Avenue), opened their shop in 1920, and it closed in 1983. See

Donald C. Dickenson, *Dictionary of American Antiquarian Book Dealers* (Westport, Conn.: Greenwood, 1998), 44–45.

4. Austrian Emperor Ferdinand Maximilian, during the time in which he reigned in Mexico City, was called "Maximilian I," as opposed to "Ferdinand Maximilian," which was his previous title.
5. Dates for the Apache Wars and Navajo Wars can vary, as numerous conflicts and battles are covered by these broader terms. The dates for the Apache Wars most often begin with 1861, though it could also be argued that 1851, with the conflicts that began that year, is the beginning of those wars. The dates offered here for the Navajo Wars refer to conflicts between Navajos and Americans that began with the 1846 signing of the Bear Springs Treaty, which was not considered legitimate or binding by many Navajos, and ending with the 1868 signing of the Navajo Treaty. See Peter Cozzens, *The Earth Is Weeping: The Epic Story of the Indian Wars for the American West* (New York: Vintage Books, 2017).
6. On June 1, 1868, the Navajo Treaty was signed by twenty-nine Diné "headmen," General Sherman, and Colonel Tappan, and was witnessed by a number of other army officers, an Indian agent, and an interpreter. Beginning in June 1868, after the signing of the treaty, the Diné returned to a greatly reduced portion of their ancestral lands.
7. Brian R. Hamnett, "Benito Juárez, Early Liberalism, and the Regional Politics of Oaxaca, 1828–1853," *Bulletin of Latin American Research* 10, no. 1 (1991): 3, doi:10.2307/3338561.
8. Reséndez, *The Other Slavery*, 8.
9. Andrés Reséndez, "North American Peonage," *Journal of the Civil War Era* 7, no. 4 (2017): 597–619.
10. For an overview of the Santa Fe Ring, see David L. Caffey, *Chasing the Santa Fe Ring: Power and Privilege in Territorial New Mexico* (Albuquerque: University of New Mexico Press, 2014).
11. Frederick W. Nolan, *The Lincoln County War: A Documentary History* (Santa Fe: Sunstone Press, 2009); Paul Cool, *Salt Warriors: Insurgency on the Rio Grande* (College Station: Texas A&M University Press, 2008), 5, 35–39; and W. W. Mills, *Forty Years at El Paso: 1858–1898: Recollections of War, Politics, Adventure, Events, Narratives, Sketches, etc.* (Chicago: W. B. Conkey, 1901), 30, 143, 145.
12. While the majority of the photographs in this album most certainly would have been taken in 1866, it is likely that a few, particularly some of the photographs of forts, were taken in 1865.
13. Jeff L. Rosenheim, *Photography and the American Civil War* (New York: Metropolitan Museum of Art, 2013), 22.
14. Marth A. Sandweiss, *Print the Legend: Photography and the American West* (New Haven, Conn.: Yale University Press, 2004), 124.
15. *The Universal Encyclopaedia* (New York: D. Appleton, 1895), 590.
16. Bruce Warren, *Photography: The Concise Guide* (Boston: Wadsworth/Cengage Learning, 2012), 195.
17. Michel Frizot, ed., *A New History of Photography* (Cologne: Konemann Verlags, 1999), 92, 99, 233.
18. Descriptions and weights of equipment for the process of collodion wet-plate vary. The description offered here is based on the amalgamation of two sources in relation to the *Souvenir* album itself and what type of equipment must have been necessary

to produce some of the images. Sandweiss, *Print the Legend,* 127; and David Daniels, "Photography's Wet-Plate Interlude in Arizona Territory: 1864–1880," *Journal of Arizona History* 9, no. 4 (Winter 1968): 173–74.

19. That camera is now in the collection of the Smithsonian Institution National Museum of American History, ID Number PG*000004, Accession Number 20341, Catalogue Number 4. In the spring of 1839, Samuel Morse met with Louis Daguerre in his Paris studio and saw the daguerreotype process firsthand. He wrote an article for the *New York Observer* about the invention and provided America with its first description of the process; he then returned to America with the camera. Sarah Kate Gillespie, *The Early American Daguerreotype: Cross-Currents in Art and Technology* (Cambridge, Mass.: MIT Press, 2016), 23–29.
20. Angélico Chávez, *But Time and Chance: The Story of Padre Martínez of Taos, 1793–1867* (Santa Fe: Sunstone Press, 1981); and Van Deren Coke, *Photography in New Mexico: From the Daguerreotype to the Present* (Albuquerque: University of New Mexico Press, 1979), 2.
21. Because the terrain around the capital of the New Mexican Territory was so mountainous, a railroad link connecting Santa Fe to transcontinental railway lines took a long time to get built—a spur from Lamey (at that time called Galisteo Junction) opened on February 9, 1880, finally connecting Santa Fe to the rest of the country by rail. See Marta Weigle, with Frances Levine and Louise Stiver, eds., *Telling New Mexico: A New History* (Santa Fe: Museum of New Mexico Press, 2009), 234.
22. Richard Rudisill, *Photographers of the New Mexico Territory, 1854–1912* (Santa Fe: Museum of New Mexico, 1973), 53; Coke, *Photography in New Mexico*, 2; and Peter Palmquist and Thomas Kailbourn, *Pioneer Photographers of the Far West: A Biographical Dictionary, 1840–1865* (Stanford, Calif.: Stanford University Press, 2001), 485.
23. Rudisill, *Photographers of the New Mexico Territory,* 41; and Palmquist and Kailbourn, *Pioneer Photographers of the Far West*, 391.
24. Rosenheim, *Photography and the American Civil War*, vii, 15.
25. Rebecca Solnit, *River of Shadows: Eadweard Muybridge and the Technological Wild West* (New York: Penguin Books, 2010), 42.
26. Sandweiss, *Print the Legend*, 183.
27. The photographer Nicholas Brown worked in Brady's New York studio as an operator until 1857, and George A. Gaige also worked in Brady's New York studio sometime after 1859, likely leaving for Kansas City, Missouri the same year, relocating to Albuquerque in 1861. See William Garrett Piston and Thomas Sweeney, *Portraits of Conflict: A Photographic History of Missouri in the Civil War* (Fayetteville: University of Arkansas Press, 2009), 4, 7; and *Western Journal of Commerce*, April 9, 1859, and January 4, 1861.
28. Karen Current and William R. Current, *Photography and the Old West* (New York: Abradale Press/Harry N. Abrams, in association with the Amon Carter Museum of Western Art, 1986); and Laurence E. Keefe Jr. and Dennis Inch, *The Life of a Photograph: Archival Processing, Matting, Framing, and Storage* (Boston: Focal Press, 1984), 252.

CHAPTER 1. FACES AND PLACES

1. Fort Bliss is a U.S. Army post that currently is located in the states of New Mexico and Texas. Initially, in 1848, a post was established across the Rio Grande from

El Paso del Norte, Mexico, which was occupied until 1854, when Fort Bliss was established at the post of El Paso at Magoffinsville, remaining at this location for fourteen years. In 1861, Confederate forces took the fort but abandoned it after their defeat in the Battle of Glorieta Pass and in the face of Carleton's advancing column. In 1865, the Fifth Infantry Regiment arrived at the fort and rebuilt it, as described later in this book. The Fifth Infantry was relieved of their post at Fort Bliss on August 12, 1866, by the Twenty-Fifth Infantry Regiment, a regiment of Buffalo Soldiers, who do not figure in any photographs in the *Souvenir* album, another indication of the time frame of the photographs. After Fort Bliss was severely flooded in May of 1867, it was subsequently relocated to Camp Concordia. See Leon C. Metz, *Desert Army: Fort Bliss on the Texas Border* (El Paso: Mangan Books, 1995).

2. Los Pinos, at Bosque Farms, New Mexico, originally known as Camp Peralta (1860–62), was a Union quartermaster depot and remount station (for the provision of horses to army units that needed new mounts) from 1862 to 1866. Fort Craig (1853–85), located along the Camino Real in Socorro County, was the largest fort in the Southwest in 1861, and the important Civil War battle of Valverde happened very near this fort. Fort Marcy (1846–94), built on a hill, was established just after the Mexican-American War began (1846–48) and just after General Stephen W. Kearny took Santa Fe.
3. What today is El Paso, Texas, is here called Franklin to avoid confusion with El Paso del Norte (now Ciudad Juárez, Mexico). Franklin was an early American settlement in Texas, established after the Treaty of Guadalupe Hidalgo that ended the Mexican-American War. Franklin was officially renamed El Paso in 1852, when a post office opened there. The name El Paso was further established when in 1859 Anson Mills put the name on a map. However, confusion over the name of the city would remain until 1888, when El Paso del Norte on the Mexican side of the Rio Grande was renamed Ciudad Juárez. See Wilbert Timmons, *James Wiley Magoffin: Don Santiago—El Paso Pioneer* (El Paso: Texas Western Press, 1984), 8.
4. James F. Meline, *Two Thousand Miles on Horseback, Santa Fe and Back: A Summer Tour through Kansas, Nebraska, Colorado, and New Mexico in the Year 1866* (New York: Hurd and Houghton, 1867), 111.
5. University of Arizona Libraries, Bloom Southwest Jewish Archives Photograph Collection, Box 7, photograph: "Original store of Samuel Schutz and his brother (Franklin [now El Paso]; ca. 1865)." This image is the same as Plate 33. "Samuel Schutz Passes Away," *Albuquerque Evening Citizen,* March 5, 1906, 5; Gretchen Dickey and Sara Flores, "Solomon C. Schutz Helped Bring Law and Order to El Paso," *Borderlands* 23 (2004–5), https://epcc.libguides.com/c.php?g=754275&p=5406060.
6. Andrea Cuarterolo, "The Social Construction of the Photographic Portrait in 19th-Century Rio de la Plata," *Oxford Research Encyclopedia of Latin American History*, December 2015, http://latinamericanhistory.oxfordre.com/view/10.1093/acrefore/9780199366439.001.0001/acrefore-9780199366439-e-105.
7. It is true that in this era, photographers sold equipment, props, negatives, and prints to other photographers, but the poor quality of the painted backdrop makes it an unlikely candidate for reuse by another photographer. Furthermore, an appearance of one of the women portrayed in the second grouping in this set (plate 51) in a portrait found in another collection, set against, yet again, this same backdrop

(discussed later in the book) makes it even more likely that all three groupings in this set are related and were taken by the same photographer or team of photographers.

8. Though research and publications about the French Intervention in Mexico have been undertaken and circulated, aside from the recent publication of Michael Hogan's *Abraham Lincoln and Mexico: A History of Courage, Intrigue and Unlikely Friendships* (Guadalajara, Jalisco, Mexico: Fondo Editorial Universitario, 2016), Robert Ryal Miller is the only scholar to have written to any great degree about the participation of the U.S. Army and American involvement in the French Intervention in Mexico. See Miller, "Arms across the Border: United States Aid to Juárez during the French Intervention in Mexico," *Transactions of the American Philosophical Society* 63, no. 6 (1973): 38, doi:10.2307/1006291. Regarding the larger topic of the French Intervention in Mexico, in addition to the publications listed in footnote number two, see Jack Dabbs, *The French Army in Mexico, 1861–1867: A Study in Military Government* (The Hague: Mouton, 1963); Alfred Jackson Hanna and Kathryn Abbey Hanna, *Napoleon III and Mexico: American Triumph over Mexico* (Chapel Hill: University of North Carolina Press, 1971); David Crook, *The North, the South and the Powers, 1861–65* (New York: Wiley, 1974); José Villalpando, *El juicio de la historia: Maximiliano: Los hechos frente a nuestro presente* (Barcelona, Spain: Grijalbo, 2017); and Michele Cunningham, *Mexico and the Foreign Policy of Napoleon III* (New York: Palgrave Macmillan, 2001).
9. For example, regarding dates, some of the titles or ranks given to the military men help bracket dates, while the moniker "Pistol Bullet" on Manuelito's portrait (plate 48) or the use of the word "Thieves" on the Navajo double portrait of men (plate 57b) offers insight into how the person making the annotations might have viewed the sitters, as enemy captives for example.
10. Willard J. Brown, *The Signal Corps, U.S.A. in the War of the Rebellion* (Baltimore, Md.: Butternut and Blue, 1996).
11. General Order No. 3, as found in "General Orders, Special Orders, and Circulars of the War Department and Quartermaster Department, 1832–36, 1860–69, and 1904–20" (entry 195) in Record Group 92, National Archives and Records Administration (hereafter NARA). By which all officers of the Quartermaster's Department were to provide drawings of all the hospitals, barracks, quarters, or other buildings. Those "drawings" could be a "sketch, either made by hand, or by the photograph. . . . If a photograph, it should be mounted on stiff paper, but should be upon thin paper." The thin paper on stiff paper indicated an albumen print was required. Further indication of the purpose of this order is found in the Annual Report of the Quartermaster General, where it states that it is hoped this information can be obtained and compiled, "for which an accurate statement of the number, cost and proceeds of sale of such structures, as also of the amount of rents paid for buildings used for the public service, may be prepared. It was proposed to obtain this information, in part, from the investigations of the officers recommended to examine the accounts of officers of this department at the treasury." *Report of the Quartermaster General of the United States Army to the Secretary of War, for the Year Ending June 30, 1865, 1898–1900* (Washington, D.C.: Government Printing Office, 1865), 176.
12. William Blackmore Collection, Album 9, #AM, A9.91, British Museum, London.
13. See the "J. G. Gaige" file in the photographer's files at the New Mexico History Museum, Palace of the Governors Photo Archives.

14. During research for this book, I located and contacted Jane Blyth and Jennifer Schmandt, the great-granddaughters of Charles T. Jennings and daughters of Joanna and Jon Blyth. They provided helpful information about the photograph that was photocopied in the Gaige file in the Palace of the Governor's Archives (but at the time of this printing, it has not been located in the Museum of New Mexico collection, where it was donated), and about related objects that their parents, along with their uncle William Charles Jennings and their aunt Eleanor Savastano, donated to the Museum of Indian Arts and Culture in Santa Fe, New Mexico. The record number for a Navajo weaving donated by the Blyths/Jennings/Savastano is MIAC object number 54594.01. See also note 45, this chapter.
15. Five of the Navajo portraits (plates 47, 48, 55, 56, and 62) that are found as copy prints at the Library of Congress seem to be the sources for numerous commercial reproductions of these images on items such as posters, shower curtains, mugs, pillows, yoga mats, and more, which are available for purchase on the internet through a number of online retailers.
16. In the American Philosophical Society Library, the image number is graphics 3043, APSimg5478; it is part of the A. Zeno Shindler American Indian Photograph Collection (Mss.970.1.Sh6).
17. Anthony Hamber, *Collecting the American West: The Rise and Fall of William Blackmore* (East Knoyle, Salisbury, U.K.: Hobnob Press, 2010), 154, 241–45.
18. Ibid., 64.
19. Ibid., 293; Dolores Kilgo, *Likeness and Landscape: Thomas M. Easterly and the Art of the Daguerreotype* (St. Louis: Missouri Historical Society Press, 1994), 141. For the transfer of Blackmore papers and other items from New Mexico by the anthropologist Barbara Freire-Marreco Aitken to the Historical Society of New Mexico, now part of the Fray Angélico Chávez History Library, see Mary Ellen Blair, *A Life Well Led: The Biography of Barbara Freire-Marreco Aitken, British Anthropologist* (Santa Fe: Sunstone Press, 2008), 276.
20. Hamber, *Collecting the American West,* 8, 91.
21. The identifying number for this image in the Taylor scrapbook at the National Anthropological Archives is NAA INV 01605601. Also at the archives, the identifying number of the glass plate negative for a single image of the same man, labeled "Barboncito," is NAA INV 06402000 OPPS NEG 02441.
22. Virginia M. Simmons, *The Ute Indians of Utah, Colorado, and New Mexico* (Boulder: University Press of Colorado, 2000), 104, 110, 114, 147, 170–1, 213. The story behind Duhem's photographs of Pfeiffer is that on August 18, 1869, a group of prospectors, under the command of Col. Pfeiffer, left Fort Garland in southern Colorado to prospect for gold and precious metals. Pfeiffer, who had trouble with his vision, got separated from the group and got very lost. He was found several days later, wandering on foot, by none other than Constant Duhem, who was out taking landscape photographs. The portrait of Pfeiffer in figure 10 depicts the moment of that rescue. Duhem brought Pfeiffer to safety in Denver, as reported in the article "Lost Prospectors," *Carson Daily Appeal* (Carson City, Nev.), October 29, 1869, 2.
23. National Anthropological Archives, *The James E. Taylor Album,* 114 (4605–223), http://collections.si.edu/search/results.htm?q=set_name:%22James+E.+Taylor+scrapbook+of+the+American+West+1863-1900%22.
24. The identifying number for this image in the Peabody Museum of Archaeology and Ethnology at Harvard University is 2004.29.4270.

25. The complexities of these various copies of photographs housed in the archives of the Smithsonian were first investigated and laid out in Paula Richardson Fleming, *Native American Photography at the Smithsonian: The Shindler Catalogue* (Washington, D.C.: Smithsonian Books, 2003).
26. The identifying number for this image in the Peabody Museum of Archaeology and Ethnology at Harvard University is 2004.29.4244.
27. Margaret Schevill, "From the Desk of Washington Matthews," *Journal of American Folklore* 73, no. 290 (1960): 318.
28. The identifying number for this image in the Netherlands Photo Museum is WMR-900588_NB.
29. Charles T. Jennings enrolled in the First Regiment of the California Volunteer Cavalry in Stockton, Calif., on March 11, 1863, joining at the rank of second lieutenant, and a couple of months later, transferred to Company M. He was promoted to first lieutenant and regimental quartermaster in December of the same year. See California, Adjutant General's Office, *Records of California Men in the War of the Rebellion, 1861 to 1867* (Sacramento, Calif.: Sacramento State Office, 1890), 142.
30. James Bailey Blackshear, *Fort Bascom: Soldiers, Comancheros, and Indians in the Canadian River Valley* (Norman: University of Oklahoma Press, 2016), 136–7.
31. In the process of researching this book, the descendants of Charles T. Jennings were located and contacted. Two of his great-great-granddaughters and one of his great-grandsons recalled that two blankets Charles T. Jennings acquired while he had his trading post at Hatch's Ranch were donated to the Museum of Indian Arts and Culture (MIAC) in Santa Fe. The record for one of the blankets, object number 54594.01, indicates that "Jennings family oral history claims this chief's blanket was Manuelito's. Collected by Charles T. Jennings, great, great grandfather of the donors, at Fort Sumner." The Charles T. Jennings diary, a copy of which is also in the MIAC collection, relates that on July 11, 1867, he received a Navajo blanket, which could very well be the blanket now at MIAC. Most likely the photographs belonging to Charles T. Jennings were also donated to a museum in New Mexico, though they have yet to be located.
32. Lieutenant John Gaw Meem (grandfather of the architect) is found in the Confederate Muster Roll, 1861, Record Group 109, NARA Catalog ID 586957, Publication Number M324.
33. *Bury My Heart at Wounded Knee,* written by Dee Alexander Brown in 1970, is a work of nonfiction about Native Americans in the American Southwest in the late nineteenth century. Brown discusses the Navajos in his first chapter, addressing roughly the same time period as discussed in this book.
34. Bradley W. Richards and C. R. Savage, *The Savage View: Charles Savage, Pioneer Mormon Photographer* (Nevada City, Calif.: Carl Mautz Vintage Photography and Publishing, 1995).
35. James E. Babbitt, "From Albuquerque to Tucson in 1867: The Kansas Pacific Railway Survey Photographs of William A. Bell," *Journal of Arizona History* 39, no. 3 (Autumn 1998), 289–306.
36. A letter from General J. Carleton, headquartered in Santa Fe, orders Capt. William Hemphill Bell, who had been serving at Fort Union, to report to Santa Fe, to take a post that reports in Santa Fe but is stationed at Fort Sumner, "where, until further orders he will be charged with the especial duty of providing subsistence for all Navajo and Apache Indians who may now be at the reservation at the Bosque

Redondo, or who are, or may be, *en route* to that point from the country where they are taken, or voluntarily give themselves up." *Condition of the Indian Tribes: Report of the Joint Special Committee Appointed under Joint Resolution of March 3, 1865* (Washington, D.C.: Government Printing Office, 1867), 240.

37. James C. Faris, *Navajo and Photography: A Critical History of the Representation of an American People* (Salt Lake City: University of Utah Press, 1996), 53–91.
38. Ibid., 63–67.
39. Coke, *Photography in New Mexico*, 2; and Palmquist and Kailbourn, *Pioneer Photographers of the Far West*, 126–28.
40. Piston and Sweeney, *Portraits of Conflict*, 4.
41. Matthew J. Gallman and Gary W. Gallagher, eds., *Lens of War: Exploring Iconic Photographs of the Civil War* (Athens: University of Georgia Press, 2015), 181.
42. Palmquist and Kailbourn, *Pioneer Photographers of the Far West*, 255, 256; Peter Palmquist and Thomas Kailbourn, *Pioneer Photographers from the Mississippi to the Continental Divide: A Biographical Dictionary, 1839–1865* (Stanford, Calif.: Stanford University Press, 2005), 272; and Piston and Sweeney, *Portraits of Conflict*, 7.
43. *Santa Fe Gazette* (Santa Fe, N.Mex.), November 15, 1862, 2, c1.
44. Palmquist, and Kailbourn, *Pioneer Photographers of the Far West*, 255, 256; Palmquist, and Kailbourn, *Pioneer Photographers from the Mississippi to the Continental Divide*, 272.
45. Piston and Sweeney, *Portraits of Conflict*, 7.
46. *Western Journal of Commerce*, April 9, 1859; January 4, 1861.
47. Palmquist and Kailbourn, *Pioneer Photographers of the Far West*, 255.
48. Ibid.
49. Ibid., 255, 256.
50. *The Weekly Arizonian* (Tucson), July 10, 1869, p. 3: "Died—J. G. Gaige, the efficient photographic artist and accomplished gentleman, (illegible) left this city a few weeks since, died at Camp Goodwin on the 2nd inst."
51. Jeremy W. Pye, "Living on the Border: Health, Environment, and Multiculturalism in 19th Century Tucson" (PhD diss., University of Florida, 2013), 330.
52. *Journal of the Legislative Council of the Territory of New Mexico: of the session begun and held in this city of Santa Fe, Territory of New Mexico, on Monday the second day of December,* A.D. *one thousand eight hundred and sixty-seven, it being the seventeenth Legislative Assembly for the said territory* (Santa Fe: Manderfield and Tucker, Public Printers, 1866), 250.
53. A copy of Smith's diary, long missing (see Palmquist and Kailbourn, *Pioneer Photographers of the Far West*, 256n4, for "A. G. Gaige" for mention of Smith's missing diary), was recovered during research for this book at the Palace of the Governors Photo Archives.
54. Palmquist and Kailbourn, *Pioneer Photographers of the Far West*, 507.
55. Ibid.
56. *Western Journal of Commerce*, April 9, 1859; June 10, 1866.
57. "Death Takes C. L. Duhem," *Oroville Mercury* (Oroville, Calif.), April 26, 1933, 1. This obituary contains a good deal of detailed and fascinating information, some of it uncorroborated.
58. Two of Constant Duhem's roll cards, from November 27, 1864, show him mustering out in Las Cruces, being "entitled to one hundred dollars bounty, as per act of Congress." Carded Records Showing Military Service of Soldiers Who Fought in

Volunteer Organizations during the American Civil War, compiled 1890–1912, documenting the period 1861–1866, Record Group 94, NARA Catalog ID 300398.

59. Richard H. Orton, *Records of California Men in the War of the Rebellion, 1861 to 1867* (Charleston, S.C.: Nabu Press, 2010), 414 (note that Victor Duhem's last name is misspelled as "Duhern, Victor"). Victor Duhem's U.S. Army Muster Roll, Carded Records Showing Military Service of Soldiers Who Fought in Volunteer Organizations during the American Civil War, compiled 1890–1912, documenting the period 1861–1866, Record Group 94, NARA Catalog ID 300398. An enlistment ledger with both Constant's and Victor's reenlistment is noted consecutively in the ledger. Victor Duhem's U.S. Army pension files also indicate his two enrollments. See Registers of Enlistments in the United States Army, compiled 1798–1914, Record Group 94, NARA Catalog ID 575272; and Organization Index to Pension Files of Veterans Who Served between 1861 and 1900, compiled 1949–1949, Documenting the Period 1861–1942, Record Group 15, NARA Catalog ID 2588825.
60. Income Tax Records of the Civil War Years, New Mexico, 1862–70, 1 roll, NARA M782.
61. The Duhem photograph of Brotherton is in the collection of historian J. Dale West and originally appeared in "'Regulars, By God!,'" *Military Images* 24, no. 1 (August 2002): 8, http://www.jstor.org/stable/44033957. The Duhem brothers had a studio in Albuquerque from August 1866 to July 1867. An account of the departure of Manuelito and his followers from Fort Wingate is found in a letter from Capt. Edmond Butler, Commander at Fort Wingate, to Maj. Cyrus H. DeForrest at Headquarters in Santa Fe on September 9, 1866. See J. Lee Correll, *Through White Men's Eyes: A Contribution to Navajo History: A Chronological Record of the Navajo People from Earliest Times to the Treaty of June 1, 1868*, vol. 5. (Window Rock, Ariz.: Navajo Heritage Center, 1979), 368.
62. James Aarons, *Index to the Reports of Committees of the House of Representatives for the First and Second Sessions of the Forty-Sixth Congress 1879–'80: In Six Volumes* (Washington, D.C.: Government Printing Office, 1880), report No. 633. Victor Duhem's witness statement is in Papers Relating to Citizens, compiled 1861–1867, Record Group 109, NARA M345, Documents Relating to Civilians Who Came into Contact with the Army during the Civil War, including Deserters, Thieves, and Spies, Roll 0032.
63. Boylan's testimony, Papers Relating to Citizens, compiled 1861–1867, Record Group 109, M345, NARA Catalog ID 2133278; King's affidavit is in Documents Relating to Civilians Who Came into Contact with the Army during the Civil War, including Deserters, Thieves, and Spies, Roll 0032.
64. Aarons, *Index to the Reports of Committees of the House of Representatives*, report no. 633; and Boylan's testimony, Papers Relating to Citizens, compiled 1861–1867, Record Group 109, M345, NARA Catalog ID 2133278, Documents Relating to Civilians Who Came into Contact with the Army during the Civil War, including Deserters, Thieves, and Spies, Roll 0032.
65. Photograph of the Duhem brothers' studio by the Duhem brothers in the collection of the Denver Public Library, Photo album 139, Identifier: F10848 DPLW. The record for the photo also gives the address of the studio.
66. "Bankruptcy Notice," *Rocky Mountain News* (Denver), January 3, 1877.

67. "C. Duhem, photographer, has succeeded in making an admirable picture of the yard and garden of Hon. H. S. Stevens. The yard beyond doubt is one of the most handsome in Tucson," *Arizona Weekly Citizen* (Tucson), December 3, 1882, p. 4; and *Arizona Daily Star* (Tucson), July 30, 1882, p. 4.
68. *Arizona Daily Star* (Tucson), May 11, 1883, p. 4.
69. Record Group 94, Catalog ID 575272, Registers of Enlistments in the United States Army, compiled 1798–1914, Roll MIUSA1798-102908, Roll number 49, NARA.
70. Herman ten Kate, Pieter Hovens, William J. Orr, and Louis A. Hieb, *Travels and Researches in Native North America, 1882–1883* (Albuquerque: University of New Mexico Press, 2004), 202.
71. Ibid., 215.
72. The information on Alfredo Laurent's date and place of birth comes from a private collector.
73. Ten Kate et al., *Travels and Researches*, 164.
74. It is not clear if Laurent ever worked in Tucson, though he did partner with a photographer named Hodapp, and some of their photographs are of a well-known Tucson family. The portraits that Laurent and Hodapp made are of the Ronstadt family. Fred (né Federico José María) Ronstadt was from Sonora, but he moved to Tucson in 1882 to work with the wagon makers Dalton and Vasquez (originally from Sonora, arriving in Tucson via California), suggesting at the very least that there was some sort of circulation and social network of people between Tucson and Sonora and that Laurent and Hodapp were part of that. Some family photographs of the Ronstadt family, taken by Laurent, are located at the University of Arizona. Observations about Laurent are from Hannah Abelbeck, of the Palace of the Governors Photo Archives, New Mexico History Museum, who first noticed two of the *Souvenir* images in a book from the Netherlands. Hodapp (first name unknown) partnered at one time with Laurent, and then later with William Zuber, active initially in California, to form Hodapp y Zuber on Calle de Diana across from the Herrería Francesa (French Blacksmiths) in Mazatlán, Sinaloa, Mexico. Zuber likely bought Laurent's business after his death in 1886. The work of Hodapp and Laurent was also highlighted in the exhibition *"Memorias de plata y luz" Rumbo a la Fototeca de Sonora* that was part of the Fotoseptiembre 2015 festival held at the Instituto Sonorense de Cultura. See Palmquist and Kailbourn, *Pioneer Photographers from the Mississippi to the Continental Divide*, 611; and Anneke Groenveld and Pieter Hovens, *Odagot: Indianen Gefotografeerd, 1860–1920* (Amsterdam: Fragment; Rotterdam: Museum voor Volkenkunde, 1992); and *El Fronterizo* (Tucson), 1881, 1.
75. Another possibility, much smaller, is that if Gaige is the photographer, Laurent obtained his negatives either directly from Gaige or through the Duhems, who could have been in possession of Gaige's negatives, which were sold after his death.

CHAPTER 2. GOVERNMENT IN EXILE

1. Inventory of the I. S. Bartlett Papers, 1866–circa 1964, Collection No. 00979, American Heritage Center, University of Wyoming, https://rmoa.unm.edu/docviewer.php?docId=wyu-ah00979.xml.
2. Ichabod S. Bartlett, "President Juárez at Old El Paso," in *Bulletin of the Pan American Union*, vol. 41 (Washington, D.C.: Union of the American Republics, 1915), 648, 656, 658.

3. Ibid., 643–46.
4. Dana B. Shoaf, "'For Every Man Who Wore the Blue': The Military Order of the Loyal Legion of the United States and the Charges of Elitism after the Civil War," in *Union Soldiers and the Northern Home Front: Wartime Experiences, Postwar Adjustments,* ed. Paul A. Cimballa and Randall M. Miller, 463–75 (New York, N.Y.: Fordham University Press, 2002), 465.
5. It should be noted that in the MOLLUS-Massachusetts Commandery Civil War Photographs Collection, there are portraits of both Clark and Carleton. The portrait of Carleton in the MOLLUS album is identical to the portrait found as a negative in the Library of Congress collection (figure 7), which also appears to be from the same sitting as the Carleton portrait in the *Souvenir* album (plate 7).
6. Mary Dowell Phillips Memoirs, MS 031, C. L. Sonnichsen Special Collections Department, The University of Texas at El Paso Library.
7. Nancy Hamilton, *Ben Dowell: El Paso's First Mayor* (El Paso: Texas Western Press, 1976), 5–59.
8. Ibid.
9. Nancy Hamilton, "Memoirs Describe Elegant 1866 El Paso Ball," *El Paso Herald-Post*, August 10, 1973, p. B1.
10. Ichabod Bartlett, "When Juarez Rallied His Men in El Paso to Free Mexico," *El Paso Herald*, June 5, 1909, 1–29.
11. The history of Fort Bliss begins with the stationing of U.S. Army troops at Coon's Ranch in 1848, established to defend the newly authenticated border with Mexico and to protect settlers and those bound for California during the gold rush from Indian attack. In 1854, the command was established in Magoffinsville, and was named Fort Bliss that same year. In 1861, the fort was surrendered to the Confederates, but it was retaken by the Union Army in mid-1862 by Carleton and his California Column. After the reoccupation, rebuilding of the fort began, though it was ultimately destroyed for good, when it washed away in a flood in 1867.
12. Hamilton, "Memoirs Describe Elegant 1866 El Paso Ball," p. B1.
13. Ibid.
14. Bartlett, "President Juarez at Old El Paso," 641–59
15. The list of those who attended included some of the most important names in southwestern history from this era, from both sides of the border, including Mariano and Carmen Samaniego; Juan Ruiz; the Daguerre family; Colonel James Albert Zabriskie and his wife, Juana Adelaida (Stephenson) Zabriskie; Mrs. Leonor Percy, daughter of Hugh Stephenson, renowned trader and businessman, and wife of Frederick Augustus Percy; Mrs. Elena (Miranda) Stephenson; Mrs. Carmelita (Magoffin) Lightner; Máximo Aranda; the family of Rómulo Varela (also spelled Barela), of the Rómulo Barela Land Grant; Albert A. French and his wife, Bernancia (Stephenson) French; José María Uranga and family; Anson Mills; Henry J. Cuniffe and his wife, Francisca Lujan Cuniffe. Hamilton, "Memoirs Describe Elegant 1866 El Paso Ball," p. B1.
16. Cool, *Salt Warriors*, 35.
17. Ibid., 5, 35–39; and Mills, *Forty Years at El Paso*, 30, 143, 145.
18. Oscar J. Martínez, *Border Boom Town: Ciudad Juárez since 1848* (Austin: University of Texas Press, 2011), 21–23.
19. The second edition of Mills' *Forty Years,* appendix IV, has an image, courtesy of "Mrs. Evelyn Rosen," with the caption: "This rare photograph presents to Benito

Juárez, Henry J. Cuniffe, W. W. Mills and two unidentified men playing cards. Cuniffe is seated left, Mills follows and Don Benito in the center," though the person in the center is clearly not Juárez and is perhaps José María Uranga. W. W. Mills, *Forty Years at El Paso: 1858–1898: Recollections of War, Politics, Adventure, Events, Narratives, Sketches, Etc.* (Chicago: W. B. Conkey, 1962), 198–99.

20. Nancy Hamilton, "Pioneer Wagon Train Operator Rescued E. P. Caravan," *El Paso Herald-Post*, January 27, 1974, p. B1.
21. Ibid., 29.
22. Cool, *Salt Warriors*, 36.
23. Gordon Owen, *The Two Alberts: Fountain and Fall* (Las Cruces: Yucca Tree Press, 1996), 42.
24. Ibid.
25. Roderic Ai Camp, ed., *The Oxford Handbook of Mexican Politics* (New York: Oxford University Press), 43.
26. Jay Kinsbruner and Erick D. Langer, *Encyclopedia of Latin American History and Culture* (Detroit: Charles Scribner's Sons, 2008), 3:51.
27. Miller, "Arms across the Border," 5, 10, 13–14.
28. Hamnett, "Benito Juárez," 5–6.
29. Peter Guardion, *The Time of Liberty: Popular Political Culture in Oaxaca, 1750–1850* (Durham, N.C.: Duke University Press, 2005), 213–16; Hamnett, "Benito Juárez," 5–6; Kathryn Sloan, *Runaway Daughters: Seduction, Elopement, and Honor in Nineteenth-Century Mexico* (Albuquerque: University of New Mexico Press, 2008), 24–25.
30. Hamnett, "Benito Juárez," 4.
31. Kinsbruner and Langer, *Encyclopedia of Latin American History and Culture*, 3:52–53.
32. Ridley, *Maximilian and* Juárez, 73.
33. Kinsbruner and Langer, *Encyclopedia of Latin American History and Culture*, 3:183.
34. Hamnett, "Benito Juárez," 4.
35. Gorhamm D. Abbot, *Mexico and the United States: Their Mutual Relations and Common Interests: With Portraits on Steel of Juárez and Romero, and Colored Maps* (New York: G. P. Putnam and Son, 1869), 171.
36. Hamnett, "Benito Juárez," 5; and Abbot, *Mexico and the United States*, 171–73.
37. Abbot, *Mexico and the United States*, 173.
38. Frank A. Knapp, *The Life of Sebastián Lerdo de Tejada, 1823–1889: A Study of Influence and Obscurity* (New York: Greenwood Press, 1968).
39. Kinsbruner and Langer, *Encyclopedia of Latin American History and Culture*, 3:404, 409; and Donna L. Chollett, *Neoliberalism, Social Exclusion, and Social Movements: Resistance and Dissent in Mexico's Sugar Industry* (Lanham, Md.: Lexington Books, 2013), 35.
40. Brian Hamnett, "The Comonfort Presidency, 1855–1857," *Bulletin of Latin American Research* 15, no. 1 (1996): 81–100, doi:10.1111/j.1470-9856.1996.tb00023.x; and Kinsbruner and Langer, *Encyclopedia of Latin American History and Culture*, 3:175.
41. Jesús González Ortega, *The Presidency of Mexico: Protest of General Jesus Gonzales Ortega, President of the Supreme Court of Justice against the Decrees of Senor Benito Juárez, Ex-president of the Mexican Republic, Issued November 8th,*

1865, and His Address to the Mexican Nation, to Which Are Appended Letters in Ratification of His Position (New York: Russell's American Steam Printing House, 1866); and Kinsbruner and Langer, *Encyclopedia of Latin American History and Culture,* 3:175.

42. McAllen, *Maximilian and Carlota*, 367, 381.
43. Kinsbruner and Langer, *Encyclopedia of Latin American History and Culture,* 3:175.
44. Ibid., 4:51.
45. Ridley, *Maximilian and Juárez*, 73.
46. "The Siege and Fall of Puebla," *New York Times*, June 13, 1863; and Abbot, *Mexico and the United States*, 150, 151.
47. Abbot, *Mexico and the United States*, 150, 151.
48. Hogan, *Abraham Lincoln and Mexico*, 144, 147–48; and Miller, "Arms across the Border," 5, 10, 13–14.
49. Hogan, *Abraham Lincoln and Mexico*, 134–39.
50. Miller, "Arms across the Border," 7.
51. Hogan, *Abraham Lincoln and Mexico*, 141–42.
52. Ibid.
53. Miller, "Arms across the Border," 11.

CHAPTER 3. HARDSHIP AND GREED

1. George H. Pettis, "The California Column," in *The Stone Idols of New Mexico: A Description of Those Belonging to the Historical Society,* by Historical Society of New Mexico, (Santa Fe: New Mexican Printing, 1908), 11:5.
2. Glen Sample Ely, "What to Do about Texas?: Texas and the Department of New Mexico in the Civil War," *New Mexico Historical Review* 85, no. 4 (Fall 2010): 380.
3. Ibid.
4. Ibid.
5. Jerry D. Thompson, *A Civil War History of the New Mexico Volunteers and Militia* (Albuquerque: University of New Mexico Press, 2015), 211, 360.
6. Ibid., 86, 211, 212, 310, 317, and 318.
7. Reséndez, *The Other Slavery*, 6, 11; Ely, "What to Do about Texas?," 380 and 381; and E. Susan Barber and Charles F. Ritter, "Dangerous Liaisons: Working Women and Sexual Justice in the American Civil War," *European Journal of American Studies* 10, no. 1 (2015): 10, doi:10.4000/ejas.10695.
8. Ely, "What to Do about Texas?," 381.
9. Ibid.
10. Ibid.
11. Mills, *Forty Years at El Paso*, 24.
12. Ray E. Boomhower, *The Sword and the Pen: A Life of Lew Wallace* (Indianapolis: Indiana Historical Society Press, 2005), 96.
13. Bartlett, "President Juárez at Old El Paso," 646.
14. Ibid.
15. Hogan, *Abraham Lincoln and Mexico,* 143.
16. Ibid., 142.
17. Ely, "What to Do about Texas?," 388.
18. Ibid.

19. Capt. D. H. Brotherton to Gen. J. H. Carleton, May 3, 1865; and statement of William J. Davis, March 3, 1865, both in Daniel Lamont, *The War of the Rebellion; A Compilation of the Official Records of the Union and Confederate Armies* (Washington, D.C.: Government Printing Office, 1894), 374–76. In these letters between Brotherton, Carleton, and Inspector General Nelson H. Davis, a plot is revealed, whereby Spruce M. Baird, formerly a lawyer in New Mexico Territory and a Confederate sympathizer, had been raising an army—nine full companies with eighty-four men in total—to attack New Mexico, with the hope of retaking it.
20. Assistant Inspector General N. H. Davis to Capt. D. H. Brotheron, May 4, 1865; and Brigadier General James H. Carleton to Captain David H. Brotherton, May 9, 1865, in ibid., 376–77.
21. Ely, "What to Do about Texas?," 388.
22. 1880 Federal Census, Las Cruces, Dona Ana, New Mexico, Roll 802, p. 276A, Enumeration District 011.
23. Jerry D. Thompson, ed., *New Mexico Territory during the Civil War: Wallen and Evans Inspection Reports, 1862–1863* (Albuquerque: University of New Mexico Press, 2008), 255; and Mills, *Forty Years at El Paso,* 91. Additionally, Cuniffe's daughters, Anna and Mary, also held the position of postmaster in Las Cruces, Anna in 1877 and Mary in 1882 and 1897; see "Dona Ana County Post Office History," nmahgp.genealogyvillage.com/donaana/post_office_history.htm; and the 1880 Federal Census for the listing of Anna and Mary as Henry Cuniffe's daughters.
24. In 1860, six years before his *Souvenir* portrait was taken, Cuniffe owned real estate valued at $6,000 and personal property worth $20,000. See Thompson, *New Mexico Territory during the Civil War,* 255; and Mills, *Forty Years at El Paso,* 91.
25. Thompson, *New Mexico Territory during the Civil War,* 252 and 262; and Mills, *Forty Years at El Paso,* 20.
26. Robert W. Frazer, *Forts of the West: Military Forts and Presidios, and Posts Commonly Called Forts, West of the Mississippi River to 1898* (Norman: University of Oklahoma Press, 1965), 108; and Thompson, *New Mexico Territory during the Civil War,* 151.
27. Thompson, *New Mexico Territory during the Civil War,* 151.
28. Darlis A. Miller, "The Perils of a Post Sutler: William H. Moore at Fort Union, New Mexico, 1859–1870," *Journal of the West* 32, no. 2 (April 1993): 7–18.
29. Ely, "What to Do about Texas?," 383.
30. Thompson, *New Mexico Territory during the Civil War,* 150.
31. This photo is found in appendix IV of Mills, *Forty Years at El Paso,* 199, 200. The caption does not name everybody correctly.
32. Thompson, *New Mexico Territory during the Civil War,* 263–64; and F. Stanley, *The Civil War in New Mexico* (Santa Fe: Sunstone Press, 2011), 379, 380.
33. Bartlett, "President Juárez at Old El Paso," 653.
34. Bartlett, "When Juarez Rallied His Men in El Paso to Free Mexico," *El Paso Herald,* June 5, 1909, 27.
35. Ibid., 29.
36. Rex Strickland, *Six Who Came to El Paso: Pioneers of the 1840's* (El Paso: Texas Western Press, University of Texas at El Paso, 1979), 36.
37. William H. Seward, *Papers Relating to Foreign Affairs, Accompanying the Annual Message of the President to the Second Session of the Thirty-ninth Congress, Part III* (Washington, D.C.: Government Printing Office, 1867), 76–78.

38. Miller, "Arms across the Border," 5.
39. Letters and Their Enclosures Received by the Commission Branch of the Adjutant General's Office, 1863–70, Record Group 94, Catalog ID 300360, M1064, Roll 0258, NARA; Andrew E. Masich, *The Civil War in Arizona: The Story of the California Volunteers, 1861–1865* (Norman: University of Oklahoma Press, 2006), 16–17; and Nolan, *The Lincoln County War*, 462.
40. Nolan, *The Lincoln County War*, 38.
41. Clifford R. Caldwell, *John Simpson Chisum: Cattle King of the Pecos Revisited* (Santa Fe: Sunstone Press, 2010), 90.
42. Frederick W. Nolan, *The West of Billy the Kid* (Norman: University of Oklahoma Press, 1998), 107; and Caffey, *Chasing the Santa Fe Ring*, 151–2.
43. Nolan, *The Lincoln County War*, 135.
44. Blackshear, *Fort Bascom*, 27.
45. Caffey, *Chasing the Santa Fe Ring*, 140.

CHAPTER 4. SORROW

1. The Mescalero Apaches were the first to be imprisoned at Bosque Redondo when their chief, Cadete, surrendered to the U.S. Army rather than being wiped out, as General James H. Carleton had ordered Kit Carson to kill any Apache man who resisted. The Mescaleros escaped from the Bosque in 1865, during the night, returning to their home in the Sacramento Mountains. See Thompson, *A Civil War History*, 60–61; Almer N. Blazer, *Santana: War Chief of the Mescalero Apache*, ed. by A. R. Pruit (Rancho de Taos, N.Mex.: Dog Soldier Press, 2000), 15–16.
2. Numbers of how many Navajos were interned at Bosque Redondo vary but are generally estimated at between 8,000 and 11,000, though the number of Mescalero Apaches (five hundred) is well agreed upon. The figure of 11,000 Navajos comes from Jennifer Denetdale. She makes a compelling case for the higher number, indicating that by November 1864, the beginning of the Long Walk, 8,570 Navajos were reported at Bosque Redondo, and her estimate of upward of 11,000 takes into account that many more Navajos were brought there over the next four years. She likewise makes the point that it is hard to account for the numbers who died along the way or the number of prisoners who were stolen by slave raiders who followed the forced march. Jennifer Denetdale, *The Long Walk*, 49.
3. Robin Riley Fast, "The Land Is Full of Stories: Navajo Histories in the Work of Luci Tapahonso," *Women's Studies* 36, no. 3 (2007): 195, doi:10.1080/00497870701255388.
4. Various sources cite the number of Navajos who died from smallpox in the first months of 1865 as "2,321." However, those sources do not indicate where that number comes from. For example, see Edward Spicer, *Cycles of Conquest: The Impact of Spain, Mexico, and the United States on the Indians of the Southwest, 1533–1960*, 220. However, as a primary source, Theodore H. Dodd's report of August 28, 1866, covering his first year as Indian agent for the Navajos, a report he wrote to Col. A. B. Norton, Superintendent of Indian Affairs in Santa Fe, indicates that in his first year as Indian agent there was a decrease of 1,576 Navajos, which he attributed to death and desertion. Dodd arrived when the smallpox epidemic was well under way, so it could be that hundreds more were already dead, and the number of deaths from smallpox could indeed have been greater than 2,000. See United States, Office of Indian Affairs, *Annual Report of the Commissioner of*

Indian Affairs for the Year 1866 (Washington, D.C.: Government Printing Office, 1866), 150–51.

5. Thompson, *A Civil War History*, 299.
6. Gerald Thompson, *The Army and the Navajo: The Bosque Redondo Reservation Experiment, 1863–1868* (Ann Arbor, Mich.: Books on Demand, 1997), 12; Tom Dunlay, *Kit Carson and the Indians* (Lincoln: University of Nebraska Press, 2005), 318; and Trudy I. Scee, *Rogues, Rascals, and Other Villainous Mainers* (Camden, Maine: Down East Books, 2014), 59.
7. William J. Bauer, *California through Native Eyes: Reclaiming History* (Seattle: University of Washington Press, 2016), 102.
8. James Henry Carleton, *To the People of New Mexico. This Paper Sets Forth Some of the Principal Reasons Why the Navajo Indians Have Been Located upon a Reservation at the Bosque Redondo* (n.p., 1864), 12.
9. Gerald E. Thompson, "'To the People of New Mexico': Gen. Carleton Defends the Bosque Redondo," *Arizona and the West* 14, no. 4 (Winter 1972): 347.
10. *Condition of the Indian Tribes—Report of the Joint Special Committee Appointed under Joint Resolution of March 3, 1865* (Washington, D.C.: Government Printing Office, 1867), 110.
11. Thomas E. Farish, *History of Arizona* (Phoenix: Second Legislature of the State of Arizona, 1918), 2:102–11.
12. Thompson, *A Civil War History*, 298; Raymond Friday Locke, *The Book of the Navajo* (New York: Kensington, 2010), 347; and Keleher, *Turmoil in New Mexico, 1846–1868* (Albuquerque: University of New Mexico Press, 1982), 338.
13. Ralph E. Twitchell, *The Leading Facts of New Mexican History* (Cedar Rapids: Torch Press, 1911), 3:418.
14. Thompson, *A Civil War History*, 267–68.
15. Ibid., 307–8.
16. J. Lee Correll, *Through White Men's Eyes: A Contribution to Navajo History: A Chronological Record of the Navajo People from Earliest Times to the Treaty of June 1, 1868* (Window Rock, Ariz.: Navajo Heritage Center, 1979), 5:295–96; Kelli Carmean, *Spider Woman Walks This Land: Traditional Cultural Properties and the Navajo Nation* (Walnut Creek, Calif.: AltaMira Press, 2002), 17; and Thompson, *A Civil War History*, 331.
17. Correll, *Through White Men's Eyes*, 267–68.
18. Denetdale, *The Long Walk*, 56; and David Remley, *Kit Carson: The Life of an American Border Man* (Norman: University of Oklahoma Press, 2012), 230.
19. Flannery Burke, *A Land Apart: The Southwest and the Nation in the Twentieth Century* (Tucson: University of Arizona Press, 2017), 108.
20. Locke, in *The Book of the Navajo*, states that the Navajos were forced to work the fields at gunpoint, but he does not cite his sources. Other sources (e.g., Lynn R. Bailey, *Bosque Redondo: The Navajo Internment at Fort Sumner, New Mexico, 1863–1868* [Tucson: Westernlore Press, 1998]; Chris J. Magoc and David C. Bernstein, *Imperialism and Expansionism in American History: A Social, Political, and Cultural Encyclopedia and Document Collection*, vol. 2 [Santa Barbara, Calif.: ABC-CLIO, 2015]; etc.) indicate that the Navajos were forced to work the fields at bayonet point. Sources do seem to corroborate that Navajos were forced to work the fields under threat of violence, and there is no question that 1867 was the third year in a row that crops failed, as indicated in reports of the time, including Sherman's 1868 report.

Locke, *The Book of the Navajo,* 347 and 380; Bailey, *Bosque Redondo*, 223.

21. Denetdale, *Reclaiming Diné History: The Legacies of Navajo Chief Manuelito and Juanita* (Tucson: University of Arizona Press, 2007), 75.
22. James E. Farmer and Dale F. Giese, *My Life with the Army in the West: The Memoirs of James E. Farmer, 1858–1898* (n.p., 1993), 109–10.
23. Iverson and Roessel, *Diné*, 59.
24. Some Navajo had metalworking skills, particularly ironworking, which they had learned to do from Mexican blacksmiths before going to Bosque Redondo. Perhaps as many as several dozen were employed as blacksmiths at Bosque Redondo. A letter from Assistant Adjutant-General Ben. C. Cutler, on August 22, 1864, to the commanding officer at Fort Sumner, relays that the chief quartermaster " will direct that a set of blacksmith tools, complete, and some iron, be sent to Fort Sumner for the use of the Navajoes." See *The Miscellaneous Documents of the House of Representatives for the Second Session of the Fifty-Second Congress, 1892–'93* (Washington, D.C.: Government Printing Office, 1893), 812. For more on the topic, also see Margery Bedinger, *Indian Silver: Navajo and Pueblo Jewelers* (Albuquerque: University of New Mexico Press, 1974), 9–14; and Locke, *The Book of the Navajo,* 371.
25. Locke, *The Book of the Navajo*, 371–72.
26. Locke, *The Book of the Navajo*, 282; and Reséndez, *The Other Slavery*, 279.
27. Reséndez, *The Other Slavery*, 330.
28. Michael Steck to William Dole, January 13, 1864, Record Group 75, OIA, M234, LR, NMS, Roll 552, NARA.
29. Thompson, *A Civil War History*, 344.
30. Brooks, *Captives and Cousins*, 309.
31. Reséndez, *The Other Slavery*, 283, 287; Oscar H. Lipps, *A Little History of the Navajos* (Albuquerque: Avanyu, 1989), 54–55; and Correll, *Through White Men's Eyes*, 23.
32. Thompson, *A Civil War History*, 346.
33. Gen. Sherman, when negotiating with Barboncito, mentions the Peonage Act of 1867 to assure him that the U.S. government was serious about ending peonage and captive slavery of Navajos and others in the territory. See William Kiser, *Borderlands of Slavery: The Struggle over Captivity and Peonage in the American Southwest* (Philadelphia: University of Pennsylvania Press, 2017), 86. See also William Wirt Howe, "The Peonage Cases," *Columbia Law Review* 4, no. 4 (April 1904): 279–86; and United States Statutes at Large, 39th Cong., 2nd Sess., Ch. 187 (1866–67), 546.
34. Union Provost Marshal's File of Paper Relating to Civilians, 1864, Record Group 75, OIA, M345, LR, NMS, Roll 0100, NARA.
35. Union Provost Marshal's File of Paper Relating to Civilians, 1865, Record Group 75, OIA, M345, LR, NMS, Roll 0270, NARA.
36. *Executive Documents Printed by Order of the House of Representatives, during the Third Session of the Fortieth Congress 1868–'69, in Fourteen Volumes* (London: Forgotten Books, 2016), 620; and C. L. Sonnichsen, *The Mescalero Apaches* (Norman: University of Oklahoma Press, 1982), 134–35.
37. Amendment to the Indian Depredations Act, February 7, 1914, Report 311, of the 63rd Cong., 2nd Sess., House of Representatives, 9.
38. Both "Mackinaw blankets" and "Mexican blankets" were ordered in volume by the U.S. Army, but seemingly the Mackinaw blankets were intended for Navajos

and the "Mexican blankets" for Utes and Apaches. See Joe B. Wheat, *Blanket Weaving in the Southwest*, edited by Ann Lane Hedlund (Tucson: University of Arizona Press, 2003), 76; and Keleher, *Turmoil in New Mexico*, 498.

39. A description of this type of everyday pouch, as opposed to a Jish, a pouch for holding medicine, is discussed at length in Charlotte Frisbie, *Navajo Medicine Bundles or Jish: Acquisition, Transmission and Disposition in the Past and Present* (Albuquerque: University of New Mexico Press, 1987).
40. Denetdale, *Reclaiming Diné History*, 5.
41. Thompson, *A Civil War History*, 353–54; and Correll, *Through White Men's Eyes*, 90–92.
42. Carleton to Shaw, March 23, 1865, cited in Correll, *Through White Men's Eyes*, 94–95.
43. This account is related in three letters written by Capt. Edmond Butler, commander at Fort Wingate, who wrote variously to the Asst. Adj. General, to the Commanding Officer at Los Pinos, and to Carter, cited in Correll, *Through White Men's Eyes*, 295–96.
44. A letter from Capt. Edmond Butler, Commander at Fort Wingate, to Maj. Cyrus H. DeForrest at Headquarters in Santa Fe on September 2, 1866. See Correll, *Through White Men's Eyes*, 368.
45. A letter from Capt. Edmond Butler, Commander at Fort Wingate, to Maj. Cyrus H. DeForrest at Headquarters in Santa Fe on November 11, 1866. See Correll, *Through White Men's Eyes*, 393–94.
46. *Santa Fe Gazette*, November 17, 1866.
47. Thompson, *A Civil War History*, 409.
48. Correll, *Through White Men's Eyes*, 368.
49. Brown, *Bury My Heart at Wounded Knee*, 33; Lawrence D. Sundberg, *Red Shirt: The Life and Times of Henry Lafayette Dodge* (Santa Fe: Sunstone Press, 2013), 573; Keleher, *Turmoil in New Mexico*, 298; and Laurance D. Linford and Floyd A. O'Neil, *Tony Hillerman's Navajoland: Hideouts, Haunts, and Havens in the Joe Leaphorn and Jim Chee Mysteries* (Salt Lake City: University of Utah Press, 2016), 100.
50. Valerie Rangel, "The Story of Manuelito" (n.d., People menu), *New Mexico Office of the State Historian*, http://newmexicohistory.org/people/the-story-of-manuelito.
51. For context on Apaches with Manuelito's group, a letter from Capt. Edmond Butler to Maj. Cyrus H. DeForrest, which relays an account given by the Navajo man "Billi Lani? 'Many Horse,'" on July 28, 1866, indicates that many Apache were with him; see Correll, *Through White Men's Eyes*, 358–60. Regarding the most likely location for these photographs to have been taken, given that those portrayed in the Navajo *Souvenir* album portraits were seemingly all part of the surrendering party of Manuelito, and, for example, neither Barboncito nor any of his surrendering band are presented, it seems that the portraits would have had to have been taken sometime between when Manuelito's band surrendered on September 1 at Fort Wingate and when they arrived at Bosque Redondo about one month later. This is deduced by the seeming absence of anyone other than individuals from Manuelito's surrendering band being portrayed, and the fact that the portraits were made against a backdrop of an itinerant photographer, as opposed to in a studio or in the landscape of Fort Sumner or Bosque Redondo. That being the case, it can be further deduced that the portraits were most likely taken en route, either

in Santa Fe, at Fort Union, or more likely in Albuquerque, where the Duhems had their studio, or perhaps another place where Manuelito's band stopped on their way to Fort Sumner.

52. Paula Richardson Fleming and Judith Luskey, *The North American Indians in Early Photographs* (New York: Calmann and King, 2000), 109–11.
53. Gordon Maitland, "The *Two Sides* of the *Camera Lens: Nineteenth Century Photography* and the *Indigenous People* of the *South Pacific*," *Photofile: South Pacific* 6, no. 3 (1988): 47–60.
54. For a larger overview of slavery of indigenous people in New Mexico in this era, see Reséndez, *The Other Slavery*. For more on the representation of indigenous women by others, see Denise K. Lajimodiere, "American Indian Females and Stereotypes: Warriors, Leaders, Healers, Feminists; Not Drudges, Princesses, Prostitutes," *Multicultural Perspectives* 15, no. 2 (2013): 104–9, doi:10.1080/15210960.2013.781391; or Max Quanchi, *Photographing Papua: Representation, Colonial Encounters and Imaging in the Public Domain* (Newcastle, U.K.: Cambridge Scholars, 2007), 66.
55. Correll, *Through White Men's Eyes*, 121.
56. Carolyn Epple, "A Navajo Worldview and Nádleehí: Implications for Western Categories," in *Two-Spirit People: Native American Gender Identity, Sexuality, and Spirituality,* edited by Sue-Ellen Jacobs (Urbana: University of Illinois Press, 2005), 174–91.
57. The use of this image as representative of "two spirit" can generally be dated to 2009, with the release of Lydia Nibley's 2009 documentary *Two Spirit,* which features the image. The documentary centers on the story of the murder of sixteen-year-old *nádleehí* Fred Martínez.
58. Information regarding the three young Navajo men, their arrival at Carlisle, their ages, and the dates of their deaths is narrated in numerous volumes from 1883 of *The Morning Star* (Carlisle, Pa.), vol. 3, no. 12, July 1883; vol. 3, no. 1, August 1883, p. 3, mentioned in a letter from Denis M. Riordan (Indian agent for the Navajo, Fort Defiance Reservation, December 1882–December 1883) to Captain Richard Henry Pratt (Superintendent of the Carlisle Indian School), written September 27, 1883. See Louise Lockard, "No One Remembers a Winter Like This: A Year at the Navajo Agency, 1882–1883," February 2000 (https://eric.ed.gov/?id=ED454013), 270–71, as well as the Student Information Cards from Carlisle, archived at the National Archives. An account of Riordan's visit to Carlisle with Henry Chee Dodge, Ganado Mucho, and Capt. Tom can be found in *The Morning Star*, vol. 4, no. 8, March 1884, p. 4, which makes the identification of "Navajo Jack" in the photograph, as it is labeled in the Smithsonian National Anthropological Archives, somewhat problematic, though Riordon did visit Carlisle between January 1883 and July 1883, so it is possible that the photograph does portray "Navajo Jack" if taken before March of 1883, when he died.
59. While the captions in the *Souvenir* album do not indicate corn husking is happening in these images, the captions that go with these same images as found at the National Archives indicate that that's what they are doing. See Robert A. Roessel, *Pictorial History of the Navajo from 1860 to 1910* (Rough Rock, Ariz.: Navajo Curriculum Center, Rough Rock Demonstration School, 1980), 38, 40.
60. Ibid., 37.

BIBLIOGRAPHY

Aarons, James. *Index to the Reports of Committees of the House of Representatives for the First and Second Sessions of the Forty-Sixth Congress, 1879–'80: In Six Volumes*. Washington, D.C.: Government Printing Office, 1880.

Abbot, Gorham D. *Mexico and the United States: Their Mutual Relations and Common Interests: With Portraits on Steel of Juárez and Romero, and Colored Maps*. New York: G. P. Putnam and Son, 1869.

Babbitt, James E. "From Albuquerque to Tucson in 1867: The Kansas Pacific Railway Survey Photographs of William A. Bell." *Journal of Arizona History* 39, no. 3 (Autumn 1998): 289–306.

Bahr, Howard M., ed. *The Navajo as Seen by the Franciscans, 1898–1921: A Sourcebook*. Lanham, Md.: Scarecrow Press, 2004.

Bailey, Lynn R. *Bosque Redondo: The Navajo Internment at Fort Sumner, New Mexico, 1863–1868*. Tucson: Westernlore Press, 1998.

"Bankruptcy Notice." *Rocky Mountain News* (Denver), January 3, 1877.

Barber, E. Susan, and Charles F. Ritter. "Dangerous Liaisons: Working Women and Sexual Justice in the American Civil War." *European Journal of American Studies* 10, no. 1 (2015): 2–19. doi:10.4000/ejas.10695.

Bartlett, Ichabod S., ed. *History of Wyoming*. Vol. 1. Chicago: S. J. Clarke, 1918.

———. "President Juarez at Old El Paso." In *Bulletin of the Pan American Union*. Vol. 41, 641–59. Washington, D.C.: Union of the American Republics, 1915.

———. "When Juarez Rallied His Men in El Paso to Free Mexico." *El Paso Herald*, June 5, 1909.

Bauer, William J. *California through Native Eyes: Reclaiming History*. Seattle: University of Washington Press, 2016.

Bedinger, Margery. *Indian Silver: Navajo and Pueblo Jewelers*. Albuquerque: University of New Mexico Press, 1974.

Blackshear, James Bailey. *Fort Bascom: Soldiers, Comancheros, and Indians in the Canadian River Valley*. Norman: University of Oklahoma Press, 2016.

Blair, Mary Ellen. *A Life Well Led: The Biography of Barbara Freire-Marreco Aitken, British Anthropologist*. Santa Fe: Sunstone Press, 2008.

Blazer, Almer N. *Santana: War Chief of the Mescalero Apache*. Edited by A. R. Pruit. Rancho de Taos, N.Mex.: Dog Soldier Press, 2000.

Boomhower, Ray E. *The Sword and the Pen: A Life of Lew Wallace*. Indianapolis: Indiana Historical Society Press, 2005.

Brooks, James F. *Captives and Cousins: Slavery, Kinship, and Community in the Southwest Borderlands*. Chapel Hill: Omohundro Institute of Early American History and Culture and the University of North Carolina Press, 2011.

Brown, Dee Alexander. *Bury My Heart at Wounded Knee: An Indian History of the American West*. New York: Rinehart and Winston, 1979.

Brown, Willard J. *The Signal Corps, U.S.A. in the War of the Rebellion*. Baltimore: Butternut and Blue, 1996.

Burke, Flannery. *A Land Apart: The Southwest and the Nation in the Twentieth Century*. Tucson: University of Arizona Press, 2017.

Caffey, David L. *Chasing the Santa Fe Ring: Power and Privilege in Territorial New Mexico*. Albuquerque: University of New Mexico Press, 2014.

Caldwell, Clifford R. *John Simpson Chisum: Cattle King of the Pecos Revisited*. Santa Fe: Sunstone Press, 2010.

California, Adjutant General's Office. *Records of California Men in the War of the Rebellion, 1861 to 1867*. Sacramento, Calif.: Sacramento State Office, 1890.

Camp, Roderic Ai, ed. *The Oxford Handbook of Mexican Politics*. New York: Oxford University Press, 2012.

Carleton, James Henry. *To the People of New Mexico: This Paper Sets Forth Some of the Principal Reasons Why the Navajo Indians Have Been Located upon a Reservation at the Bosque Redondo*. N.p., 1864. https://catalog.hathitrust.org/Record/009563033.

Carmean, Kelli. *Spider Woman Walks This Land: Traditional Cultural Properties and the Navajo Nation*. Walnut Creek, Calif.: AltaMira Press, 2002.

Chávez, Angélico. *But Time and Chance: The Story of Padre Martínez of Taos, 1793–1867*. Santa Fe: Sunstone Press, 1981.

Chollett, Donna L. *Neoliberalism, Social Exclusion, and Social Movements: Resistance and Dissent in Mexico's Sugar Industry*. Lanham, Md.: Lexington Books, 2013.

Coke, Van Deren. *Photography in New Mexico: From the Daguerreotype to the Present*. Albuquerque: University of New Mexico Press, 1979.

Condition of the Indian Tribes: Report of the Joint Special Committee Appointed under Joint Resolution of March 3, 1865. Washington, D.C.: Government Printing Office, 1867.

Cool, Paul. *Salt Warriors: Insurgency on the Rio Grande*. College Station: Texas A&M University Press, 2008.

Correll, J. Lee. *Through White Men's Eyes: A Contribution to Navajo History: A Chronological Record of the Navajo People from Earliest Times to the Treaty of June 1, 1868*. Vol. 5. Window Rock, Ariz.: Navajo Heritage Center, 1979.

Cozzens, Peter. *The Earth Is Weeping: The Epic Story of the Indian Wars for the American West*. New York: Vintage Books, 2017.

Crook, David. *The North and the South and the Powers, 1861–65*. New York: Wiley, 1974.

Cuarterolo, Andrea. "The Social Construction of the Photographic Portrait in 19th-Century Rio de la Plata." *Oxford Research Encyclopedia of Latin American History*. December 2015. http://latinamericanhistory.oxfordre.com/view/10.1093/acrefore/9780199366439.001.0001/acrefore-9780199366439-e-105.

Cunningham, Michele. *Mexico and the Foreign Policy of Napoleon III*. New York: Palgrave Macmillan, 2001.

Current, Karen, and William R. Current. *Photography and the Old West*. New York: Abradale Press/Harry N. Abrams, in association with the Amon Carter Museum of Western Art, 1986.

Dabbs, Jack Autrey. *The French Army in Mexico, 1861–1867: A Study in Military Government*. The Hague: Mouton, 1963.

Daniels, David. "Photography's Wet-Plate Interlude in Arizona Territory: 1864–1880." *Journal of Arizona History* 9, no. 4 (Winter 1968): 171–94.

"Death Takes C. L. Duhem." *Oroville Mercury* (Oroville, Calif.), April 26, 1933, 1.

Denetdale, Jennifer. *The Long Walk: The Forced Navajo Exile*. New York: Chelsea House, 2008.

———. *Reclaiming Diné History: The Legacies of Navajo Chief Manuelito and Juanita*. Tucson: University of Arizona Press, 2007.

Dew, Charles B. *Apostles of Disunion: Southern Secession Commissioners and the Causes of the Civil War*. Charlottesville: University of Virginia Press, 2017.

Dickenson, Donald C. *Dictionary of American Antiquarian Book Dealers*. Westport, Conn.: Greenwood, 1998.

Dickey, Gretchen, and Sara Flores. "Solomon C. Schutz Helped Bring Law and Order to El Paso." *Borderlands* 23 (2004–5). https://epcc.libguides.com/c.php?g=754275&p=5406060.

"Dona Ana County Post Office History." https://nmahgp.genealogyvillage.com/donaana/post_office_history.htm.

Dunlay, Tom. *Kit Carson and the Indians*. Lincoln: University of Nebraska Press, 2005.

Dunmire, William W. *New Mexico's Spanish Livestock Heritage: Four Centuries of Animals, Land, and People*. Albuquerque: University of New Mexico Press, 2014.

Ely, Glen Sample. "What to Do about Texas?: Texas and the Department of New Mexico in the Civil War." *New Mexico Historical Review* 85, no. 4 (Fall 2010): 375–408.

Epple, Carolyn. "A Navajo Worldview and Nádleehí: Implications for Western Categories." In *Two-Spirit People: Native American Gender Identity, Sexuality, and Spirituality*, edited by Sue-Ellen Jacobs, Wesley Thomas, and Sabine Lane, 174–91. Urbana: University of Illinois Press, 1997.

Executive Documents Printed by Order of the House of Representatives, during the Third Session of the Fortieth Congress 1868–'69, in Fourteen Volumes. London: Forgotten Books, 2016.

Faris, James C. *Navajo and Photography: A Critical History of the Representation of an American People*. Albuquerque: University of New Mexico Press, 1996.

Farish, Thomas Edwin. *History of Arizona*. Vol. 2. Phoenix: Second Legislature of the State of Arizona, 1918.

Farmer, James E., and Dale F. Giese. *My Life with the Army in the West: The Memoirs of James E. Farmer, 1858–1898*. N.p., 1993.

Fast, Robin Riley. "The Land Is Full of Stories: Navajo Histories in the Work of Luci Tapahonso." *Women's Studies* 36, no. 3 (2007): 185–211. doi:10.1080/00497870701255388.

Faust, Drew Gilpin. *This Republic of Suffering: Death and the American Civil War*. New York: Vintage, 2008.

Fleming, Paula Richardson. *Native American Photography at the Smithsonian: The Shindler Catalogue*. Washington, D.C.: Smithsonian Books, 2003.

Fleming, Paula Richardson, and Judith Luskey. *The North American Indians in Early Photographs*. New York: Calmann and King, 2000.

Fogel, Marshall. "The History of Goudey Gum Company." *Professional Sports Authenticator,* July 8, 2003. http://www.psacard.com/articles/articleview/3886/history-goudey-gum-company.

Foner, Eric. *Reconstruction: America's Unfinished Revolution, 1863–1877.* New York: Harper and Row, 1988.

Frazer, Robert Walter. *Forts of the West: Military Forts and Presidios, and Posts Commonly Called Forts, West of the Mississippi River to 1898.* Norman: University of Oklahoma Press, 1965.

Frisbie, Charlotte Johnson. *Navajo Medicine Bundles or Jish: Acquisition, Transmission, and Disposition in the Past and Present.* Albuquerque: University of New Mexico Press, 1987.

Frizot, Michel, ed. *A New History of Photography.* Cologne: Konemann Verlags, 1999.

Gallman, J. Matthew, and Gary W. Gallagher, eds. *Lens of War: Exploring Iconic Photographs of the Civil War.* Athens: University of Georgia Press, 2015.

Gillespie, Sarah Kate. *The Early American Daguerreotype: Cross-Currents in Art and Technology.* Cambridge, Mass.: MIT Press, 2016.

Gonzales-Berry, Erlinda, and David R. Maciel, eds. *The Contested Homeland: A Chicano History of New Mexico.* Albuquerque: University of New Mexico Press, 2000.

González Ortega, Jesús. *The Presidency of Mexico: Protest of General Jesus Gonzales Ortega, President of the Supreme Court of Justice against the Decrees of Senor Benito Juarez, Ex-president of the Mexican Republic, Issued November 8th, 1865, and His Address to the Mexican Nation, to Which Are Appended Letters in Ratification of His Position.* New York: Russell's American Steam Printing House, 1866.

Groenveld, Anneke, and Pieter Hovens. *Odagot: Indianen Gefotografeerd 1860–1920* [Photographs of American Indians 1860–1920]. Amsterdam: Fragment; Rotterdam: Museum voor Volkenkunde, 1992.

Guardion, Peter. *The Time of Liberty: Popular Political Culture in Oaxaca, 1750–1850.* Durham, N.C.: Duke University Press, 2005.

Hamber, Anthony. *Collecting the American West: The Rise and Fall of William Blackmore.* East Knoyle, Salisbury, U.K.: Hobnob Press, 2010.

Hamilton, Nancy. *Ben Dowell: El Paso's First Mayor.* El Paso: Texas Western Press, 1976.

———. "Memoirs Describe Elegant 1866 El Paso Ball." *El Paso Herald-Post,* August 10, 1973, sec. B, p. 9.

———. "Pioneer Wagon Train Operator Rescued E. P. Caravan." *El Paso Herald-Post,* January 10, 1974, sec. B.

Hamnett, Brian R. "Benito Juárez, Early Liberalism, and the Regional Politics of Oaxaca, 1828–1853." *Bulletin of Latin American Research* 10, no. 1 (1991): 3–21. doi:10.2307/3338561.

———. "The Comonfort Presidency, 1855–1857." *Bulletin of Latin American Research* 15, no. 1 (1996): 81–100. doi:10.1111/j.1470–9856.1996.tb00023.x.

Hanna, Alfred Jackson, and Kathryn Abbey Hanna. *Napoleon III and Mexico: American Triumph over Mexico.* Chapel Hill: University of North Carolina Press, 1971.

Hogan, Michael. *Abraham Lincoln and Mexico: A History of Courage, Intrigue and Unlikely Friendships.* Guadalajara, Jalisco, Mexico: Fondo Editorial Universitario, 2016.

Howe, William Wirt. "The Peonage Cases." *Columbia Law Review* 4, no. 4 (April 1904): 279–86.

Iverson, Peter, and Monty Roessel. *Diné: A History of the Navajos*. Albuquerque: University of New Mexico Press, 2003.

Kate, Herman ten. *Travels and Researches in Native North America, 1882–1883*. Translated by Pieter Hovens et al. Albuquerque: University of New Mexico Press, 2004.

Keefe, Laurence E., Jr., and Dennis Inch. *The Life of a Photograph: Archival Processing, Matting, Framing, and Storage*. Boston: Focal Press, 1984.

Keleher, William Aloysius. *Turmoil in New Mexico, 1846–1868*. Albuquerque: University of New Mexico Press, 1982.

———. *Violence in Lincoln County, 1869–1881: A New Mexico Item*. Albuquerque: University of New Mexico Press, 1982.

Kilgo, Dolores A., and Thomas Martin Easterly. *Likeness and Landscape: Thomas M. Easterly and the Art of the Daguerreotype*. St. Louis: Missouri Historical Society Press, 1994.

Kinsbruner, Jay, and Erick D. Langer. *Encyclopedia of Latin American History and Culture*. 6 vols. Detroit: Charles Scribner's Sons, 2008.

Kiser, William S. *Borderlands of Slavery: The Struggle over Captivity and Peonage in the American Southwest*. Philadelphia: University of Pennsylvania Press, 2017

Knapp, Frank A. *The Life of Sebastián Lerdo de Tejada, 1823–1889: A Study of Influence and Obscurity*. New York: Greenwood Press, 1968.

Lajimodiere, Denise K. "American Indian Females and Stereotypes: Warriors, Leaders, Healers, Feminists; Not Drudges, Princesses, Prostitutes." *Multicultural Perspectives* 15, no. 2 (2013): 104–9. doi:10.1080/15210960.2013.781391.

Lamont, Daniel. *The War of the Rebellion; A Compilation of the Official Records of the Union and Confederate Armies*. Washington, D.C.: Government Printing Office, 1894.

Linford, Laurance D. *Tony Hillerman's Navajoland: Hideouts, Haunts, and Havens in the Joe Leaphorn and Jim Chee Mysteries*. Salt Lake City: University of Utah Press, 2016.

Link, Martin A. *Navajo: A Century of Progress, 1868–1968*. Window Rock, Ariz.: K. C. Publications with the Navajo Tribe, 1968.

Lipps, Oscar H. *A Little History of the Navajos*. Albuquerque: Avanyu, 1989.

Lockard, Louise. "No One Remembers a Winter Like This: A Year at the Navajo Agency, 1882–1883." February 2000. https://eric.ed.gov/?id=ED454013.

Locke, Raymond Friday. *The Book of the Navajo*. New York: Kensington, 2010.

"Lost Prospectors." *Carson Daily Appeal* (Carson City, Nev.), October 29, 1869.

Magoc, Chris J., and David C. Bernstein, eds. *Imperialism and Expansionism in American History: A Social, Political, and Cultural Encyclopedia and Document Collection*. Vol. 2 of 4 vols. Santa Barbara, Calif.: ABC-CLIO, 2015.

Maitland, Gordon. "The Two Sides of the Camera Lens: Nineteenth Century Photography and the Indigenous People of the South Pacific." *Photofile: South Pacific* 6, no. 3 (1988): 47–59.

Martin, Percy F. *Maximilian in Mexico: The Story of the French Intervention (1861–1867)*. New York: Charles Scribner's Sons, 1914.

Martínez, Oscar J. *Border Boom Town: Ciudad Juárez since 1848*. Austin: University of Texas Press, 2011.

Masich, Andrew E. *The Civil War in Arizona: The Story of the California Volunteers, 1861–1865*. Norman: University of Oklahoma Press, 2006.

McAllen, M. M. *Maximilian and Carlota: Europe's Last Empire in Mexico*. San Antonio, Tex.: Trinity University Press, 2015.

McNitt, Frank. *Navajo Wars: Military Campaigns, Slave Raids, and Reprisals.* Albuquerque: University of New Mexico Press, 1990.

McPherson, James M. *Battle Cry of Freedom: The Civil War Era.* New York: Oxford University Press, 1988.

Meline, James F. *Two Thousand Miles on Horseback, Santa Fe and Back: A Summer Tour through Kansas, Nebraska, Colorado, and New Mexico in the Year 1866.* New York: Hurd and Houghton, 1867.

Metz, Leon C. *Desert Army: Fort Bliss on the Texas Border.* El Paso: Mangan Books, 1995.

Miller, Darlis A. "The Perils of a Post Sutler: William H. Moore at Fort Union, New Mexico, 1859–1870." *Journal of the West* 32, no. 2 (April 1993): 7–18.

Miller, Robert Ryal. "Arms across the Border: United States Aid to Juárez during the French Intervention in Mexico." *Transactions of the American Philosophical Society* 63, no. 6 (1973): 1–68. doi:10.2307/1006291.

———. "Lew Wallace and the French Intervention in Mexico." *Indiana Magazine of History* 59, no. 1 (March 1963): 31–50. https://scholarworks.iu.edu/journals/index.php/imh/article/view/8957.

Mills, W. W. *Forty Years at El Paso: 1858–1898.* Illustrated by Tom Lea. El Paso: C. Hertzog, 1962.

———. *Forty Years at El Paso: 1858–1898: Recollections of War, Politics, Adventure, Events, Narratives, Sketches, etc.* Illustrated by Tom Lea. Chicago: W. B. Conkey, 1901.

The Miscellaneous Documents of the House of Representatives for the Second Session of the Fifty-Second Congress, 1892–'93. Washington, D.C.: Government Printing Office, 1893.

Nolan, Frederick W. *The Lincoln County War: A Documentary History.* Rev. ed. Santa Fe: Sunstone Press, 2009.

———. *The West of Billy the Kid.* Norman: University of Oklahoma Press, 1998.

Nott, Charles C., and Archibald Hopkins. *Cases Decided in the Court of Claims at the December Term, 1875, and the Decisions of the Supreme Court in the Appealed Cases, from October, 1875, to May, 1877.* Washington, D.C.: Government Printing Office, 1877.

Owen, Gordon. *The Two Alberts: Fountain and Fall.* Las Cruces, N.Mex.: Yucca Tree Press, 1996.

Palmquist, Peter E., and Thomas R. Kailbourn. *Pioneer Photographers from the Mississippi to the Continental Divide: A Biographical Dictionary, 1839–1865.* Stanford, Calif.: Stanford University Press, 2005.

———. *Pioneer Photographers of the Far West: A Biographical Dictionary, 1840–1865.* Stanford, Calif.: Stanford University Press, 2001.

Papers Relating to the Foreign Relations of the United States, Transmitted to Congress, with the Annual Message of the President, December 3, 1877. Washington, D.C.: Government Printing Office, 1877.

Pettis, George H. "The California Column." In *The Stone Idols of New Mexico. A Description of Those Belonging to the Historical Society,* by Historical Society of New Mexico, 11:5–45. Santa Fe: New Mexican Printing, 1908. https://archive.org/details/stoneidolsofnewmoohistrich.

Picard, Sarah M. "Racing Jules Lion." *Louisiana History* 58, no. 1 (Winter 2017): 5–37.

Piston, William Garrett, and Thomas P. Sweeney. *Portraits of Conflict: A Photographic History of Missouri in the Civil War.* Fayetteville: University of Arkansas Press, 2009.

Pye, Jeremy W. "Living on the Border: Health, Environment, and Multiculturalism in 19th Century Tucson." PhD diss., University of Florida, 2013.

Quanchi, Max. *Photographing Papua: Representation, Colonial Encounters and Imaging in the Public Domain.* Newcastle, U.K.: Cambridge Scholars, 2007.

Remley, David A. *Kit Carson: The Life of an American Border Man.* Norman: University of Oklahoma Press, 2012.

Report of the Quartermaster General of the United States Army to the Secretary of War, for the Year Ending June 30, 1865, 1898–1900. Washington, D.C.: Government Printing Office, 1865.

Reséndez, Andrés. "North American Peonage." *Journal of the Civil War Era* 7, no. 4 (2017): 597–619.

———. *The Other Slavery: The Uncovered Story of Indian Enslavement in America.* Boston: Houghton Mifflin Harcourt, 2016.

Richards, Bradley W., and C. R. Savage. *The Savage View: Charles Savage, Pioneer Mormon Photographer.* Nevada City, Calif.: Carl Mautz Vintage Photography and Publishing, 1995.

Ridley, Jasper Godwin. *Maximilian and Juárez.* London: Phoenix Press, 1992.

Rodríguez, José Antonio. "Práctica de la fotografía en el noroeste mexicano." *Alquimia* 8, no. 22 (2004): 9. http://mediateca.inah.gob.mx/repositorio/islandora/object/articulo:8982.

Roessel, Robert A. *Pictorial History of the Navajo from 1860 to 1910.* Rough Rock, Ariz.: Navajo Curriculum Center, Rough Rock Demonstration School, 1980.

Rosenheim, Jeff L. *Photography and the American Civil War.* New York: Metropolitan Museum of Art, 2013.

Rudisill, Richard. *Photographers of the New Mexico Territory, 1854–1912.* Santa Fe: Museum of New Mexico, 1973.

Sandweiss, Martha A. *Print the Legend: Photography and the American West.* New Haven, Conn.: Yale University Press, 2004.

Scee, Trudy Irene. *Rogues, Rascals, and Other Villainous Mainers.* Camden, Maine: Down East Books, 2014.

Schevill, Margaret. "From the Desk of Washington Matthews." *Journal of American Folklore* 73, no. 290 (1960): 317–25.

Shoaf, Dana B. "For Every Man Who Wore the Blue": The Military Order of the Loyal Legion of the United States and the Charges of Elitism after the Civil War." In *Union Soldiers and the Northern Home Front: Wartime Experiences, Postwar Adjustments,* edited by Paul A. Cimbala and Randall M. Miller, 463–75. New York, N.Y.: Fordham University Press, 2002.

Simmons, Virginia M. *The Ute Indians of Utah, Colorado, and New Mexico.* Boulder: University Press of Colorado, 2000.

Sloan, Kathryn A. *Runaway Daughters: Seduction, Elopement, and Honor in Nineteenth-Century Mexico.* Albuquerque: University of New Mexico Press, 2008.

Solnit, Rebecca. *River of Shadows: Eadweard Muybridge and the Technological Wild West.* New York: Penguin Books, 2010.

Sonnichsen, C. L. *The Mescalero Apaches.* Norman: University of Oklahoma Press, 1982.

Spicer, Edward. *Cycles of Conquest: the Impact of Spain, Mexico, and the United States on the Indians of the Southwest, 1533–1960*. Tucson: University of Arizona Press, 1962.

Stanley, F. *The Civil War in New Mexico*. Santa Fe: Sunstone Press, 2011.

Strickland, Rex W. *Six Who Came to El Paso: Pioneers of the 1840's*. El Paso: Texas Western Press, University of Texas at El Paso, 1979.

Sundberg, Lawrence D. *Red Shirt: The Life and Times of Henry Lafayette Dodge*. Santa Fe: Sunstone Press, 2013.

Thompson, Gerald. *The Army and the Navajo: The Bosque Redondo Reservation Experiment, 1863–1868*. Ann Arbor, Mich.: Books on Demand, 1997.

———. "'To the People of New Mexico': Gen. Carleton Defends the Bosque Redondo." *Arizona and the West* 14, no. 4 (Winter 1972): 347–66.

Thompson, Jerry D. *A Civil War History of the New Mexico Volunteers and Militia*. Albuquerque: University of New Mexico Press, 2015.

———, ed. *New Mexico Territory during the Civil War: Wallen and Evans Inspection Reports, 1862–1863*. Albuquerque: University of New Mexico Press, 2008.

Timmons, Wilbert H. *James Wiley Magoffin: Don Santiago—El Paso Pioneer*. El Paso: Texas Western Press, 1984.

Twitchell, Ralph E. *The Leading Facts of New Mexican History*. Vol. 3. Cedar Rapids, Iowa: Torch Press, 1911.

The Universal Encyclopaedia. New York: D. Appleton, 1895.

United States Office of Indian Affairs. *Annual Report of the Commissioner of Indian Affairs for the Year 1866*. Washington, D.C.: Government Printing Office, 1866. http://digital.library.wisc.edu/1711.dl/History.AnnRep66.

Villalpando, José Manuel. *El juicio de la historia: Maximiliano: Los hechos frente a nuestro presente*. Barcelona, Spain: Grijalbo, 2017.

Wadsworth, Nelson B. *Set in Stone, Fixed in Glass: The Mormons, the West, and Their Photographers*. Salt Lake City: Signature Books, 1996.

Warren, Bruce. *Photography: The Concise Guide*. Boston: Wadsworth/Cengage Learning, 2012.

Weigle, Martha, with Frances Levine and Louise Stiver, eds. *Telling New Mexico: A New History*. Santa Fe: Museum of New Mexico Press, 2009.

Wheat, Joe Ben. *Blanket Weaving in the Southwest*. Edited by Ann Lane Hedlund. Tucson: University of Arizona Press, 2003.

INDEX

Page numbers followed by an *f* indicate figures, those followed by a *p* indicate plates, and page numbers in *italics* indicate additional information in a caption.